"Hear O Israel"

STUDIES IN RHETORIC AND COMMUNICATION
General Editors:
E. Culpepper Clark
Raymie E. McKerrow
David Zarefsky

"Hear O Israel"
The History of American Jewish Preaching, 1654–1970
Robert V. Friedenberg

A Theory of Argumentation
Charles Arthur Willard

Robert V. Friedenberg

"Hear O Israel"

The History of American Jewish
Preaching, 1654–1970

The University of Alabama Press   Tuscaloosa and London

BM730
A4
U64
1989

Library of Congress Cataloging-in-Publication Data
Friedenberg, Robert V.
    "Hear O Israel" : the history of American Jewish preaching,
1654–1970 / Robert V. Friedenberg.
    p. cm.—(Studies in rhetoric and communication)
    Bibliography: p.
    Includes index.
    ISBN 0-8173-0422-3
    1. Preaching, Jewish—United States—History.   2. Judaism—United
States—History.   I. Title   II. Series.
BM730.A4U64 1989
296.4′2′0973—dc19   88-20954
                                                                              CIP

British Library Cataloguing-in-Publication Data available

———————————

With all my Love, to Emmy

Contents

Preface

This work constitutes the first comprehensive rhetorical examination of an entire group of significant American speakers: the American rabbinate. Consequently, it was written with the expectation that it might prove of interest and value to both scholars in the fields of speech communication and Judaic studies.

Moreover, it was written with the added expectation that it might prove instructive to individuals seeking information about a group of American clergy who have overcome unique obstacles in developing a meaningful preaching tradition. Such individuals might well be rabbis, clergy of all faiths, as well as laypersons.

Mindful of these two distinct scholarly audiences, as well this third broader audience, I have tried to write in a style that will prove accessible to all and provide a flavor of the preaching being discussed. To this end, I have also provided the reader with a glossary of both Hebrew and rhetorical terms.

A work such as this cannot possibly treat all preachers in the history of American Judaism, nor even all of the outstanding preachers in that history. I have therefore tried to focus on those key figures whose preaching best illustrates the evolution of American Jewish preaching from its inception to the present. No doubt some readers will feel that individual rabbis or sermons have been slighted. I apologize in advance for any such slights.

If this book serves as a comprehensive history of American Jewish preaching anywhere near as well as preaching has served the American Jewish community, and indeed the American community at large, it will have been well worth the effort.

Acknowledgments

In 1981, I received a phone call from Professor Lowell McCoy of the Cincinnati campus of Hebrew Union College-Jewish Institute of Religion, inviting me to teach a speech course at HUC-JIR, replacing a faculty member who had taken ill. I accepted his invitation and have been invited back each year since. Prior to 1981, most of my own research had been in the fields of American public address and American political rhetoric. Hence, in those first years at HUC-JIR, I frequently found myself responding to class questions by observing, "I'm not sure how a rabbi would handle that, but many speakers, such as political figures, handle it by . . . " To better answer those classroom questions, I began to research the history of American Jewish preaching. I wish to express my deepest appreciation to Professor McCoy, whose invitation first caused me to think seriously about American Jewish preaching and who has remained a constant source of guidance. I also wish to thank my students at HUC-JIR, whose questions stimulated my inquiries into the subject.

As I began my research, I soon found that no comprehensive book-length study of American Jewish preaching existed and, indeed, that the preaching of relatively few rabbis had ever been studied by trained rhetoricians. Beginning my own studies, I again realized the value of the graduate education I had received in the speech department at Temple University in the late 1960s. The training and experience I received, particularly while a student of Doctors Donald

Ecroyd and Ralph Towne, helped me enormously in this endeavor, as it has throughout my professional career.

One of my mentors at Temple, Dr. DeWitte Holland, was actively involved not only in the study of American preaching but also in the development of the Religious Speech Communication Association. Members of this ecumenical organization of communication scholars have provided me with considerable encouragement and often served as sounding boards for preliminary versions of several portions of this work.

As my research progressed, I was fortunate to be awarded the Margarite R. Jacobs Post-Doctoral Fellowship in American Jewish History by the American Jewish Archives, enabling me to spend the summer of 1984 utilizing the resources of that remarkable institution. The work done that summer is reflected here, particularly in chapters one through four. The archives staff, particularly administrative director Dr. Abraham Peck, has been a continual source of help during each phase of my studies.

In 1985, I received a Miami University faculty research grant, the results of which are evident in chapter six and the epilogue. Moreover, I would be remiss without acknowledging the supportive environment Miami University has provided me throughout the years.

The staff of The University of Alabama Press has been uniformly cooperative. Judith Knight, manuscript editor Trinket Shaw, and their associates have done all that any author could request. Moreover, an early draft of this work was reviewed by Professors David Zarefsky of Northwestern University and Marc E. Saperstein of Washington University. The incisive comments that they made contributed appreciably to any strengths evident in this work.

Yet all of the associations I have had the good fortune to make and all of the support I have had the good fortune to receive while working on this book pale in comparison to the support and encouragement I have received from my family. My wife, Emmy, has often found herself inconvenienced by the demands that this project has required of my time and effort. Nevertheless, her help as critic, proofreader, and indexer, and in countless other ways, has been enormous. Finally, the help of my son, David, age six, and my daughter, Laurie, age three, simply cannot be ignored. When the tedium of research and writing grew too great, no author could have asked for more enjoyable breaks than those I had playing baseball, checkers, or ticktacktoe with David and reading all about Pat the Bunny and the Cat in the Hat with Laurie.

"Hear O Israel"

1

Jewish Preaching in Colonial and Revolutionary America

On October 28, 1636, the general court of Massachusetts "agreed to give four hundred pounds towards a school or college."[1] With this act the Massachusetts legislature, a body that had been in existence less than eight years, serving a colony that had itself existed for less than ten years, founded a college. Two years later that college was offering instruction. The impetus behind the founding of Harvard, and subsequently virtually every other early American university, was religion. The Puritans of Massachusetts and the leaders of many other religious faiths that found refuge in the New World opened colleges primarily to educate the clergy.

In contrast, it was not until October of 1875, fully 237 years after Harvard began to offer instruction to potential Puritan clergymen, and 221 years after the first Jews arrived in colonial America, that Hebrew Union College, the first rabbinic seminary in the New World, opened its doors to nine students.[2] It took the Puritans of Massachusetts ten short years to develop the resources necessary to sponsor a college and successfully mount an attempt to train young men for the clergy. It took the Jews of the United States well over two hundred years to do the same. That contrast exemplifies the problems faced by Jews in colonial America and suggests the difficulties encountered by early American Jews in both observing their faith and developing a preaching tradition.

Developing a Preaching Tradition

The development of a preaching tradition necessitates three minimum requirements: a religion that is hospitable to the concept of preaching and sermonizing; an audience desirous of listening to preachers and sermons; and clergymen able to preach. Each of these requirements was, in large part, lacking in the Jewish communities of colonial America.

American Judaism, as it existed in the eighteenth century, was not hospitable to preaching. Vernacular sermons had been a continuing tradition of Jewish life until the outset of the eighteenth century, when they gradually disappeared from Jewish services in large parts of Europe. As a rule, Jewish worship services in Europe, primarily excepting Holland, did not include vernacular sermons when the first European Jews immigrated to the colonies. From the early 1700s until 1808, when German Jews began to reestablish the sermon as part of their services, few European Jews used vernacular sermons. Consequently, the first few generations of colonial Jews arrived in the New World with very little preaching tradition.

The widespread absence of sermons in many European Jewish communities was a temporary aberration in the long history of Judaism. Though the biblical prophets have often been called preachers, Jewish leaders drew a clear distinction between their addresses and sermons. The prophets did not speak in the context of a normal religious service, nor did they prepare extensively in advance. Moreover, the prophets were not necessarily interpreting scripture. For these reasons, the biblical prophets, though renowned for their speaking, did not give rise to a sermonic or preaching tradition in Judaism.[3]

Rather, the early Jewish sermonic tradition was born out of the destruction of the ancient Temple. With the destruction of the Temple and much of national life, Jewish leaders felt that their faith in the Torah could best be preserved by combining prayer with instruction. Thus, worship services included sermons that served to instruct. The preaching tradition had been well established in Judaism during the biblical period, predating Christianity, and long before the New World was explored and colonized.[4]

Biblical passages indicate that, as early as the return to Palestine from Babylon, Hebrew was no longer understood by the masses. This necessitated the use of vernacular translations to explain the law. The first translators of Hebrew into Aramaic were known as meturgemen. It was not very long before the meturgemen began to supplement their verse-by-verse translations of the Torah with personal illustrations and other forms of amplification and explanation. Though the office of meturgeman eventually was discredited, it gave rise to the use of the vernacular within the Hebrew service. The drashah, or sermon, was an outgrowth of the meturgemen's vernacular, often embellished, translations of the Torah. The drashah was not simply an embellished vernacular translation but comes from the Hebrew *darah*, "to search" and "to investigate." The preacher searched and investigated for truth. He then presented his findings to his congregants in the form of a sermon.[5] Hence, the sermon had been a well-established aspect of Jewish services for generations before the New World's existence was even recognized.

However, for reasons that have never been fully explained, sermons largely disappeared from European Jewish services in the late seventeenth and eighteenth centuries. The immigrant Jews of colonial and revolutionary America, excepting perhaps those of Dutch New Amsterdam, had grown up observing their faith with services that did not include sermons. In a religion in which customs and tradition are exceedingly important, most American Jews brought to the New World a Judaism void of sermons. The Jewish religious services of colonial and revolutionary America were conducted in Hebrew, and vernacular sermons were largely nonexistent. The sermon was not a part of the normal Sabbath or holiday service in most parts of Europe. Hence, the practice of preaching was not widespread in the colonies.

A second factor inhibited the development of preaching among colonial Jews. Even if preaching had been a common practice of immigrant Jews, a prospective Jewish preacher would have had difficulty in finding an audience in colonial and revolutionary America. Such was the scarcity of Jews in the colonies.

In 1654, the Dutch colony of Brazil fell to a Portuguese army. Many Dutch residents, including twenty-three Sephardic Jews, fled to New Amsterdam, bringing with them an incipient preaching tradition. The twenty-three Jews who pioneered Jewish settlements of the United States were not immediately joined by large numbers of their coreligionists.[6] On the eve of revolution, 220 years later, the total Jewish population in the colonies was only approximately twenty-five hundred. By 1730, European Jews other than those with a Sephardic tradition composed the majority of colonial Jewry.

The scarcity of Jews in the colonies made the establishment of minyans for worship and synagogues in which to worship unusually difficult. Although Jews had arrived in New Amsterdam in 1654, ten years before it became British and was renamed New York, it was not until 1730 that the first synagogue building was established in New York. This synagogue was home to Shearith Israel (Remnant of Israel), and by 1776, its pulpit was occupied by Gershom Mendes Seixas.

The largest concentration of Jews in colonial America could be found in Newport, Rhode Island, a colony founded by Roger Williams as a haven for religious dissenters. The hospitality of Rhode Island caused almost half the entire Jewish population of the United States to locate in Newport by 1776. While this meant that Newport did have a thriving Jewish community, which erected a synagogue in 1768, it also meant that Jews could scarcely even be found in many other colonies. Maryland, Virginia, and North Carolina, for example, had virtually no Jewish citizens at the time of the Revolution. In addition to New York and Rhode Island, by 1776, there were only organized Jewish communities in three other colonies: Pennsylvania, South Carolina, and Georgia. At the outset of the Revolution, approximately three thousand houses of worship existed in the United States. Of them, only five were synagogues.[7] While there was no lack of potential immigrants among the approximately two million Jews in the world at this time, few of those two million had both the financial means and the willingness to risk a dangerous voyage to a questionable new land.

The third factor inhibiting the development of preaching among colonial Jews was the lack of preachers. Colonial American synagogues were able to do nicely without rabbis. It was not until the 1840s, when Abraham Rice served the Baltimore Jewish community, that a fully ordained rabbi headed an American synagogue. The failure of American synagogues to either import or train rabbis illustrates the role of Jewish religious leaders during the two hundred years from the first Jewish settlements in the colonies, until Rice's arrival in the 1840s. The role of those leaders was such that a well-prepared layperson was normally able to handle the job. Such individuals, who took the title of hazzan, served as cantors and readers. But hazzans were not trained rabbis. The importance of this distinction for the development of a preaching tradition cannot be overlooked.[8]

The hazzans were not ordained. They had not studied Jewish laws and traditions. They were exceptionally proficient in Hebrew and normally could translate it into English and, often in the early synagogues founded by Sephardic Jews, Spanish. However, their knowledge of Judaism was limited. The power that was vested in them came from the lay leadership of the synagogue that employed them, not from any formal recognition of their scholarship, such as seminary graduation or ordination. Hence, they were ill prepared to preach. The typical hazzan had no formal training in subjects that he might turn to for sermons, such as the Talmud, Midrash, and other Jewish literature. Moreover, he had no training in speaking itself.

Finally, hazzans were employed by colonial synagogues without the expectation or desire on the part of the lay leadership that they preach. Given the low wages paid to hazzans, they could scarcely be expected to increase their duties. Making a living as a hazzan was difficult. Normally, it could only be done by supplementing one's salary with a variety of other occupations.[9] Adding preaching to the tasks of the hazzan made no sense: the hazzan was ill prepared for the task; the synagogues were not desirous of the service; and the hazzan needed time to hold other jobs to make a living.

The lack of a preaching tradition in many European Jewish communities during the colonial period carried over to the New World. Coupled with the scarcity of Jews in the New World, the difficulty in gathering minyans for worship, much less developing synagogues, and the lack of rabbinic leadership, the preaching tradition of colonial American Jewry was, not surprisingly, extremely limited.

Initiating the American Jewish Preaching Tradition

The motivation for delivering sermons from Jewish pulpits during the colonial period often did not come from within the Jewish community. Rather, colonial Jewish sermons were often motivated by the civil authorities. Importantly, civil authorities suggested, and Jewish synagogue leadership voluntarily complied. The New World was not Europe.

The first vernacular Jewish sermon given in the American colonies was probably delivered by the Reverend Joseph Jeshurun Pinto, hazzan of Shearith Israel Congregation in New York. Pinto was descended from a well-known rabbinic family and had come to New York from London. He knew English, and it is likely that his sermons were in English, the language with which all his congregants were familiar.[10] However, he might have personally preferred Spanish or Portuguese, with which he was more familiar, and which might have been more pleasing to many members of his Sephardic congregation. Pinto preached several times in the 1760s.[11] Certainly, on August 15, 1763, he preached a sermon of thanksgiving.[12]

Importantly, the first sermons delivered from Jewish pulpits in this country, of which we have records, were occasioned by civil authorities. Pinto's sermon of August 15, 1763, and evidently sermons he may have preached prior to that, were an outgrowth of civil declarations of days of thanksgiving. The English victory over the

French at Montreal and the subsequent surrender of French Canada evidently gave rise to Pinto's sermons. The signing of the peace treaty that ended the French and Indian wars gave rise to Pinto's August 1763 sermon. On this occasion, a day of thanksgiving had been proclaimed for the province of New York by the civil authorities.[13] It was widely observed through religious celebrations and prayers. Like its Christian counterparts, Shearith Israel held a special service, at which Pinto preached, taking as his text Zechariah 2:10:[14]

> Ho, ho, flee then from the land of the north,
> saith the Lord, for I have spread you abroad
> as the four winds of the heaven, saith the Lord.

The French had been forced to flee from the north, from Canada, and the British colonies gave thanks.

The fact that Pinto's sermon was part of a special service, and not part of a normal Sabbath or holiday service, is significant. This appears to be the typical pattern. Virtually every known sermon issuing from a Jewish pulpit in the United States prior to 1830 was given as a consequence of some special event. During the colonial period, sermons were given as a consequence of such things as days of thanksgiving, humiliation, or fasting, which were promulgated by the civil government and gave rise to special religious services of all denominations, including the Jews. One other type of special event gave rise to sermons during the colonial period. On occasion, rabbis from Europe or the holy land visited the colonies, often seeking charitable support for some venture, and these visits were celebrated with a sermon.

The total number of sermons that were delivered from Jewish pulpits during the colonial period is difficult to estimate. Nathan Kagnoff suggests that, as late as 1820, that number may not have exceeded twenty-eight.[15] The number of sermons actually preserved in writing, or written about in the contemporary literature, may be only a fraction of the total number delivered. Those that were preserved or commented upon dealt with matters of interest to non-Jews as well as Jews. The lack of primary sources, as well as the fragmentary nature of existing scholarship, makes it impossible to determine whether preaching took place during normal Jewish services in colonial America. The absence of sermons preached during Sabbath or other services does not conclusively prove that none were preached. The presence of a preaching tradition in a segment of colonial American Jewry, the Sephardic, at least suggests the plausibility of some preaching during this period. However, the number of sermons preached from Jewish pulpits during the colonial period

Gershom Mendes Seixas (1746–1816). Courtesy, American Jewish Archives, Cincinnati, Ohio

is clearly far less than what would be expected from a comparable group of colonial Christian churches and clergymen.

Gershom Seixas: Early Preaching

The outstanding Jewish preacher in prerevolutionary America was Gershom Mendes Seixas, the first native-born hazzan to serve in the colonies. He was born in New York City on January 15, 1746.[16] His father had emigrated from England, hoping to engage in business in the colonies. We know little about Seixas prior to his 1768 election as cantor or hazzan of the Spanish-Portuguese Shearith Israel Congregation, the only synagogue in New York. However, we do know that his father was descended from a family of wealth and learning and that his brother, Benjamin, helped found the New York Stock Exchange.[17] Seixas studied Hebrew and became bar mitzvah at age thirteen, and as a teenager he was apprenticed to learn mechanical trades. No doubt his election was due both to his knowledge of Hebrew and his family connections.

Seixas was not only the preeminent preacher of the early American Jewish pulpit, but he also added new dimensions to the job of hazzan. Prior to Seixas, the principal responsibility of the hazzan was to lead the Hebrew prayers and chants during services. Depending on the community and synagogue, hazzans might also circumcise male children, teach and prepare them for bar mitzvah, and act as shohatim.

By the time that Seixas became hazzan of Shearith Israel in 1768, the influence of the Protestant minister as a role model for religious leaders had begun to permeate the American Jewish community. In Europe the Jewish communities were often largely independent, having relatively little contact with the world around them. The role of the rabbi as scholar and teacher was well defined and maintained. But in the colonies Jews mingled freely and equally with other citizens. They perceived the roles that ministers played, not only as scholars and teachers, but also as counselors to their congregants, as social workers, and as agitators for social change. Particularly in these last capacities, the sermon was the major tool utilized by the Protestant minister. With models of this nature, the responsibilities of the hazzan began to change in the decades immediately preceding the revolution.

Those changes were primarily in two areas. First, the hazzan gradually became more of a pastor, concerning himself with the personal and spiritual welfare of his congregants. Seixas was among the first hazzans to concern himself actively with these matters.

Whether his concern was a consequence of the influence of his Christian contemporaries, whose pastoring activities constituted a major portion of their jobs, or whether it was because of his warm personality is hard to judge. Presumably, both factors entered into his assumption of these extra duties. Regardless of the cause, Seixas became immersed in these activities. He provided leadership to the community when epidemics struck. He worked on behalf of the needy by establishing a major charitable organization. Often he utilized sermons to advance the causes he supported. Frequently, when epidemics struck or when charity was particularly necessary, he used the occasion for a special service, which included a sermon.[18]

The second change in the hazzan's responsibilities involved the use of sermons even more than the growing pastoral role. During the late colonial period and in the years that followed, the civil authorities frequently called on the nation's religious leaders for support. When the colonial or state legislatures or the federal government declared days of fasting, penitence, thanks, humiliation, or celebration, they invariably asked the clergy to participate by leading special services. In the Jewish communities the responsibility to direct such services fell on the hazzan. Slowly but surely, he became the spokesperson of the Jewish community to the rest of society. It was in response to these civilly inspired occasions that Gershom Seixas became the outstanding Jewish pulpit orator of the revolutionary and early national periods of American history.

Though Seixas delivered many sermons, including an annual sermon on behalf of Kalfe Sedaka, the charity he founded, he is perhaps best known for his sermons given during the midst of civilly inspired services. The first such sermon of which we have a written record is undated, but it must have been given during the revolutionary war. This "Prayer for Peace" probably lasted no more than five to seven minutes, and information about the circumstances of its delivery cannot be found. Nevertheless, references to George Washington as "commander of the army of these states" at least indicate its wartime delivery.[19]

Seixas's "Prayer for Peace" is a predictable speech. There is virtually nothing in it that would mark it as uniquely Jewish. Rather, it is a prayer that might have been offered by virtually any clergyman supporting the revolution. Seixas opens by calling on God to "save and prosper the men of these United States who have gone forth to war."[20] He continues, asking the Lord to fight for and protect the patriot troops who serve on land and ship, as well as their rulers, their leaders, and their allies. "We beseech thee, O most gracious and merciful King to whom peace pertaineth," says Seixas in his conclusion, that thou wilt cause us to enjoy a firm Peace and Tranquility and spread over us the Tabernacle of peace everlastingly, speedily permit that amongst us may be heard the voice of him who bringeth glad tidings, announcing that the Reedemer cometh to Zion. Amen, so may it be.[21]

This prayer does evidence some of the positive characteristics of Seixas's preaching. He utilizes vivid language and seems to have a sense of rhythm. But it is surely not an exceptionally masterful work. Given the theme, the content is highly predictable.

Though he had counseled for peace, with the onset of the revolution, Seixas immediately sided with the colonials.[22] In the summer of 1776, with the British occupation of New York imminent, Seixas and many other revolutionary sympathizers fled the city. Tradition, fostered in part by Seixas's descendants, has it that by August of 1776, with the British landing on Long Island and with New York City within range of British artillery, Seixas gave a vehement address, calling on the Jewish community to leave New York and stand with the revolutionaries. Whether he actually gave such an address seems to be a matter of conjecture.[23] Nevertheless, most of the Jewish community of New York, including its hazzan, sympathized with the Revolution and fled. Seixas, taking the synagogue scrolls and ornaments for safekeeping, fled to Stratford, Connecticut, and subsequently to Philadelphia. During his stay in Philadelphia he was elected hazzan of Mikveh Israel. Hence, Seixas had the distinction of at one time heading both of the leading congregations in the new nation. He returned to New York in 1784, to again serve Shearith Israel, remaining there for the rest of his life.[24]

Gershom Seixas: Preaching for a New Nation

Seixas's sermon to Shearith Israel on the first Thanksgiving illustrates his speaking at midcareer. Coming nine months after the first presidential election, seven months after the creation of the Department of State, and two months after the creation of the Treasury Department and the office of attorney general, the new nation had much for which to be thankful. It had successfully challenged the British Empire and won. It was in the process of successfully creating a new government. No less than Thomas Jefferson, who coined the phrase, American Jews perceived their new nation as an "Empire for Liberty."[25] They enthusiastically joined their Christian neighbors in honoring the president's proclamation that Thursday,

November 26 "be observed as a day of Public Thanksgiving and Prayer."[26]

The Thanksgiving service that Seixas prepared for his congregants had six sections:

1. Chanting of five psalms
2. Discourse [Seixas's sermon]
3. Prayer for the rulers of the United States
4. Prayer for the Congregation
5. Portions of the Festive Morning Service from Kol Israel to the end of Adon Olam
6. Final Prayer[27]

Seixas's sermon evidences several characteristics that were typical of his speaking. It is clearly organized, it makes good use of vivid, concrete language, and it illustrates an awareness of rhythm.

No doubt because of the similarity between many of the situations in which he delivered sermons, Seixas frequently utilized the same basic thesis. This sermon is no exception. Like many of his sermons, the thesis of this one is that few, if any, nations have been as good for Jews and Judaism as the United States. As a consequence, Jews should actively support the government of the United States.[28]

Seixas develops this thesis by following what was his standard pattern of organization. He opens with a thesis, drawn from text. For this speech he uses Psalm 100, in which King David asks all to make a "joyful noise unto the Lord" and "enter into his presence with singing."[29]

Having presented his text and thesis, Seixas moves to the body of his speech. Typically, he utilizes three major points in the body of his sermons. In this sermon the first point he develops in the body is that the outcome of the revolution and the adoption of the Constitution has resulted in making Jews "equal partakers of every benefit that results from this good government." As a consequence, he continues, we must ask, "How can we show our gratitude?"[30] This question serves as a transition to his second point.

David, Seixas tells his audience, concluded that the only way he could show gratitude to the Lord was to acknowledge his dependence on the Lord and the benefits he received from the Lord by proclaiming his greatness. Seixas points out that this has been a characteristic of Jewish history and offers repeated examples of occasions when Jews gave public thanks to the Lord for his aid. After this seven-page review of Jewish history, the most extensive section of the sermon, he concludes, "From the foregoing you will naturally observe the duties we owe our Creator."[31] Clearly, he suggests, days of public thanksgiving are entirely consistent with Jewish history and tradition.

Seixas's third major point is that, in addition to the duties we owe our creator, there are also "duties we owe to ourselves and the community to which we belong."[32] He finds two such duties. First,

it is necessary that we, each of us in our respective situation behave in such a manner as to give strength and stability to the laws entered into by our representatives; to consider the burden imposed on those who are appointed to act in the executive department, to contribute, as much as lays in our power, to support that government which is founded upon the strictest principles of equal liberty and justice.[33]

The second duty that Jews owe to themselves and to the community, claims Seixas, is to become "living evidences of his divine power and unity. . . . to live as Jews ought to do in brotherhood and amity, to seek peace and pursue it."[34]

In effect, the conclusion of Seixas's sermon is the prayer for the government, which follows in the program. That prayer calls upon God "to bless, preserve, guard, and assist the President and Vice President of the Union, The Senate and House of Representatives of the United States of America, the Governor, Lt. Governor, and People of this State, the Judges and Magistrates of this city and all Kings and Potentates in alliance with these States."[35]

This sermon is highly characteristic of Seixas's civilly inspired sermons. The basic message of the sermon is that the United States has been good to Jews and that Jews in turn should be productive citizens of the United States. It opens with a textual passage that is amplified into the thesis. The body illustrates the thesis through three clear divisions. The conclusion is brief but appropriate. Although Seixas's delivery may have been somewhat formal and stiff,[36] the sermon clearly makes its major points. The language is appropriate, and when read aloud, the sermon suggests Seixas's sense of rhythm and timing.

Seixas's thanksgiving sermons, given on national days of thanksgiving or, as in 1799 and 1804, when New York City or the state called for a day of thanksgiving, were either highly patriotic or were centered around charity. He frequently used a thanksgiving service as an occasion to call for charitable acts from his congregation. His sermon of December 20, 1804, illustrates this type of sermon.

In the winter of 1804, several parts of the country were hit by an epidemic. Fortunately for Seixas and his congregants, the epidemic did not reach New York City. As a consequence, the city government recommended that all clergy lead their congregations in services of public thanksgiving and prayer on December 20.

Seixas's introduction was based on Psalm 62: "to thee O Lord is loving kindness, and Thou wilt requite each according to his deeds."[37] Seixas amplifies this passage to develop his thesis.[38] His explanation of the passage relates it to the good fortune of New York City in being spared by the epidemic. He concludes that his congregation should be thankful and should express their thanks by performing God's duties. "Among the various duties we owe to our heavenly Father," he continues, "there are none perhaps more important than attending to the poor, the widow, and the orphan."[39]

Having established his thesis, Seixas then proceeds to illustrate it from scripture. He cites the actions of Moses, Jeremiah, and David to illustrate the importance of charity. He then concludes that charity is a complex term, with at least three meanings. These meanings form the threefold division of the topic, which constitutes the remainder of the sermon.

The original Hebrew term for charity, Seixas claims, involved three different "lights": charity, justice, and righteousness.[40] Charity, he continues, makes both the giver and the recipient feel good. Justice demands that we utilize charity for those in distress. Righteousness suggests that we have the most honorable of motives and do not benefit in giving. All three of the "lights" should guide our charitable acts. Moreover, unless we are charitable, Seixas suggests, we may face trouble in the next world.[41]

Seixas closes by summarizing his major points. As in his Thanksgiving sermon of 1789, he moves directly into a prayer for Congress and other government agencies, including in this case, the schools. The prayer effectively serves as the sermon's conclusion.

This sermon is typical of Seixas's preaching in several ways: it was prompted by the civil authorities, and it dealt with one of his two basic themes, charity. Although the introduction is unusually long, it follows his basic organizational pattern that incorporates an introduction utilizing a text, a body involving a threefold division of the topic, and a conclusion making use of a final prayer.

While most of Seixas's civilly inspired sermons were given on occasions for which it was appropriate to utilize one of his two major themes—the patriotic responsibilities of American Jews toward a land that had been kind to them, and the desirability of charity—these themes were not always appropriate. On May 9, 1798, in response to President John Adams's call for a day of fasting, prayer, and national humiliation, Seixas gave one of the rare sermons that deviated from his two principal themes.

In 1796 and 1797, France had seized at least 316 American merchant ships and mistreated many of their crews. The French had claimed that these vessels, loaded fully or in part with goods of British manufacture, were providing aid and assistance to Britain in its conflict with France. Americans felt that these seizures were a clear violation of their rights as a neutral nation.[42]

President John Adams sent a diplomatic mission to France, seeking to resolve the difficulties. However, the French continued their attacks upon American shipping and even tried to extort money from the American diplomats, suggesting that France would cease its hostile actions and would sign a treaty to that effect only if the United States made a $12,800,000 loan to France and also paid bribes of $250,000 to several key figures in the French Ministry of Foreign Affairs.[43]

News of this attempt at bribery quickly became public. The three French agents who had suggested the bribe were dubbed agents X, Y, and Z by President Adams, and the entire episode took on that name. The XYZ affair gave rise to the slogan "Millions for defense, but not one cent for tribute." However, while Americans generally reacted negatively to the entire affair, many still remembered the help France had provided in the war for independence and still harbored resentment toward the British. The Federalist, pro-British Congress passed the Alien and Sedition Acts, limiting freedom of speech and of the press. These acts also put restrictions on aliens and made naturalization much more difficult. All of these Federalist acts were aimed at French sympathizers, who generally supported their political opposition, the Republicans. Hence, the XYZ affair triggered considerable political controversy. The very constitutionality of these acts, the political repression that they created, and the continuing unofficial naval war with France all gave rise to deep public rifts. In this context, with a new nation experiencing for the first time sharp internal divisions at home as it sought to deal with the rest of the world, President Adams declared May 9, 1798, a day of fasting, prayer, and humiliation.

Shearith Israel, similar to the churches of the day and to the nation as a whole, also had its share of both Federalists and Republicans. However, Seixas's remarks would not have offended either group. Indeed, he did not discuss the immediate events that had precipitated Adams's designation of May 9 as a day of fasting, prayer, and humiliation. He avoided attacking the French, nor did he comment on the naval war or other events of the day. In this respect Seixas differed markedly from his contemporaries in the Christian pulpit.

Christian pulpits had, from the very inception of the country, utilized current events as subjects for sermons. Well before the

American Revolution, and especially in the years immediately preceding the Revolution, Christian clergymen preached on secular issues. However, American Jewish preachers virtually never spoke on secular issues. Again, in 1798, Seixas made no attempt to sermonize on the issues of the day.

The service at Shearith Israel was divided into seven sections, as follows:

1. Prayers by the Reader—Repeated by the Congregation
2. Psalms XLVI and LI Chanted by the Reader and then the Congregation
3. Prayer by the Reader
4. The Discourse in English
5. Prayer for the United States and Administrators of the Government
6. Prayer for the Congregation
7. Psalms 120, 121, 130, and 20 Chanted jointly by Reader and Congregation[44]

Seixas opened his sermon by quoting Psalm 133: "Behold how good and pleasant it is for brethren to dwell together in Unity."[45] From this starting point, he develops his thesis, that "union in society" should "be deemed one of the greatest blessings."[46] Seixas amplifies his passage from the psalm, and develops his thesis by drawing on aspects of King David's life. With the thesis clearly stated, he then notes that he will not "enter into any civil or political discussion." Instead, he will confine himself "to the nature and consequences of such actions as are consistent with the true spirit and principle of religion."[47]

Seixas develops the body of his sermon by observing that we must seek strength from within ourselves, and to attain that strength we must first confess our sins and turn from evil. Second, we must seek peace. Finally, we must supplicate ourselves.[48] Each of these three points is developed in the body of his sermon.

In calling on his congregation to confess their sins and turn from evil, Seixas is specifically concerned with sins in which one's own interests and excessive pride are placed ahead of society's larger interests. He utilizes biblical examples of ill-fated rebellions against Moses and Aaron to make his point.[49] He amplifies his second major point, that we must seek peace, or more precisely "union in society," by calling on his congregation to strictly adhere "to the grand principles of benevolence towards all our fellow creatures."[50] This is the most extensive section of the sermon. He discusses Jeremiah, the second book of Kings, Leviticus, and several psalms, in an attempt to illustrate the principles of benevolence that, if followed by all, will create union in society. From his examination of these works, he concludes that the principles of benevolence include charity, mercy, and piety.[51]

The final point that Seixas develops in the body of his sermon is that we must supplicate ourselves to God, "to promote the welfare of these states."[52] Here Seixas returns to a favorite theme, stressing that in America Jews possess "every advantage that other citizens of these states enjoy and which is as much as we could in reason expect."[53] Hence, he feels, Jews should certainly be willing to promote the welfare of the United States. He stresses that this is important not just for the present generation of American Jews, but also for future generations of Jews who might also enjoy the blessings of America.[54]

The blessings America has provided her Jewish citizens— economic and political equality—should not, Seixas argues in this sermon, lull American Jews into forgetting that they are still exiles from Zion. As Raphael Mahler has illustrated, Seixas suggests in several of his patriotic sermons that, by being patriotic Americans, Jews can also expedite the return to Zion.[55] In this sermon Seixas applies his text, "Behold how good and how pleasant it is for brethren to dwell together in Unity," not only to domestic national unity, but also to the situation confronting Jews scattered throughout the Diaspora. If American Jews behave in the fashion that Seixas has described in this sermon, contributing to American society "a gathering of mankind . . . composed of all classes and types of human beings, gathered from different lands, and in which everyone brings with him the ancient statutes of the government in which he was educated," then, Seixas argues, they will be paving the way for God to fulfill what is written in Ezekiel: "and I will take you from the nations and gather you from all the lands and bring you to your land."[56] Thus, Seixas uses his patriotic sermons to suggest that the success of the unique American experiment in democracy and the contribution of American Jews to that success are linked to the eventual return of Jews to their own homeland.

Seixas concludes this sermon as he began it, by returning to his theme that brethren should dwell together in unity. This thesis differs from the two principal themes that Seixas normally developed in his civilly inspired sermons, though even in this thesis the patriotic duty of American Jews to their new nation is evident in his third major point. Otherwise, this sermon is highly analogous to his other preaching: it opens with a text, which is then amplified into the thesis; the thesis is followed by a body consisting of a threefold analysis of the text; his conclusion leaves the audience with a clear sense of closure; and his language is clear and vivid.

Gershom Seixas: Charity Sermons

Seixas's charity sermons evidence the same basic characteristics of his patriotic sermons. They were not part of the normal Sabbath or holiday services. Typically, they were given on two types of occasions: first, as we have seen, in response to special events which the civil authorities felt warranted commemoration; second, on special days his congregation designated for the collection of charity. Normally, Seixas delivered a sermon on behalf of tzedakah on such occasions. Typical of such sermons was his sermon of January 11, 1807. Seixas notes that he preached "in compliance with the request of the trustees [of Shearith Israel], for the sake of the fund appropriated to private charity."[57]

Seixas's charity sermons are organized identically to his patriotic sermons. They make use of a text at the outset, which is then amplified into the thesis. In his sermon of 1807, Seixas selects Psalm 41 as his text: "blessed is he who considereth the poor, in the day of evil the Lord will deliver him."[58] This text is then explained and illustrated by several biblical passages, allowing Seixas to state his thesis that charities must be supported.[59]

Having introduced his sermon with a text and developed the text into his thesis, Seixas then develops the body of the sermon by examining three major aspects of his thesis. This threefold analysis of the thesis in charity sermons is identical to his procedure in patriotic sermons.

In this instance Seixas finds that his congregation must practice and support charity "in respect to religion," "in respect to morality," and "in respect to society."[60] Charity must be supported for religious reasons, he argues, because we must observe God's commandments and express thanks for his blessings and mercy by considering the poor "with benevolence."[61] Charity must be supported for moral reasons, he argues, because "uniting morality with principles of religion teaches us to do unto others what we would they should do unto us."[62] Our worldly riches, he observes, should be used according to moral doctrines in works of charity.[63] Charity must be supported for social reasons, he argues, because when we enter into society with others we take on responsibilities for our fellow man.[64] Each of these three points is fully developed in the fifteen-page body of this sermon.

Finally, as in his patriotic sermons, Seixas has a clear and distinct conclusion. In this instance, he closes with a call for contributions.[65] Seixas cites Job, Moses, King David, and others who have done what his audience should do.[66]

Gershom Mendes Seixas became the outstanding American Jewish preacher of his day. However, the paucity of preaching in American Judaism at this time meant that the total number of sermons he delivered in his entire life was probably less than an active Christian minister might have delivered in one year. Moreover, Seixas was called to his position of leadership without a rabbinic education, a college education, or even a high school education. Most of the outstanding Christian clergymen of his day were far better educated than Seixas. For understandable reasons such as these, Seixas's sermons do not have the artistic merit that the sermons of many of the outstanding Christian clergymen of his time evidence.

Seixas's sermons are workmanlike, but they do not compare favorably with those of a Jonathan Mayhew, a Jonathan Edwards, a Samuel Seabury, a John Witherspoon, or others who might represent the very best of American Christian preaching of this era. They lack the artistic merit of the sermons of such men as these. Put bluntly, Seixas's basic mastery of the English language was not equal to his most outstanding Christian contemporaries. Often his sentence structure makes passages of his sermons awkward and difficult. While his overall organizational structure is clear, his three major points often lack any guiding or coherent principle to unify them. Little is known of his ability to deliver sermons, but the very absence of any widespread commentary suggests that as a speaker he did little to excite his audiences. This is not to suggest that his oral delivery was poor. Rather, the lack of comments by his audiences likely speaks more to the infrequency of his sermons and the probability of his workmanlike delivery. In sum, it is unfair to even attempt to compare Seixas to his Christian counterparts. They came from a tradition that valued, encouraged, and fostered outstanding preaching. Seixas did not. They were provided weekly, if not more frequent, opportunities to preach. Seixas was not. Perhaps most importantly, they had extensive formal educations. Seixas had none. Yet Seixas served his congregation well.[67] Shearith Israel called on him to preach on a limited number of occasions and in well-defined situations. Though his sermons were often similar in theme, support material, and language, it is likely that they were well received.[68] Gershom Seixas helped to lay the groundwork for the development of the American Jewish preaching tradition. He is best remembered not as the most skilled or outstanding practitioner of that tradition, but rather as a pioneer.

2

Jewish Preaching in
Jacksonian America

Between the death of Gershom Seixas, in July of 1816, and the year 1830, American Jewish preaching underwent little outward change. However, in Europe the first three decades of the nineteenth century were filled with changes that were subsequently to have a dramatic impact on the American Jewish community. Not the least of those changes involved preaching.

European Influences on American Preaching

The end of the eighteenth century and the first decades of the nineteenth century saw the rise of Reform Judaism in Europe, particularly in Germany. While practices differed from community to community, the most typical reforms introduced into the practices of German Jewry during this period involved fundamental changes in both beliefs and customs.[1]

Reform beliefs ultimately found expression in the work of Abraham Geiger, who claimed, along with others, that Judaism was a living institution. As such, its heart and spirit were not to be altered. But as with all living things, its form was subject to change. Thus, Jews had two responsibilities. They had a responsibility to be true to the heart of Judaism, its fundamental beliefs, but they also had a duty to delve into their faith and modify those beliefs, customs, and traditions in ways appropriate for each generation. Among the major beliefs that underwent change was one that was ultimately to have special importance for American Reform Judaism. German Reformers deleted all reference to the restoration of a national homeland in Zion from their prayer book. These deletions no doubt were to suggest that German Jews had found a home in Germany. As we will see, American Reform Judaism ultimately adopted a similar attitude toward a national homeland.

The German Reform movement altered a variety of Jewish customs. It advocated a more relaxed observance of both the Sabbath and the rules of Kashruth. Moreover, it made a variety of reforms in the service itself. Among the major changes advanced were shortening services, replacing much of the Hebrew with German, seating women with men, adding organ music to the service, and, perhaps most importantly, adding a vernacular sermon to the normal Sabbath and holiday services.

The addition of a vernacular sermon to the service was a consequence of a variety of influences. At the end of the eighteenth century, many German Jewish schools had developed the practice of providing students with "devotional hours." A religious address became an essential part of these devotional hours. Gradually, the audiences for these addresses grew to include not simply the students, but also their parents and friends.[2]

A second pervasive influence was the Christian community. Just as Seixas had been influenced by the clergymen around him to transform the role of the hazzan, so too were German Reformers influenced by the Protestant clergymen around them.[3] Prior to the rise of German Reform Judaism, the primary function of the rabbi was to serve as an authority on Jewish law and as a teacher. The functions of preacher and pastor were not part of the rabbi's duties. The typical rabbi spoke only twice a year, almost exclusively on a talmudic subject. Hence, as Michael A. Meyer argues, "at the turn of the nineteenth century the rabbinate in Germany consisted of men trained to this traditional role and quite unwilling and, indeed, incapable of preaching a vernacular sermon."[4]

However, Reform-minded Jews, primarily found in the larger cities, desired services more analogous to their Christian neighbors. Hence, they sought a new type of leader. Many of these synagogues were soon headed by both a rabbi, who served the traditional functions, and a prediger, who assumed the sermonic and pastoral duties.[5] Gradually, as the older generation of rabbis died, a new generation of men, trained in both sermonic and pastoral functions as well as Jewish law, emerged to unify the leadership of the German Reform congregations under rabbis who could not only argue Jewish law, but who could also preach. This transformation was essentially completed in the German Reform pulpits by 1830.[6]

A third influence contributing to the development of preaching in German Reform Judaism was the influence of civil authorities. On March 17, 1808, Napoléon's government required rabbis in those areas of Germany occupied by France to know the language of the country. Moreover, that same edict specified that preaching would be among the rabbi's duties.[7]

A final influence on the development of preaching in German Reform Judaism was the influence of the early Reform preachers themselves. They set precedents that were soon followed by many others. Joseph Wolf is credited with initiating the sermon in 1808, in the Reform synagogue at Dessau. Wolf delivered his initial sermon in 1808 on the occasion of the fiftieth jubilee of Duke Leopold, with the duke himself present in the synagogue.[8] However, unlike the many civilly inspired sermons delivered prior to 1808 in America, this sermon was used by Wolf to initiate regular German language preaching in Dessau. Wolf's preaching and his coediting of a journal that frequently argued on behalf of preaching[9] contributed to the push toward making sermons a normal feature of the German Reform service.

In little over two decades, between 1808 and 1830, German language sermons had also spread to some conservative and orthodox German Jewish communities. In 1827, Bavarian authorities required an examination in rhetoric for all rabbinic candidates. In the decade 1830–40, preaching in German had become an established feature of Jewish services in many communities of Germany, including Würzburg, Bernburg, Offenbach, Wiesbaden, Magdeburg, Königsberg, Dresden, Teplitz, Breslau, and Berlin.[10]

The sermons preached in German Reform temples during the period 1808–40 were substantially different from the traditional Jewish drashah.[11] First, the topics dealt with by the German Reform preachers were different from those dealt with by their predecessors. Traditional Judaism was minimized. Rather, a religion of rational humanity, based on Enlightenment philosophy, developed from these sermons. Topics that were specifically Jewish were rarely treated. Rabbinic literature was rarely used. A more universal faith, based on reason and biblical scripture, emerged from these sermons.[12] Such a faith suggested that Jewish concerns were similar to Christian concerns and that Jewish reaction to those concerns was somewhat similar to Christian reaction. Such sermons no doubt aimed, in part, at integrating German Jews into their predominantly Christian community.

While the Reform sermon was the predominant mode of German Jewish preaching to which several American Jewish preachers of the Jacksonian period were exposed, it was not initially transplanted into America. Rather, the few English language preachers that followed Seixas remained true to their more orthodox Jewish faith.

Though there is no evidence that Isaac Leeser or any of the handful of English language sermonists of Jacksonian America ever heard Leopold Zunz preach, they had more in common with his approach than with many of the German Reformers. Zunz attempted to reestablish a strong Jewish tradition in the content of the German Jewish sermon.[13]

However, Zunz often practiced the second distinction between the German Reform sermons and the traditional drashah: the utilization of largely Protestant models in sermon organization and form. The widespread availability of prescriptive homiletics and treatises on preaching designed for the Christian clergyman and the lack of similar materials for the rabbi, the apparent effectiveness of many Christian clergymen with their audiences, and, indeed, the willingness of some Christian clergy to instruct young Jewish preachers all combined to make the early German Jewish sermon similar in form to those that were popular in the Christian churches.[14] Alexander Altmann provides us with an insightful description of the distinction between this new sermon form and the traditional drashah when he writes that the sermons of Germany

had evolved into a type of pulpit oratory decidedly different from the genre of the homily. It was not to be an exegetical discourse on scriptural verses loosely strung together but was to be a disquisition on some definite theme based on a text and presented according to a well-defined pattern of component parts. It was to be "synthetic" as distinct from the "analytic" homily. It had to avoid the scholastic aspects of the older dogmatic sermon, and the preacher was advised to shun subject matters and terms of too technical a nature. Its purpose was to "edify" the congregation, and it was to achieve this aim by observing the rules laid down in the manuals of homiletics. The customary parts of the sermon were the exordium, the prayer, the exposition, and the blessing.[15]

This was the type of sermon that early nineteenth-century German Jewish preachers attempted to imitate. Again, their American Jewish counterparts did not follow their lead.

Though the American Jewish preachers of the Jacksonian period did not adopt the major changes in the drashah that German Reformers were introducing into their sermons, the very fact that German Reformers had popularized the sermon by the decade 1820–30 and had made changes to it ultimately had an impact on American Judaism. The fact that vernacular preaching was a common practice in German Jewish communities no doubt made it far easier for American advocates of vernacular sermons to persuade reluctant members of their synagogues to allow preaching in the normal Sabbath and holiday services. Additionally, while such preachers as Isaac Leeser were to reject the principal changes made by German Reform Jews when they introduced English language sermons into American Sabbath and holiday services, later American Jewish preachers were more prone to accept many of the German innovations.

By the 1830s, with the publication of Leopold Zunz's *Sermons of the Jews* and the homiletic work of Ludwig Philippson, German Jewry was making a conscious effort to produce a uniquely Jewish sermon.[16] Since sermons were used in an ever-increasing number of German synagogues, they were patterned less and less upon Christian models and more and more upon the traditional Jewish homily, or drashah. Gotthold Salomon, preaching at the Reform Temple of Hamburg, is credited with bringing to fruition a new Jewish homiletic. By 1850, Salomon and others were preaching sermons that relied on rabbinic literature and traditions as well as biblical traditions. They were uniquely Jewish and were widely accepted. Thus, though the Jewish sermon had been fostered primarily by the Protestant example in the first portion of the nineteenth century, by the middle of the century, German Jewish sermons were uniquely Jewish in content and structure.

The use of sermons in Germany spread to other parts of Europe in the first half of the nineteenth century. Importantly for a study of American Jewish sermons, the practice of preaching crossed the English Channel by November 19, 1817. On that date Tobias Goodman gave what is generally accepted as the first English language sermon as part of a service in Great Britain. More importantly, in 1828, a committee of elders of the Bevis Marks Sephardic Synagogue of London, perhaps the most prestigious synagogue in England, was established to determine how services might be improved. Among their recommendations was the suggestion that an English sermon be delivered every Saturday afternoon. Such a sermon, the elders recommended, should be based on a text taken from scripture and should be approved by a committee of three elders before delivery, to ensure that it contain no statements hostile or contrary to either Jewish doctrine or the institutions of Great Britain.[17]

The circumstances surrounding the introduction of regular weekly sermons at Bevis Marks illustrate two aspects of sermon making that affected American preachers of this period as well. First, perhaps in response to the perceived excesses of German Reformers, the sermons delivered at Bevis Marks were clearly under the control of a committee of lay leaders. Conflicts between lay leaders and spiritual leaders of the synagogue were to plague many congregations in the United States. Often that conflict arose over sermon content. Second, the sermons delivered at Bevis Marks were to be based specifically on a text from scripture. Though this practice was followed by many American Jewish preachers during the period 1830–50, the appropriateness of grounding a sermon on other materials and on treating contemporary social and political events from the pulpit was an issue of controversy in America.

By 1830, the practice of having a sermon delivered in the vernacular as a part of a normal Sabbath or holiday service, though still a part of the entire Reform-Orthodox controversy, had became reasonably established at many European synagogues and was on its way toward far more universal acceptance by midcentury. Nevertheless, the very desirability of such preaching was itself still a controversy. Moreover, additional controversies, such as those over the content and form of such sermons, existed. Yet in little over two decades, preaching had become a relatively common practice in many Jewish services throughout Europe. Such was the practice of preaching with which many Jewish immigrants to the United States were familiar in the first decades of the nineteenth century.

Isaac Leeser: Background

One such immigrant from Germany was Isaac Leeser, who was destined to become the most significant American Jewish figure of the first half of the nineteenth century. Leeser was born in Neunkirchen, a small town in Prussian Westphalia, on December 12, 1806. His mother died when he was seven, but through the efforts of relatives, he received a good education. Living in Düelmen and Münster, Leeser studied Hebrew, Latin, and German, in part at German Catholic gymnasiums.[18] Nevertheless, by the age of eighteen, Leeser did not have an especially promising future in Germany. Hence, in 1824, when his uncle Zalma Rehine, a successful Richmond, Virginia, merchant urged him to come to the United States and start a career in business, Leeser did so.

He arrived in the United States at a time when the entire American Jewish community probably numbered no more than seven to ten thousand.[19] The religious leader of the Richmond Jewish community at the time of Leeser's arrival in 1824 was Isaac Seixas, a nephew of Gershom Seixas.

Isaac Leeser (1806–1868). Courtesy, American Jewish Archives, Cincinnati, Ohio

Perhaps because Leeser's uncle had married into the Seixas family, the young immigrant, who had quickly mastered English, was soon directing the religious school of Isaac Seixas's synagogue. In 1828, Leeser responded, in fluent English, to articles in *The Richmond Whig* that were critical of British Jewry. Leeser's response was well received and was widely circulated in American Jewish circles. This caused the governing board of Congregation Mikveh Israel of Philadelphia to invite Leeser to apply for their vacant position as hazzan. Leeser did so, and based on the recommendations he received from the Jewish community in Richmond and on his reputation as a writer, he was awarded an initial three-year contract.

Leeser later recalled the circumstances surrounding his appointment as hazzan of Mikveh Israel:

I was at that time only a few months over twenty-two years old, and had not thought of ever becoming the minister of any congregation, and was induced solely under the persuasion that by being in public life I could become useful to the Jewish community.[20]

Leeser noted that his duties as hazzan "were confined to the conducting of the public worship in the synagogue and elsewhere, and it was not expected that he [the hazzan] should be at the same time a preacher and exhorter."[21] However, Leeser observed that

it had appeared to me as an incongruity, that words of instruction formed no part of our regular service; and having been summoned on account of some literary efforts produced in Richmond to accept the trust with which the voice of a large majority of the Israelites of Philadelphia honoured me, I had indulged the hope that I would be requested immediately after my election to give discourses on our religion in the language of the country.[22]

Leeser's background prior to serving as hazzan was as a religious schoolteacher and director. His desire to provide instruction within the framework of the service seems to be a natural outgrowth of this perspective. Moreover, Leeser recalled that as a boy in Europe he had heard sermons and that those sermons had left a strong impression upon him.[23] Presumably, he hoped that by introducing English sermons to American services he might inculcate lessons into American Jewish youth and set an example that other Jewish leaders might follow.[24] Moreover, Leeser believed that preaching was justified by Jewish tradition. He claimed that oratory was cultivated in the schools of the prophets, soon after the schism of Israel and Judah.[25]

English Sermons Win Acceptance in America

Nine months after assuming his duties at Mikveh Israel, Leeser sent a letter to the synagogue Board of Adjuncts, asking them if his speaking in the synagogue would meet with their consent. Though a formal meeting was not held, a majority of the adjuncts sent unofficial personal responses indicating their approval.[26] Hence, on June 2, 1830, Isaac Leeser became the first American Jewish leader to preach on a regular basis during normal services. Initially, Leeser prepared and delivered an English language sermon every two weeks and on some special occasions.

The introduction of English sermons into the weekly service was not the occasion for as great a controversy in the United States as the use of vernacular sermons had been in many of the synagogues of Europe. In Europe the use of vernacular sermons was intimately bound to the Reform movement. Typically, vernacular sermons were part of a large group of changes by which Reformers effected both the manner of observing Judaism and some of the principal tenets of Jewish belief.

But in the United States the English sermon was introduced into the service by a staunch defender of the Orthodox tradition. In the pages of his paper, in his many public speeches, and, indeed, in virtually every aspect of his life, Isaac Leeser personified the Orthodox Jewish tradition. His *Occident and Jewish Advocate*, the first Jewish paper in the United States, was the primary organ of Orthodox Judaism in this country. Its pages were repeatedly marked by Leeser's clashes with the Reformers, particularly Isaac M. Wise.

As Lance Sussman has persuasively argued, Leeser might be characterized as having "Protestanized" the outward form of American Judaism. He did so by the introduction of such features as the sermon, Sunday schools, and attempts to upgrade the standards of religious leadership. However, his reforms were almost invariably of Jewish practices, not beliefs.[27] They were pragmatic attempts to meet the exigencies created by living in a predominantly Christian country, far removed from the centers of Jewish learning and scholarship. Leeser rarely deviated from preaching Orthodox Judaism.

Leeser felt that Orthodox Judaism was in perfect harmony with reason. "Thought and reflection," he claimed,

are a duty which we, as rational beings destined for ulterior happiness owe to our heavenly Father. Besides this, brethren, religion, such a religion at least as we possess, may be investigated, may be sifted, and exposed, and the freest inquiry cannot injure it.[28]

Leeser's orthodoxy was not that of a blind adherent to old traditions. Rather, it was that of an individual who believed in man as a rational being. But unlike the German Reformers, Leeser utilized reason not to undermine traditional Orthodox beliefs and practices but to champion them.[29] The strict traditional views he espoused in his sermons clearly dissociated the introduction of English language sermons in the United States from the basic Reform-Orthodox controversy with which vernacular sermons had been connected in Europe.

Moreover, regarding his sermons, Leeser engaged in at least three practices that also reduced the possibility of any controversy. First, he no doubt reduced the controversy that might have surrounded the introduction of English sermons into the service by placing them at the very end of the service. Those who did not wish to hear the sermon or who thought it inappropriate might leave before the sermon, and they would have still attended a complete religious service.

Leeser concluded the entire Hebrew service and then offered a prayer in English. This English prayer was typically the opening prayer for the sermon that followed. Though later such preachers as Morris J. Raphall, and Leeser himself in later years, moved the sermon to a slightly earlier position in the service, Leeser initially placed it at the very end. The sermon was an appendage that in no fashion would interfere with the service. It was provided by Leeser for the edification of those who might wish it, though he observed at the outset of his first sermon, "I cannot deny that many members of our society are sufficiently acquainted with their duties and need not be reminded of them by any preacher, however eloquent."[30]

Second, Leeser's sermons dealt exclusively with religious themes. Leeser virtually never used the sermon to speak about current affairs or popular books. Unlike his Christian contemporaries, such as Wendell Phillips, Theodore Parker, and Henry Ward Beecher, Leeser objected to the use of politics in the pulpit. He repeatedly denied the importance of politics and current events to religion and claimed that they were not within the province of religion.[31] His sermons were essentially attempts at explaining the Torah and other biblical works, so that, in his words, "the untaught may learn, and the learned be fortified by faith."[32]

Finally, Lesser deliberately avoided announcing or publishing a sermon title in advance. Leeser claimed that to do so would suggest that some people might be drawn to the service to hear a discourse. Such a practice, he worried, might make preaching of more consequence than the service. Leeser never lost sight of the fact that the service was paramount.

On at least one occasion this last practice may have caused Leeser some difficulty. In the late 1840s and the early 1850s, he was often at odds with the leadership of Mikveh Israel. Many hazzans, who, like Lesser, were not professionally trained rabbis, were often looked upon as functionaries by synagogue leaders. Hence, hazzans often did not command the respect they thought their due. Once, when asked about the dates of his future preaching, Leeser refused to provide any information in advance. Subsequently, this action gave rise to the charge that he had a "disrespectful and uncourteous bearing towards the officers of the congregation and towards the congregation themselves."[33]

Within two decades of Leeser's pioneer sermon of June 2, 1830, sermons were an accepted feature of many American Jewish services, regardless of how Reform or Orthodox the congregation might be. However, with the influx of German Jewish immigrants in the 1840s, in many synagogues the sermons were initially given in German instead of English.

Characteristics of Leeser's Oral Delivery

Evidently Isaac Leeser approached his first sermons with more than the normal fear and trepidation that beginning speakers might be expected to have. Recalling his initial speaking, Leeser wrote:

Few but those who have been placed as I was, can imagine the embarrassment I experienced when I commenced speaking. I will briefly state, that I, in all my life, never had heard but about half a dozen addresses, either from the pulpit or elsewhere; I never myself had tried the compass of my voice; I knew that I have a considerable heaviness of speech, almost amounting to a stammer, unless I speak very deliberately or rapidly; besides all this, a first attempt before an audience, whose judgement one has to respect, and individuals whose taste is both refined and experienced, is not an easy or pleasant task.[34]

In many respects, Isaac Leeser was far less than the ideal speaker one might expect of a pioneer preacher. First, he was speaking in what was perhaps his fourth language.[35] Though he spoke and wrote in English and was the translator of what for fifty years was the definitive English language version of the Torah, English was not among his first languages. Hence, he may have spoken with an accent. Information on Leeser's actual speaking is difficult to obtain. If he had an accent, it was probably not very severe. The Sephardic congregations he served would certainly not be likely to favor a hazzan with a German accent. Yet Leeser speaks, as in the passage above, of "a considerable heaviness of speech, almost amounting to a stammer, unless I speak very deliberately or rapidly." Moreover, he began to acquire his facility with English at the age of eighteen, when an accent might be difficult to lose. Unfortunately, definitive evidence on this point is lacking, but it seems fair to suggest the possibility that, unlike Seixas, a native-born speaker, Leeser may have had a slight accent.

Second, Leeser was evidently tied very closely to his manuscripts in his first sermons. He read his first sermons and acknowledges that, as a consequence, "the declamation lost considerably in point and emphasis, and became therefore less agreeable to the public."[36] Leeser suffered from poor sight. He notes that his "shortness of vision" made his attempts at reading sermons "awkward." Nevertheless, he chose, initially, to write out his sermons in word-for-word manuscripts and then read them, because

it was to us of more importance to be correct than striking; and till we learn't like a child 'to go alone' we preferred to continue in a course wherein we had a reasonable hope of succeeding, sooner than to venture on a new experiment where a failure would have been almost certain.[37]

In later years Leeser was able to deliver his sermons without making use of a fully written out manuscript. Evidently, he dispensed with the manuscript because he had the opportunity to see what he called "approved speakers," whose addresses were "pleasing to the public" and who did not use manuscripts.[38] Leeser reports that he felt able to leave the word-for-word manuscript in later years because he grew to possess "an accumulated stock of general information," and because he relied "on the general good nature of those before whom we were called upon to speak."[39] Nevertheless, from his own remarks, it is apparent that, at least in his initial years of preaching, Leeser suffered from very poor eye contact with his audiences.

The lack of eye contact may have weakened Leeser's effectiveness for two reasons. First, the lack of eye contact between speaker and audience has been proved to undermine a speaker's credibility.[40] To the extent that he could not maintain eye contact with his audiences, Leeser may have suffered a loss of credibility, undermining his effectiveness. Particularly at the outset of his career, before his many and varied accomplishments, this shortcoming may have hurt. As his career progressed, his enormous accomplishments—publisher of *The Occident and Jewish Advocate*, translator of the definitive English language version of the Torah, founder of the first Jewish publication society in the United States, author of the first religious school textbooks for American Jews, and guiding force of the first Jewish seminary in the United States—no doubt established his credibility with audiences. But when Leeser first undertook to deliver sermons, these accomplishments were all in the future.

Second, the lack of eye contact would have made it impossible for Leeser to adapt his sermons to any audience feedback.[41] Leeser's sermons are not easy to understand. Their organization is complex and often awkward. Leeser's sentence structure is also often difficult. One suspects that portions of his messages were difficult for his audience to follow and may have been lost by them altogether. The lack of eye contact would have made it impossible for Leeser to sense the problems that his audiences might have been experiencing and to adjust his message to adapt to those problems.

In sum, the picture we see of Isaac Leeser delivering his first sermons is not one of a dynamic preacher, inspiring his audiences through exciting delivery. Rather it is of a small, unattractive man[42] bent over the podium with his face close to the manuscript, reading his message, perhaps with a slight accent, to an audience that listened out of respect, in the hopes of profiting from the preacher's message.[43] It is scarcely the picture we imagine when we think of the preaching of Phillips, Parker, Beecher, and many other Christian preachers of the day.

We do not know whether Leeser's audiences ever walked out on him. We do know that he placed the sermon at the end of the service so that they could do so without missing a vital aspect of the religious service. Moreover, we know that in 1850 he editorialized in the *Occident* about the fact that evidently many congregants did walk out on sermons, characterizing this as "an exhibition of public rudeness and improper behavior. . . . In any other assembly than that of Jews, such conduct would have been viewed as an unpardonable breach of politeness."[44] Such actions, he continued, have a "chilling effect" on the preacher. A man, Leeser observes, "will naturally learn to mistrust himself and his motives when he sees that others do not think favorably of him. No man is proof against indifference. . . . He must at length commence to think himself unfitted for his position."[45]

Was Leeser writing about himself? We don't know. But if so, the negative reaction to his preaching may have been largely a function of delivery. Although Leeser might not have been the most dynamic speaker, he persevered, and evidently his delivery did improve over time. Most importantly, he never faltered in his belief that sermons were the best means of educating adult American Jews. At the end of his 1850 editorial lamenting the treatment that congregations sometimes give to their preachers, he concluded by observing that "every intelligent man will tell himself without our instructing him, public addresses are the only legitimate means to produce a greater degree of religiousness in the masses of grown persons."[46]

Leeser's Sermon Preparation

Initially, Isaac Leeser preached in English every two weeks. Eventually, no doubt as his many other activities began to consume his time, he preached in English once a month. Though he deemed preaching to be an essential task, he found it to be a demanding one. "I must confess," he wrote, "that it took me always the greater part of a week, either in writing or in arranging the subject in my mind, to finish one [sermon]."[47]

Although he voluntarily initiated his own preaching, on occasion it must have seemed an especially difficult chore, on top of his many other responsibilities. In 1855, after twenty-five years of preaching, he observed that it is indeed no easy thing to be a good Hazan or Reader; it requires years of study to become properly qualified for the office; but it surely ought to be the province of all congregations, having the ability to engage a suitable person as teacher of religion and Hebrew in addition to their Hazan who will have enough of ministerial duties, including visiting the people, as this seems lately to be viewed, though with doubtful propriety, as part of the Hazan's functions, to perform, without the superadded labor of preaching and giving instruction. If anyone had been present in a large synagogue in a certain city on the last day of atonement he could easily have satisfied himself that the minister was taxed enough to read the Kol Nidre, Shascharith, Moosaph, half Miniachah, Neila, and the concluding evening service, besides an almost endless number of offerings and Hashsaboth without expecting a sermon of him in addition.[48]

This passage no doubt reflects the continuing struggle Leeser, and other hazzans, had with the lay leadership of their synagogues in defining the precise nature of the job. But it also reflects the many demands placed upon him by his synagogue, not to mention his numerous other community and scholarly activities. In light of all of these demands, Leeser's insistence on delivering sermons on a regular basis indicates the vital importance he attached to them.

Leeser valued sermons because he perceived them as the keystone of a congregation's attempts at adult education. Moreover, because of the often inadequate Jewish background of many of his American coreligionists, he felt adult education was essential. In discussing his basic rules for the sermon, he refers to sermons as "public teaching."[49]

Leeser developed two principal axioms of preaching over the course of his long career. Essentially, they relate to sermon preparation. First, he advised, if you have nothing to say, don't give a sermon.[50] Second, if you have something to say, be certain that you are knowledgeable of your topic.[51] In elaborating on this second axiom, Leeser stressed his Orthodox beliefs by stating that the preacher should "prepare himself by constant study, that he may acquire continually new ideas, which he should propound in his addresses, so as to combine novelty with the old standard doctrines and religious duties which he should expound."[52] He goes on to note that the teacher of Judaism should be inclined to adhere to what has been handed down from his forefathers.[53]

Leeser was not a rabbi. Consequently, he was comparatively unfamiliar with rabbinic literature such as the Talmud and Midrash. Rarely does he make use of materials such as these in his sermons. Rather, he bases his sermons on the Bible, with which he was highly familiar. His basic research for sermons was done in the Bible, not in supplementary rabbinic literature, such as that which would be used by an ordained rabbi. Indeed, late in his career, when ordained rabbis had immigrated to the United States and were not quite so scarce, Leeser repeatedly deferred to them on many matters, citing his lack of training and education.

It is difficult to evaluate what effect his awareness of the practices of other clergymen may have had on Leeser. As previously noted, he observed that prior to his first sermon he had heard during his life only about six real speeches, both from the pulpit and elsewhere. Moreover, he notes that he had access to only a few German Jewish sermons when he started to preach and that "their arrangement and complexion afforded us very few points of imitation. Non-Israelite productions were studiously avoided."[54] While statements such as these and the study of Leeser's sermons suggest that he utilized few, if any, models, other evidence indicates that he may have attempted to utilize models or at least to study other sermons.

Leeser was aware of the preaching of other Jews. In the introduction to the third volume of his *Discourses on the Jewish Religion*, he briefly discusses the three other English language Jewish preachers of whom he is aware.[55] In the same passage he also briefly summarizes the history of English language sermons in Judaism, as he knows it, and predicts that the practice will be widespread in the near future. His concern for English language sermons and his knowledge of what others were doing make it difficult to imagine that he was totally unaware of the sermonic practices of other preachers.

Additionally, Leeser's personal library also suggests his interest in preaching. His library contained at least two rhetorics.[56] One, George W. Bethune's *The Eloquence of the Pulpit, with Illustrations from St. Paul*, is clearly homiletic in nature. The other, Hugh Blair's *Lectures on Rhetoric and Belles Lettres*, was a major influence on Isaac M. Wise. Hugh Blair, a Scottish clergyman, includes in his book sections designed specifically for clergymen giving sermons. Leeser owned the 1826 edition.

Leeser's library also exhibited a variety of other materials that might have proved helpful to a preacher, such as a book of English synonyms. Not unsurprisingly, it included at least one book, written by an actor, that might have provided the reader with advice on gesture and voice.[57] Perhaps most revealing, though, were no less than eighteen volumes of sermons and speeches by both Christian and Jewish clergymen, given in English. Among those represented in Leeser's library were Jacob De La Motta, the Reverend E. N. Carvalho, and the Reverend Moses N. Nathan, all of whom gave English language sermons at about the same time that Leeser began to preach.[58] While many of these eighteen volumes contain sermons that were given long after Leeser had begun to preach, at least three of these volumes had been printed prior to Leeser's first sermon in 1830.[59] The dates when Leeser actually obtained the volumes and the extent to which he used them remain unknown. Yet it is difficult to imagine that a preacher, sensitive to his own lack of experience and shortcomings, would acquire several homiletic texts, and a collection of sermons, and other related material and never use any of them. Rather, it would seem that Leeser may well have had virtually no exposure to homiletics and sermons at the outset of his career but that he gradually was exposed to such works as he continued to preach. Whether those works consciously affected him remains an unresolvable question.

Leeser's First Sermon

The title of the precedent-setting sermon that Isaac Leeser delivered to introduce English sermons into the normal Sabbath services on June 2, 1830, was "Confidence in God." Leeser does not indicate why he selected this topic. But since confidence or belief in God was the premise upon which all of his religious ideas were based, it is likely that he decided to open his series of sermons or discourses by discussing what was, for him, perhaps the most fundamental concept that any Jew could hold: confidence in God.

Leeser opens in a characteristically modest fashion, observing that "it is with extreme reluctance founded upon a knowledge of my inability to advance anything which may be generally interesting, that I now, for the first time, venture to address you."[60] He continues in this humble vein, explaining that he will use sermons "to attempt teaching that which I deem to be the essential parts of our faith."[61] Having thus acknowledged the unusual nature of what he is about to embark upon, and having apologized in advance for any shortcomings that he may exhibit, Leeser then moves directly to his text. For this sermon, he utilizes the twenty-fifth chapter of Isaiah: "And it will be said on that day; Behold this is our God in whom we have trusted, and he will save us; this is the Lord in whom we have trusted, we will be glad to rejoice in his salvation."

Using his text as a basis, Leeser presents his thesis that God is all-powerful and that "if we will to receive the protection of God, we ought first to deserve it by placing an undivided confidence in his providence, and should never hesitate to do what our religion demands of us for suffering worldly loss and inconvenience."[62] He amplifies this point by first stressing the importance of making sacrifices to serve God. Second, he calls on his audience to guard against "self-sufficiency." By that he means that many people may consider themselves successful in various pursuits and as a consequence "neglect to pay due deference to religious duties."[63] This portion of the sermon is virtually the only place that Leeser makes use of any support material. He draws an analogy between the child-parent relationship and the man-God relationship, and he also presents a parable about a man and his three friends to illustrate the importance of our ultimate dependence on God and the foolishness of ever thinking ourselves self-sufficient of him.[64]

Leeser's final point is that even if we suffer repeated adversities, even if "we should be overtaken by misfortunes, if we even see our finest hopes blighted, if those we love most are torn from our embraces in the prime of youthful life," we should maintain our confidence in God.[65] He points out that afflictions have frequently beset the Jewish people, but faith in God has always enabled them to survive.[66] Leeser's conclusion is brief, consisting of a short prayer calling on God to have mercy and "give us everlasting rest from all oppression."[67]

In several respects this sermon differs from the typical Leeser sermon. First, it tends to be more unified around a central thesis than was his normal custom. For that reason, his ideas are easier to follow in this sermon than in much of his later preaching. Second, the introduction to this sermon differs from the type of introduction that he more commonly utilized in his later preaching. Typically, Leeser opened his sermons with a prayer. He was well aware of the novelty of what he was undertaking on June 2, 1830, and that awareness no doubt affected the introduction to this sermon. Third, Leeser placed his text early in the sermon, immediately following the introduction. While this was a common practice in Christian sermons, and in those few sermons delivered by Jewish leaders such as Seixas, it is unusual for Leeser. The fact that this sermon is unified around a central thesis and is easy to understand seems to result from Leeser's use of the text early in the sermon. In sum, while this sermon displays many of the characteristics typical of Leeser's preaching, as will be evident in the next section, it can be distinguished from his usual sermons by virtue of a unique introduction appropriate to this specific situation, clearer organization around one central thesis, and utilization of his text early in the sermon.

Characteristics of Leeser's Preaching

Isaac Leeser's first sermon, though distinctive from what was to follow in several ways, also evidences several characteristics that were highly typical of his preaching. First, most of his sermons, including the first, were drashah in the traditional sense: they were attempts to explain God's word as given in the Torah. Leeser, unlike his Christian counterparts, never spoke about such topics as abolition, slavery, or the social gospel. Moreover, his rejection of the use of sermons as a means of dealing with current events was largely adhered to by most Jewish preachers throughout the period 1830–1870.[68] The titles of the first group of sermons he preached, which are indicative of all that followed, were:

1. "Confidence in God"
2. "Want of Faith"
3. "Pious Energy"
4. "The Destruction of Jerusalem"
5. "The Consolation of Israel"
6. "Perfection with God"
7. "The Covenant"
8. "Sin and Repentance"
9. "The Creation"
10. "Pious Reflections"[69]

Though Leeser did speak on secular topics, he carefully avoided doing so as part of a religious service. He gave eulogies upon the deaths of Presidents Harrison and Lincoln and delivered an address in Washington at a commemorative service for Lincoln. But addresses such as these, in which he touched on contemporary events and social issues, were clearly not typical of his sermons.

A second characteristic of most Leeser sermons, shared by his first sermon, is his almost exclusive use of the Bible as a source of evidence. His heavy reliance on the Bible, almost to the complete exclusion of other sources, was a function of at least two aspects of his background. Leeser translated the Torah and was intimately familiar with it. Additionally, he was not a rabbi. He had not studied traditional Jewish sources as did most of his successors in the Jewish pulpits of America. His preaching reflected both the strengths and weaknesses of his Jewish learning.

A third characteristic of Leeser's sermons, shared by his initial effort, is their length. Although his sermons are not as excessive when judged by both his Christian and Jewish contemporaries, they are exceptionally long by today's standards. Leeser's average sermon is slightly over fifty-three hundred words long.[70] In contrast, a random selection of 115 contemporary Jewish sermons yields an average sermon length of less than half that of Leeser's typical sermon, and not one of the contemporary sermons exceeded four thousand words.[71]

A fourth characteristic that his first sermon illustrates is the complexity of his sentence structure. A commonly accepted, though somewhat rough, measure of sentence complexity is that of simple length. Most authorities suggest that when delivered orally, speeches whose sentences average twenty-one words or more in length are "fairly difficult" to follow. Speeches whose sentences average twenty-five words or more are "difficult" to follow. Speeches whose sentences average twenty-nine words or more are "very difficult" to follow.[72] Though good sense is a better arbitrator of understanding than rigid numbers, these figures provide a widely accepted rough measure of the degree of difficulty an audience might have in comprehending a speaker.

In randomly selected passages of Leeser's initial sermon, his sentences averaged forty-four words long.[73] In randomly selected samples of his speeches delivered between 1833 and 1854, the average sentence length was entirely consistent with the forty-four-word average found in his first sermon. In the sample of speeches delivered between 1833 and 1854, the shortest average sentence length was thirty-nine words, and the longest was forty-eight. The average sentence length for all samples taken during the twenty-five years following Leeser's first sermon was forty-three.[74] Clearly, Leeser's sentence structure remained consistent throughout his preaching. Moreover, if sentence length is used as a gauge, his sentences would have been exceptionally difficult for an audience to follow.

A fifth characteristic of Leeser's first sermon, which foreshadowed those that followed, was the lack of concrete language and figures of speech. The high degree of abstract language that Leeser used and the comparative absence of similes, metaphors, and other figures of speech may have made his sermons less appealing and more difficult to follow. It is possible that Leeser was aware of this shortcoming but deliberately persisted in it. In an editorial in the *Occident* written twenty-seven years after he had begun to preach, Leeser is critical of excessively flowery language, clichéd similes, and allegories.[75] While the advice Leeser offers in this editorial is justifiable, he may have taken his advice to an unwarranted extreme in his own preaching. Leeser's desire to use the sermon as a teaching tool may have caused him to treat it more as a dry lecture than did many of his Christian contemporaries and Jewish successors.[76]

Leeser's first sermon did not resemble most of his subsequent preaching in one major way. The organization of this first sermon was unified around a central thesis, which grew immediately out of the text presented early in the sermon. This was not the typical Leeser organizational pattern. Leeser described his own procedure as follows:

In place of giving out a text and stringing a sermon to the same, as is customary with most preachers, I have generally chosen to introduce it in the middle or even at the conclusion of my discourses; because I desired to illustrate a doctrinal point, and then show its consonance with the text of Scripture, believing this course less fatiguing and more interesting to the audience than the usual mode.[77]

While Leeser's goals of increasing audience interest and decreasing audience fatigue are worthy, his method of doing so is questionable. It is not an accident that most Christian clergymen of Leeser's day, and certainly most Jewish sermonists who followed him, placed the text early in the sermon. Since the explanation of the text typically gave rise to the central thesis of the sermon, such placement ensured that the audience was presented with a clear thesis statement early in the speech. While Leeser followed this pattern in his first sermon, he rarely returned to it. Rather, his sermons are often hard to follow precisely because he fails to give the listener a clear preview of the thesis and the direction he will be taking. Combined with the exceptional length of his sentences, and his lack of concrete language and figures of speech it is little wonder that one student of Leeser has called his sermons "poorly organized and diffuse."[78]

Though the artistic merit of Lesser's preaching is subject to criticism, he remains a dominant figure in the history of American Jewish preaching by virtue of his pioneering perseverance. It was Isaac Leeser who initiated widespread use of sermons in Jewish services in the United States. Motivated by his recognition of the need to provide adult education, he lived to see the practice of vernacular sermons become widespread in American Jewish religious services. Leeser was a man of enormous accomplishments, who remained proudest of his precedent-setting preaching, for he realized that, for many American Jews, preaching was the principal means "by which the untaught may learn and the learned be fortified in faith."[79]

3

Jewish Preaching in a House Divided

On December 20, 1860, South Carolina issued its ordinance of secession, signaling its defiance of the federal government and thereby virtually ensuring a civil war. Six days later, South Carolina seized all federal property in the state, except for Fort Sumter, where federal troops had established a defensive position in the Charleston harbor. Under the command of Major Robert Anderson, holding a strong defensive position and a six-weeks supply of food and arms, the federal troops at Fort Sumter soon became the focal point of the divisiveness that had brought the nation to the verge of war.

President James Buchanan made one attempt to reinforce the fort in Charleston's harbor. But when the *Star of the West* was fired on by South Carolinian shore batteries, she withdrew from her attempt to fortify Major Anderson's position, and the lame-duck president made no further attempt at helping. Rather, as Washington, Charleston, and, indeed, the entire nation was preparing for war, Buchanan, in the last days of his presidency, declared January 4, 1861, National Fast Day. It was to be observed, Buchanan hoped, with services in all the nation's houses of worship. With Lincoln elected and waiting to be sworn in, Buchanan no doubt hoped for one last surge of patriotic sentiment that might enable the North and South to reconcile their differences.

But Buchanan's National Fast Day did not prompt a surge of patriotism that would overcome differences, as he might have hoped.

Instead, it became yet another occasion for often inflammatory speeches by partisans defending and attacking slavery.

The time had passed for reconciliation and compromise. The last serious attempt, the Crittenden Compromise, had been worked out by Kentucky Senator John J. Crittenden in late December. The key provision of Crittenden's proposals called for an extension of the Missouri Compromise line of thirty-six degrees thirty minutes to the Pacific, allowing slavery in territories south of that line and allowing territories north of that line the right of self-determination upon entering the Union. But Lincoln and the Republicans were no longer willing to compromise on slavery. Moreover, with the possible addition of other slave states should Cuba be admitted into the Union, as the Democratic platform suggested, Lincoln and the Republicans saw nothing but continued controversy unless decisive action against slavery was taken. Take it they did. The compromise was defeated. South Carolina issued her ordinances of nullification, talk of secession and war was everywhere, and a lame-duck president was in no position to take any action stronger than declaring January 4, 1861, a day of national fasting.

Countless speeches were made from the nation's pulpits that day. But few drew the attention of the sermon delivered by Rabbi Morris J. Raphall of New York. For, on January 4, 1861, Rabbi Raphall delivered the first Jewish sermon to receive widespread attention in the non-Jewish community. Hailed by southern sympathizers and denounced by his coreligionists and others in the North, Raphall delivered a ringing justification of slavery, challenging Henry Ward Beecher, or any abolitionist, to deny that slavery was not sanctioned by the Bible. Raphall's "Bible View of Slavery" was the most-publicized sermon ever delivered by an American Jew up to this time.

American Jewish Preaching in Transition

Between 1830, when Isaac Leeser began to deliver English language sermons regularly, and 1861, when Raphall delivered his "Bible View of Slavery," vernacular sermons had made slow but steady progress in America. Unlike in Europe, where preaching was closely associated with the Orthodox-Reform controversy, in America that was not the case. Preaching was evidently considered a symbol of reform and a harbinger of additional changes in only one American synagogue: Shearith Israel of New York. Here, preaching was rejected as an undesirable innovation, which, if accepted as a common practice, would give rise to additional reform.[1] Elsewhere, preaching made steady, though slow, progress regardless of whether the congregation perceived itself as highly traditional or more reformist.

In 1839, Samuel M. Isaacs was appointed head of Congregation B'nai Jeshurun of New York. Significantly, his contract required that he preach at least once a month and on special occasions, including Sabbath Shuvah and Sabbath Hagadol.[2] Isaacs was born in Holland and was generally a traditionally oriented clergyman. After eight years at B'nai Jeshurun, in 1847, he moved to another New York City congregation, Shaare Tefilo, largely because he felt that B'nai Jeshurun was moving toward Reform Judaism too rapidly.[3] Isaacs, like Leeser, was an editor and had cooperated with Leeser on several projects.

By the 1850s, there were at least sixty Jewish religious leaders in the country, of whom at least eighteen have left us printed sermons.[4] They included Abraham Rice of Baltimore, the first ordained rabbi to immigrate to the United States. Rice arrived in this country in 1840, and during that decade, he began to deliver English language sermons regularly, one a month, to his Baltimore congregation. Additionally, he delivered German language sermons. The pattern that Rice established, delivering an equal, if not greater, number of German language sermons, was characteristic of many American Jewish preachers of the period 1840–60.

Large-scale German immigration, starting in 1848, provided the American Jewish community with a number of well-trained religious leaders. During the period 1848–60, conditions in Europe caused approximately two million Jews, primarily German speaking, to immigrate to the United States.[5] Consequently, many well-trained Jewish leaders and large numbers of their congregants preferred German rather than English as a vernacular language when Hebrew was not used in the service.

Through the transition period of the 1840s and 1850s, sermons were becoming commonplace in American Jewish services. By 1855, a letter writer to Isaac M. Wise's *American Israelite* observed that preaching was now widely accepted in the American Jewish community, except in some Portuguese congregations. After noting that vernacular sermons had become a feature of American Jewish services virtually everywhere, the anonymous author then sarcastically observed, "and in our days—behold and astonished—the Portuguese Congregation of New York has advertised for a preacher. Heaven merciful heaven! Wickedness increased with every returning day!"[6]

Though vernacular preaching had become a well-established feature of American Judaism by the Civil War, the predominantly German background of many American Jewish leaders and the preponderance of German Jewish immigrants who arrived in the

United States between 1848 and 1860 meant that many sermons were given in German. As late as 1872, if one report is to be believed, there were only three English-preaching rabbis serving the Jewish community of New York City.[7] At that time, New York City's Jewish population numbered about sixty thousand, and the city was home to twenty-seven synagogues.[8]

While American Judaism clearly suffered from the fact that foreign-born and foreign-trained religious leaders often headed American institutions, the New York situation was probably not typical of the rest of the nation. Elsewhere, Jews tended to rely on English to a greater extent and more rapidly than in New York. The sheer number of immigrants who remained in that city tended to slow the pace of assimilation. But even in New York and other urban areas, Jewish immigrants who might get by without perfecting their mastery of English did not want their children to suffer from this handicap.

Thus, in areas where assimilation might have been slow, impetus for widespread adoption of English language sermons did exist. Outside of such areas, where immigrant Jews found it necessary to master English in order to conduct their everyday lives, impetus for widespread adoption of English language sermons was even greater. Hence, sometime during the late 1850s or the 1860s, English superseded German as the dominant language of American Jewish sermons.[9] By the coming of the Civil War the transition stage was complete. Sermons were an accepted facet of American Jewish life and most of those sermons were delivered in English.

Morris J. Raphall: Background

Morris Jacob Raphall was born into a wealthy Swedish Jewish family in 1798. His father urged him, after a serious childhood illness, to study for the rabbinate. He successfully completed his studies, and in 1825, he was elected to serve as rabbi of the Birmingham, England, congregation. Here he quickly developed a reputation as an outstanding preacher and also edited the first Jewish periodical in England, *Hebrew Review and Magazine of Rabbinic Literature*. The sermons he delivered while at Birmingham were widely praised and no doubt contributed to his election, in 1849, as rabbi of Congregation B'nai Jeshurun, perhaps the foremost congregation in New York City.[10] Raphall was among the first English language preachers in that city and quickly established a reputation as one of the foremost pulpit orators in American Judaism.

The extent of his ability as a preacher and as a writer is evident

Morris J. Raphall (1798–1868). Courtesy, American Jewish Archives, Cincinnati, Ohio

in a variety of his activities. He is perhaps the first rabbi whose educational attainments in Europe and whose mastery of English provided him with a background analogous to those of the outstanding Christian preachers of his day. Shortly after arriving in the United States, he went on a lecture tour throughout the eastern seaboard, speaking on "The Post-Biblical History of the Jews." The text of this lecture was serialized in *The Saturday Evening Post* starting on November 9, 1850.[11] This marks one of the first, if not the first, occasions that the work of an American rabbi, writing in English, appeared in a mass circulation publication aimed at the general public. Evidently, Raphall's lectures and articles were well received, for in 1855, they were published in book form with the title *Post-Biblical History of the Jews.*[12] Thus, within six years of arriving in the United States, Raphall had established a reputation as an outstanding speaker and writer. Significantly, more than Isaac Leeser, perhaps the outstanding Jewish community leader of the day, and more than Isaac Mayer Wise, whose real work was just beginning, by the 1850s, Raphall was probably the American rabbi best known in the Christian community.

Raphall was known outside of the Jewish community not only for his writing, but also because, in 1860, he was the central figure in a landmark event for American Jews. On February 1, 1860, Rabbi Morris J. Raphall delivered the opening prayer for the House of Representatives. For the first time in the history of the republic, a Jewish clergyman was selected to deliver the opening prayers for a session of Congress.

The circumstances surrounding Raphall's selection to deliver the opening prayer for the House of Representatives suggest that his reputation as an outstanding orator was one of the principal reasons he was chosen.[13] From their earliest sessions, the House of Representatives and the Senate had always opened their sessions with prayers. During the early congresses, local Washington clergymen were invited to lead the prayers. Jews were never called upon because the nation's capital lacked a synagogue. Shortly after its first sessions, Congress appointed a permanent chaplain. As a distinctly minority faith, totally lacking any presence in either body of the early congresses or in the capital city, clergymen of the Jewish faith were not likely to be selected.

However, in 1858, Congress adopted a new policy concerning opening prayers. In that year the House of Representatives adopted a resolution requesting that "the ministers of the Gospel in this city . . . attend and alternately perform this solemn duty."[14] Thus, 1858 was the first year in which it was feasible that a Jewish leader might deliver the opening prayer. Moreover, in 1852, the Washington Jewish community had begun to assemble in private homes to worship, rather than travel to the larger Jewish community in Baltimore, and in 1855, the Washington Hebrew Congregation was organized. Thus, by 1858, when Congress decided to rotate among all the local clergy the honor of opening its session, there was a functioning synagogue in the nation's capital. However, as was the case with many synagogues of this period, the Washington Hebrew Congregation's minister, S. M. Landsberg, was a newly arrived immigrant, an excellent scholar of Judaism but a man unable to present any type of discourse in English without speaking in an extremely heavy accent.[15] Evidently, the Baltimore rabbis, some of whom were delivering English sermons, suffered from the same problem.

Hence, when the Washington Hebrew Congregation was requested to send a rabbi to deliver the opening prayers for the session of the House of Representatives that opened on February 1, 1860, the congregational leadership contacted Isaac Leeser, Samuel M. Isaacs, and Morris J. Raphall, requesting that they come to Washington to deliver the opening prayers. It is impossible to know why Jonas P. Levy, the lay leader of the Washington Hebrew Congregation issued the invitation to these three men, nor are we absolutely certain that they were the only men invited. Nevertheless, it is impossible to imagine that Levy and his congregation had denied the honor to their own rabbi and those of nearby Baltimore and, instead, invited a rabbi from Philadelphia and two from New York, unless he felt that these men would be much more polished representatives of Judaism to the nation's leaders assembled in Congress. Evidently, Raphall was the first to respond affirmatively to Levy. Consequently, the honor was his.

This incident again suggests that Raphall's reputation as a speaker far transcended his local New York community. The circumstances of his invitation suggest that, in 1860, he was perceived as among the very finest English language preachers occupying any American Jewish pulpit. Certainly the reception that greeted Raphall's opening prayer enhanced his already outstanding reputation. The fact that a rabbi had delivered the opening prayers for a session of the House of Representatives was widely reported. Most papers, lacking Washington reporters, utilized the highly favorable account of the incident provided by the Associated Press. Raphall, wearing his yarmulke and tallith and utilizing Hebrew in his closing benediction, was variously described as having been "listened to with marked attention," having "produced a profound impression upon the minds of the multitudinous and intelligent and liberal Christian audience that surrounded him," and having made, for the moment, the halls of Congress his synagogue by maintaining "the perfect equality of his persuasion and of its religious practices with that of any other denomination."[16] While there were many who were critical of Congress for allowing a rabbi to deliver the opening prayer, there could be no doubt that by doing so, Rabbi Morris J. Raphall had enhanced his personal reputation.

When, on January 4, 1861, he delivered his "Bible View of Slavery,"

Raphall did not speak for American Judaism. No one could possibly do that. But to Christians he spoke as the rabbi whom the Jews themselves had selected to deliver an opening prayer to a session of Congress. He spoke as a rabbi who had published in general circulation periodicals, whose books had been published by Christian publishers, and whose work was presumably known by far more Christians than virtually any rabbi in the country. And of course, he spoke as a rabbi respected throughout the Jewish community for his knowledge and ability to preach.

Raphall's "Bible View of Slavery"

It is highly significant that the first important statement on slavery to be made from any Jewish pulpit in the United States was not made until January 1861, after South Carolina had already left the Union over the question of slavery and while six other states were in the process of deciding to do the same. Jewish preachers, as we have seen, steadfastly refused to use the pulpit as a forum for discussing most current events. The typical Jewish sermon was delivered to enable congregants to better understand their faith, not to inform or persuade them on the issues of the day.

Additionally, Jewish leaders, even those with such sharply differing views on Judaism as Isaac Leeser and Isaac Mayer Wise, were unified in their wariness of the abolitionist movement. Clearly uncomfortable with slavery, yet wary of the abolitionists, many northern Jewish preachers found it best to avoid the issue altogether from their pulpits, particularly when their pulpit tradition dictated that course of action.

The Jewish antipathy toward the abolitionist movement was a consequence of the perception by many American Jewish leaders that the movement was directed primarily by Christian clergymen who perceived the United States to be a Christian nation. The abolitionists had determined that slaveholding was un-Christian, and they were willing to go to war with their own brothers over that issue. What might extremist Christian clergymen think and do when they turned their attention to the Jews? Yet the vast majority of American Jews were sympathetic to the antislavery cause. Had the abolitionist movement utilized a common Judeo-Christian heritage in condemning slavery, as civil rights activists a century later would do in condemning racial inequality, it is possible that Jews would have been more active in the movement and that Jewish leaders and institutions would have been more supportive. While many Jews took individual actions against slavery, most Jewish leaders and institutions remained in the background, choosing not to become heavily involved. This choice was not a reflection of Jewish attitudes toward slavery as much as it was a reflection of Jewish reservations about the character of the abolitionist movement.

Jewish leaders were worried by the intolerance they perceived in many of the Christian clergymen who were at the forefront of the abolitionist movement. Christian clergymen who were so absolutely certain in their beliefs that they would be willing to go to war with their brothers, and willing to destroy the nation in order to impose those beliefs, were not attractive to most Jewish leaders. Jewish experiences with religious leaders who would make war over their beliefs had never been positive. The perception of abolitionists as religious fanatics bent on gaining political power to impose their beliefs can be more readily understood when one remembers that many Jewish Americans had fled Europe because of what they perceived to be the religious fanaticism of those who made it difficult for them to practice Judaism. Having found sanctuary in the United States, many Jews preferred to let the South alone rather than engage in civil war, believing that slavery would die of natural causes. Hence, Jewish antipathy toward the abolitionists was primarily a consequence of wishing to maintain the Union that had provided them with religious freedom, a desire reinforced by a centuries-old concern regarding militant clergymen.[17]

Thus, the thrust of the American Jewish preaching tradition, that is, to shy away from current events when speaking from the pulpit, and a natural antipathy toward the abolitionist movement combined to limit Jewish preaching on slavery. Proslavery and antislavery speakers had been arguing biblical and religious attitudes toward slavery for years by 1861. For some, particularly Fundamentalists, the biblical teachings on slavery were of paramount importance. In January of 1861, as proslavery and antislavery clergymen utilized President Buchanan's national day of fasting to promote their own causes, Morris J. Raphall, perhaps the rabbi Christian America best knew, a man of unquestioned Jewish learning, chose to deliver a major address, among the first ever made from a Jewish pulpit, on the biblical view of slavery.

Raphall opened his sermon by reading Jonah 3:5–10.[18] He likened the current situation to the situation described in Jonah. In the United States, as in Nineveh, the nation was observing a day of fasting. Both nations faced the possibility of war and destruction. The king of Nineveh called upon his subjects to turn from their ways of evil and violence. The president, "more polished, though less plain-spoken than the King of Nineveh, does not in direct terms require every one to turn from his evil way, and from violence that is in their hands."[19] But, says Raphall, in effect those who proclaim that "Cotton is King" and those who proclaim that "Thought is King" must all realize their errors. Neither cotton nor human thought is king. "The Lord alone is King."[20]

The quarrel that threatens to destroy the United States, Raphall continues, "is the difference of opinion respecting slaveholding, which the one section denounces as sinful—aye as the most heinous of sins—while the other section upholds it as perfectly lawful."[21] Statesmen must determine legality, but, says Raphall in justifying his preaching on this topic,

the question whether slave-holding is a sin before God, is one that belongs to the theologian. I have been requested by prominent citizens of other denominations, that I should on this day examine the Bible view of slavery, as the religious mind of the country requires to be enlightened on the subject.[22]

Raphall's introduction chastises both North and South for suggesting that anything other than God is King. Having taken care of that matter, he then notes the appropriateness of theologians' and his own dealing with the religious question of whether slavery is a sin. Moreover, he notes that he will do so because of requests that have been made of him. Perhaps significantly, those requests were evidently not made by members of his congregation or by other Jews.

Raphall's introduction serves the normal functions associated with a speech introduction, but it also goes beyond. The biblical passage and the criticism of both North and South equally serve to gain attention and introduce the topic. However, Raphall also uses the last portion of his introduction to build his ethos or credibility. It is perhaps significant that he felt the need to do so. He was no doubt aware that Jewish preaching on slavery was not common. Moreover, he no doubt knew that the position he was about to espouse would be unpopular among both his own congregants and the general populace of New York, where it might be reported. Hence, Raphall's statement that theologians, not statesmen, determine sin and his statement that he speaks at the request of "prominent citizens of other denominations" are attempts to go beyond the normal functions of a sermon introduction and do something that most preachers, given their favorable relationships with the audience, often do not need to do: build their own ethos. Given the rhetorical situation he confronted, Raphall's inclusion of these references seems wise.

Raphall opens the body of his sermon by indicating the three topics he will discuss. "First, how far back can we trace the existence of slavery? Secondly, is slaveholding condemned as a sin in sacred Scripture? Thirdly, what was the condition of the slave in Biblical times, and among the Hebrews?"[23]

Turning to his first topic, how old slavery is, Raphall finds "that next to the domestic relations of husband and wife, parents and children, the oldest relation of society with which we are acquainted is that of master and slave."[24] Raphall justifies this conclusion by utilizing Genesis 9:25, in which Noah places on his son Ham the curse that his descendants will be the meanest of slaves. Raphall concludes that this curse was, in effect, a prophecy and remains valid to this day.[25]

This section was a prelude to the essence of the sermon. It is not vital to Raphall's major points, and it may also be the weakest segment of the sermon. Even those Jewish authorities who were sympathetic to the South's position, or those, such as Leeser and Wise, who were ambivalent toward the abolitionists, tended to reject Raphall's claim that a biblical curse could be considered a prophecy that held valid in that day.[26]

The heart of Raphall's sermon is his answer to the second question he wishes to consider: is slaveholding condemned as a sin in sacred scripture? His answer is a resounding *no*. "How this question can at all arise in the mind of any man that has received a religious education, and is acquainted with the history of the Bible," he observes,

is a phenomenon I cannot explain to myself, and which fifty years ago no man dreamed of. But we live in times when we must not be surprised at anything. . . . The New Testament nowhere, directly or indirectly, condemns slaveholding, which indeed, is proved by the universal practice of all Christian nations during many centuries. . . . And when we next refer to the history and "requirements" of our own sacred Scriptures, we find that on the most solemn occasion therin recorded, when God gave the Ten Commandments on Mount Sinai . . . Even on that most solemn and most holy occasion, slaveholding is not only recognized and sanctioned as an integral part of the social structure, when it is commanded that the Sabbath of the Lord is to bring rest to *Ngabadecna ve Amathecha*, "Thy male slave and thy female slave" (Exodus xx. 10; Deut. v. 14). But the property in slaves is placed under the same protection as any other species of lawful property.[27]

Raphall never mentions Henry Ward Beecher by name, but he directly confronts him:

I would therefore ask the reverend gentleman of Brooklyn and his compeers—How dare you, in the face of the sanction and protection afforded to slave property in the Ten Commandments—how dare you denounce slaveholding as a sin? When you remember that Abraham, Isaac, Jacob, Job—the men with whom the Almighty conversed, with whose names he emphatically connects his own most holy name, and to whom He vouchsafed to give the character of "perfect, upright, fearing God and eschewing evil" (Job i. 8)—that all these men were slaveholders, does it not strike you that you are guilty of something very little short of blasphemy? And if you answer me, "Oh, in their time slaveholding was lawful, but now it has become a sin," I in my turn ask you, "When and by what authority you draw the line?" Tell us the precise time when slaveholding ceased to be permitted, and became sinful?[28]

Raphall continues this line of argument by pointing out that the abolitionists, by "inventing a new sin, not known to the Bible," are creating enormous division within the country, "to a degree that men who should be brothers are on the point of embruing their hands in each other's blood."[29] He claims that Beecher and the abolitionists have taken it upon themselves to render moral judgments, which they claim are clear outgrowths of scripture. However, Raphall contends that they are presumptuous to render moral judgments, particularly when their judgments have no sanction in scripture and create havoc throughout the nation.[30]

This section of Raphall's sermon was precisely what proslavery advocates wanted to hear. One of the leading rabbis in the nation, if not *the* leading rabbi in the nation, was unequivocally claiming that the Old Testament did not prohibit slavery. Indeed, he argued, it sanctioned slavery.

Raphall's denunciation of the abolitionist viewpoint may have seemed all the more credible to his audiences because of his admission "I am sorry to find, that I am delivering a proslavery discourse."[31] He explained that he was not a friend of slavery and disliked the institution. Yet he spoke as "a teacher in Israel" and hence was propounding not his own feelings, but "the word of God, the Bible view of slavery." In effect, Raphall was claiming that he was a reluctant witness on behalf of slavery. Such a statement, which need not have been made, may have made this section of the speech all the more powerful.

The final topic that Raphall treated in his well-publicized sermon was the condition of slaves in biblical times and among the Hebrews. Utilizing a variety of biblical passages, he draws a sharp distinction between the Hebrew treatment of a slave, as "a person in whom the dignity of human nature is to be respected; *he has rights*," and the southern treatment of a slave, which "reduces the slave to a *thing*, and a thing can have no rights."[32] Though this distinction clearly implies criticism of the southern system of chattel slavery, the third section of Raphall's sermon also gave southerners something about which to be happy.

Using passages from the book of Deuteronomy, including those frequently employed by the abolitionists, Raphall claims that the Bible gives sanction to the fugitive slave law. Abolitionists had claimed that Deuteronomy 23:16, "Thou shalt not surrender unto his master the slave who has escaped from his master unto thee," justified civil disobedience of the fugitive slave law. Raphall argued that this passage applied only to a slave who entered Israelite territory from abroad. It did not, he claimed, apply to the fugitive slave of an Israelite. Hence, just as the Israelite would not be bound to return a fugitive slave from another country but would be bound to return the slave of a fellow Israelite, Raphall concludes that a New Yorker would not be bound to return a fugitive slave from Cuba or Brazil but would be bound to follow the fugitive slave law and return a runaway slave from the southern states.[33] Raphall spends several pages of his sermon clearly explicating the implications of the Bible for the fugitive slave law.[34] His explanation is clear, plausible, and entirely consistent with the thrust of Hebrew commentary.[35]

Thus, in the third major section of this sermon, Raphall is critical of the way in which southerners treat their slaves, and he distinguishes southern chattel slavery from the more humane treatment Hebrew slaves received during biblical times. However, he provides the South with a biblical justification supportive of the fugitive slave law, thereby undermining the abolitionist claim that the fugitive slave law contradicts the laws of God. Raphall concludes this sermon with a prayer for peace and unity.[36]

Raphall's "Bible View of Slavery" added little to the proslavery arguments being advanced from American pulpits. Biblical justifications of slavery were quite common by the 1860s, having begun to appear in large number as early as 1830.[37] The thrust of most Christian justifications for slavery was on interpretation of the New Testament, though occasional references to the Old Testament were also made.[38] Consequently, it is unlikely that earlier justifications influenced Raphall greatly. The essence of his sermon, that the history of the Bible indicates that slaveholding is not sinful, was a well-worked theme by 1860. However, his focus on the Old Testament history might have added to the body of support materials utilized to justify this theme and might have distinguished his approach from Christian apologists for slavery.[39]

Although Raphall's basic arguments were commonplace by 1860, his sermon generated an immediate reaction from both Christians and Jews. And well it might. Because of the expertise Jews were perceived to have on the Old Testament and because Jews had remained largely silent in this controversy, a clear statement from a major Jewish figure such as Raphall was bound to be well reported and to generate widespread attention. Moreover, Raphall's sermon was a controversial one. He directly confronted one of the abolitionist movement's premier speakers. Additionally, though speaking in the North where his position was unpopular and even though he acknowledged his own uncomfortable feelings about what he was saying, Raphall seemed to place Judaism clearly behind the proslavery movement.

The "Bible View of Slavery" also reveals a highly talented American Jewish preacher, fully able to hold his own with the finest Christian pulpit speakers. Raphall's sermon evidences a speaker who is sensitive to the relationship that exists between himself and his audience and who is working to enhance his ethos. It evidences a speaker who is clearly organized and easy to follow and who has a flair for dramatic language. In sum, Morris J. Raphall's "Bible View of Slavery" was an artistically sound sermon, which compares favorably with the proslavery sermons delivered from Christian pulpits.

Responses to Raphall's "Bible View of Slavery"

Raphall's sermon was distributed throughout the country. It was reprinted in at least three major New York City newspapers, the *New-York Tribune*, the *New York Daily News*, and the *New York Herald*, the next day.[40] It was widely distributed, particularly throughout the South, in pamphlet editions and in collections of sermons preached on the national day of fasting.[41] Southern papers such as the *Richmond Daily Dispatch* and the *Charleston Mercury* both referred to Raphall's sermon as an exceedingly "powerful argument."[42] Proslavery advocates immediately publicized Raphall's sermon, asserting both that he spoke for all Jews and that as a Jewish spokesman his views warranted exceptional attention.

Abolitionist Jews were dismayed by Raphall's sermon and the reaction it generated, fearing that it appeared that he had committed their faith to support of the slavery movement. The attention that the "Bible View of Slavery" received virtually mandated a response from antislavery Jews. Responses were not long in coming. Three responses particularly warrant our attention. The first and mostpublicized Jewish response to Raphall came from a Jewish intellectual, Michael Heilprin. The second, which received the widest exposure among Christian theologians was not a direct response to Raphall. Rather, it was a scholarly, dispassionate Ph.D. dissertation by Moses Mielziner, written without any reference to the American slavery issue. Mielziner subsequently immigrated to the United States, serving as rabbi of Anshe Chesed Congregation in New York City and as a faculty member and eventually president of Hebrew Union College. The final major response to Raphall came from the pen of Rabbi David Einhorn. A passionate abolitionist who suffered personally for his stand on the issue and who was forced to flee his Baltimore home and congregation in the wake of proslavery rioting, Einhorn aimed his response to the German-speaking American Jewish community, publishing a series of articles in the paper he edited.

The fact that the principal responses to Raphall were not made in the form of sermons is revealing. First, it suggests the strength of the precedents and counsel of such men as Isaac Leeser and Isaac M. Wise, who had continually avoided dealing with controversial civil issues from the pulpit. Raphall was among a handful of American rabbis who, by 1863, on rare occasion broke from the policy of utilizing the sermon exclusively to treat Jewish themes. Most American Jewish preachers of this period did not think that even so momentous an issue as slavery warranted treatment in sermons. While David Einhorn had preached against slavery as early as 1856, and while Bernard Felsenthal had been active in the antislavery movement and had preached antislavery and pro-Union sermons prior to the war, these men were the exception.[43]

Second, it may reveal the antipathy toward the abolitionist movement shared by many Jewish religious leaders. The reasons for this have already been discussed. It may well be that some Jewish leaders feared that a strong abolitionist statement coming from the pulpit would cast them in league with the abolitionist clergymen of whom they were suspicious.

The most-publicized Jewish response to Raphall was made by Michael Heilprin, who published a lengthy three-column article in the *New-York Tribune* eleven days after Raphall's sermon. Heilprin was an intellectual of stunning attainments.[44] He had fled to the United States after taking part in the Hungarian revolution of 1848. He read eighteen languages and spoke eight of them. He was a veritable encyclopedia of historical, biographical, and geographical knowledge and, in fact, edited every entry in Appleton's *New American Cyclopedia* in those three areas. Moreover, he served as an editor of *The Nation* magazine.

Heilprin's response to Raphall displays three distinct characteristics. First, it is filled with scorn and invective. Heilprin calls Raphall and his sermon "sacrilegious," "blasphemous," "woefully mistaken," and an "absurdity."[45] Second, Heilprin questions Raphall's translations of scripture, particularly Raphall's translation of *ebed* as "slave," rather than "servant."[46] Finally, Heilprin questions Raphall's understanding of biblical history, raising numerous objections to his interpretations justifying slavery.[47]

The importance of Heilprin's refutation lies not in its accuracy or merit, but in its very existence. Few readers of the *New-York Tribune* might be expected to be in a position to judge accurately the merit of Raphall's and Heilprin's interpretations.[48] What Heilprin most likely may have accomplished was to raise reasonable doubt about the accuracy and validity of Raphall's sermon and, most importantly, to illustrate clearly that Raphall did not speak for all of American Jewry.

The second principal response to Raphall was written by Moses Mielziner. Born on August 12, 1828, Mielziner was descended from a long line of Polish rabbinic and talmudic scholars.[49] In 1858, he was ordained a rabbi in Copenhagen. In June of 1859, he submitted his thesis for his doctorate, in both Latin and German, to the regents of the University of Giessen. Mielziner wrote his dissertation, titled "The Institution of Slavery amongst the Ancient Hebrews," without any awareness of the American slavery controversy. It was accepted by the university, and in 1859, he was awarded his degree. His work was published in several languages, including Danish, and won highly favorable reviews.[50]

Mielziner's work was eventually brought to the attention of Columbia University professor and legal scholar Francis Lieber, who was a foe of slavery and a strong supporter of the Union. Lieber provided the work to the Reverend Henry B. Smith, editor of the *American Theological Review*. Now in an English language version, Mielziner's work was published in two installments in the *American Theological Review* of April 1861 and July 1861.[51] Smith wrote a brief introduction in which he claimed:

The following treatise on Hebrew slavery was published in German in Copenhagen in 1859 as a contribution to Hebrew and Jewish antiquities. Its author, we understand, is a Jew of high attainments. . . . Its use of the Rabbinic comments, as well as the Scripture text, its comprehensive treatment of the subject, and its full digest of all the points, entitle it to careful study. Nowhere else perhaps can the whole matter be found so clearly and fully presented.[52]

Six months later Mielziner's work was reprinted again, this time in the *Evangelical Review*.[53] The translator, a Columbia professor, asserted in the introduction that

the author is reputed to be the most learned Israelite now in Europe, and his treatise has attracted a great deal of attention in Germany, it being regarded in that country as on the whole the most satisfactory dissertation that we possess upon the subject of Hebrew slavery. . . . it is simply a calm scientific discussion of biblical archaeology, written without the remotest reference to American slavery.[54]

The translator noted that he had hoped that the work would be published, as it deserved to be, in book form, but publishers were reluctant to issue it for fear of offending the South. Hence, it was being reprinted in the *Evangelical Review*. The translation and reprinting of Moses Mielziner's work in two different theological journals no doubt gave it considerable exposure in American theological circles. However, it did not receive the popular exposure that Raphall's or Heilprin's works received. Moreover, all of this translation and publication of his work was being done totally without Mielziner's knowledge. Though he immigrated to the United States in 1865, he was totally unaware of what had been done with his doctorate study until 1885, when, totally by chance while browsing in a used bookstore in Cincinnati, he ran across the old issue of the *Evangelical Review* containing his work.[55] This is even more ironic in light of the fact that Mielziner had delivered at least one sermon on slavery and the Thirteenth Amendment shortly after arriving in this country in 1865.[56]

Mielziner's thesis was stated in his very first sentence: "Among the religions and legislations of antiquity none could exhibit a spirit so decidedly averse to slavery as the religion and legislation of Moses; nor could any ancient nation find, in the circumstances of its own origin, such powerful motives to abolish that institution as the people of Israel."[57] In a meticulous examination of Jewish teachings on all aspects of slavery—the Hebrew in service of the Hebrew, the slave who was not Hebrew, the duration of slavery, the treatment of slaves, and similar topics—Mielziner illustrated that though slavery had, under limited conditions, once existed among the Hebrews, for all intents and purposes it had ended with the destruction of the first Temple.[58]

Mielziner's response to Raphall, if it can be so termed, was no doubt extremely effective with those few who read it. The impartial circumstances under which it was written contributed to the positive acceptance it received. The fact that the study had been accepted as a dissertation at a German university reinforced the impression of scholarship and the intimate familiarity with the sources that is evident on almost every page. In sum, Mielziner, totally oblivious to the American controversy, had written the definitive response to Raphall. However, it received comparatively little exposure.

A somewhat similar fate befell the responses written by Rabbi David Einhorn, who is a major figure in the development of the

American Jewish preaching tradition because of his early and ardent championing of vernacular sermons. Born in Dispeck, Bavaria, November 10, 1809, he was a child prodigy of talmudic studies and was ordained a rabbi at the age of seventeen.[59] Though he had studied Orthodox Judaism, he simultaneously had exposed himself to the classics, mathematics, and similar secular studies at Bavarian universities. His interest in a diversity of subjects made him highly open to change, and by the 1840s, he had emerged as a champion of reform. While he was active in a wide variety of reform causes, his position on vernacular in the service and for sermons was spelled out when he participated in the rabbinic conference held in Frankfort on the Main in 1845. Here, Einhorn claimed that

while the Talmud leaves no doubt as to the permissibility of the vernacular in the liturgy he would urge its use in the divine service as a necessity today. Hebrew is the language of the study of the law. As long as prayer was mainly the cry of the oppressed Jew, the scarcely intelligible Hebrew sufficed. Now people need prayer as the simple expression of their innermost thoughts, convictions and sentiments. This can only be attained through the mother-tongue. . . . Sentiment is praiseworthy, but not that morbid sentimentalism which paralyzes, and kills all spiritual life. By striking the rock of a dead language we can not bring forth living waters to quench the thirst of the people.[60]

Einhorn had no problems with reading the Torah and haftorah, conducting the service, and delivering sermons in the vernacular. By the 1850s, he had become one of the leading voices of German Reform Judaism. In 1855, he was offered the spiritual leadership of Har Sinai Congregation of Baltimore. Believing America to be a land where reform could flourish, he accepted. Hence, already established as an outstanding scholar and theologian, Einhorn arrived in a city with largely southern sympathies.

As the first outstanding German Reform leader to arrive in America, David Einhorn rapidly became a controversial figure, whose ideas, many of which were far more radical than his advocacy of the use of the vernacular, were subject to frequent attacks. In 1856, he founded the *Sinai*, a journal to disseminate his ideas and respond to his critics. It was in the pages of the *Sinai* that, in 1861, David Einhorn responded to Morris J. Raphall. But the *Sinai* was a German language publication whose readership was composed almost exclusively of American Jews. Hence, Einhorn's reply to Raphall was reprinted in both pamphlet form and in New York newspapers. Though it is unlikely his response received the distribution of Raphall's sermon, Einhorn suffered for his criticism of slavery and Raphall. Confederate sentiment ran strong in Baltimore. By April of 1861, rioting had broken out. Einhorn was among many abolitionists targeted by the proslavery sympathizers. During four days of rioting he was protected by many of the men of his congregation against possible attack, but along with other abolitionist presses, those of the *Sinai* were destroyed. Finally, he concluded that his own personal safety and that of his family dictated that he leave a city with such strong Confederate sympathies as those of Baltimore. He settled in Philadelphia, where he assumed the leadership of Keneseth Israel Congregation, and subsequently he served congregations in New York, never returning to Baltimore.

Einhorn devoted four different articles to refuting Raphall.[61] The first was by far the most thorough.[62] Essentially, he argues that Raphall has mistaken the point of the controversy. The thrust of Raphall's sermon dealt with whether slavery was condemned as a sin in the Bible. But the real question, declares Einhorn, "simply is: Is slavery a moral evil or not?"[63] Coming from the German Reform tradition, Einhorn would not accept Raphall's "literal" interpretation of the Bible. The fact that the Bible might not condemn slavery as a sin does not prohibit contemporary Americans from considering it sinful.

The Bible, Einhorn believes, "merely *tolerates* this institution as an evil not to be disregarded, and therefore infuses in its legislation a mild spirit gradually to lead to its dissolution."[64] "It must be conceded," he argued,

that the Mosaic law, as in the case of blood-vengeance and the marriage of a war-prisoner, here merely tolerated the institution in view of once existing deeply-rooted social conditions, or—more correctly—evils, and recognized it in reference to civil rights even (compare Exod. 21, 10, Levit, 18,18), but never approved of or considered it pleasing in the sight of God.[65]

Einhorn points out that there are many social institutions that were once practiced and not specifically condemned in the Bible, for example, polygamy, but that these nevertheless do not deserve our current sanctions.[66] Einhorn marshals biblical history in his defense and also questions Raphall's translations of several passages. He concludes by observing that, as a Jew, one might feel that he must be tremendously thankful for "a country which grants him all the spiritual and material privileges he can wish for. He wants peace at every price and trembles for the preservation of the Union like a true son for the life of a dangerously sick mother."[67] But though our patriotic sentiments must be strong, we cannot allow them to tarnish "the spotless morality of the Mosaic principles. . . . to proclaim slavery in the name of Judaism to be a God-sanctioned institution—the Jewish-religious press must raise objections to this, if it does not want itself and Judaism branded *forever.*"[68]

Einhorn's response to Raphall is a cogent one. His basic thesis is similar to that of many Christian abolitionists. For Einhorn, as for them, the Bible cannot be taken literally. The existence of a practice in biblical times, he argues, does not necessarily make it desirable in our time. Rather, there is a higher law, a law of principles and morality, that Einhorn felt we should strive to practice today, even though it may not have always been practiced in biblical times.

Heilprin, Mielziner, and Einhorn all raised serious questions about Raphall's position, and the very existence of their responses also served to indicate that just as slavery divided Christian communities, so too did it divide the American Jewish community. Heilprin questioned Raphall's translations of Hebrew. While the questions were never decisively resolved, the very fact that a man of Heilprin's attainments in the study of languages would question Raphall's translations undermines his position. Mielziner claimed that slavery among the ancient Hebrews was an institution that was, at best, tolerated but never encouraged. Additionally, he illustrates that it disappeared with the destruction of the first Temple and was neither missed nor reestablished. The conclusion Mielziner draws from his historical study of ancient Hebrew slavery is that none of the ancient faiths "was so decidedly averse to slavery" as Judaism. In so concluding, Mielziner raises doubt about Raphall's basic claim, that biblical history seems to justify slavery. Einhorn claims that Raphall has missed the real point of the slavery question. He focuses on what he perceives to be the essence of the issue: Is slavery immoral? In sum, Raphall's critics raised serious questions about his sermon, but it is unlikely that those questions received the widespread attention that was accorded to Raphall's oft-reprinted and oft-quoted sermon.

Isaac Mayer Wise and the Americanization of the Jewish Sermon

As early as the 1820s, Jewish leaders in New York City recognized that if Judaism was to flourish in the United States it would need institutions of higher education to train and provide leaders for the American Jewish community. During the 1850s and 1860s, groups headed by both Isaac Leeser and Isaac Mayer Wise attempted to establish American rabbinic seminaries. Although their plans had merit, Lesser's hope for Maimonides College and Wise's dream for Zion College both fell through for lack of financial support.[1] Nevertheless, American Jews were fast recognizing that they could not continue to import foreign-born religious leaders.

In 1873, Wise was able to bring together twenty-eight congregations from throughout the country to form the Union of American Hebrew Congregations. Two years later, now able to draw on support from Jewish communities in twenty-eight different cities, the union opened Hebrew Union College, naming Wise as its first president. Hebrew Union College flourished and today is not only the oldest but also the largest rabbinic seminary in the United States, with campuses in Cincinnati, New York, Los Angeles, and Jerusalem. The success of the college was soon emulated by other institutions of Jewish learning, most notably the Jewish Theological Seminary and Yeshiva University.[2] However, it was Hebrew Union College and its first president, Wise, that gave great impetus to the growth of the American Jewish preaching tradition in the late nineteenth century.

Isaac Mayer Wise (1819–1900). Courtesy, American Jewish Archives, Cincinnati, Ohio

Isaac Mayer Wise: Background

Isaac Mayer Wise was born on March 29, 1819, in Steingrub, a small village near the town of Eger in Bohemia.[3] His father was a leader of the little Jewish community but made a poor living as a teacher. Wise began to attend school with his father at the age of four and was introduced to talmudic studies by the age of six.[4] But Wise's promise caused his family to send him to Durmaul, where he could stay with his grandfather and receive a better education.[5]

Wise was only twelve when his grandfather died. Already determined to be a rabbi, he moved to Prague, the center of Jewish learning in Bohemia. Though young and poor, Wise was a promising student. As was the custom, the wealthier Jewish families of Prague provided "day board" to the most deserving students. Wise remained in Prague for about two years, making the acquaintance of a variety of prominent figures in that city's Jewish community.

In 1835, at the age of sixteen, he became a student in the most outstanding Bohemian rabbinic school, which was conducted by Rabbi Aaron Kornfield. Because of government decrees concerning the required education of a rabbi, Wise not only found himself studying traditional Jewish subjects, but he soon was also studying geography, mathematics, and German poetry and literature. For several years Wise continued his studies in both secular and Jewish subjects, while working primarily as a tutor. To further his education he traveled, studying in both Hungary and Vienna. Eventually, he returned to Prague, and in 1842, at the age of twenty-three, Wise completed all of his rabbinic examinations and was ordained.

During his studies, Wise had acquired an appreciation of a variety of secular subjects. Additionally, he had lived for a brief period of time with Isaac Noah Mannheimer, perhaps the outstanding Jewish preacher in Vienna at the time. Liberal influences such as these bent his attitudes in the direction of reform.

Wise held only one rabbinic position in Europe before he immigrated to the United States. In 1843, he was elected rabbi of the congregation located in Radnitz, a small town near Pilsen, Bohemia. He immediately began to preach regularly in German. Outside of Prague, he was evidently one of the only two rabbis in Bohemia who regularly preached in the vernacular.[6]

But Wise's years in Radnitz also served to heighten his desire to leave Germany. Jews in Germany lived under a wide variety of disabilities, which ranged from limited professions and occupations in which they could make a living, to their rights to marry. Wise himself frequently violated the law by marrying Jewish couples when the groom did not have the civil authorization to marry.[7] In 1844, Wise himself married Theresa Bloch, the sister of Edward and Joseph Bloch, whom he had tutored while a student in Prague.

Though his personal life was happy, his professional life was discouraging. In 1845, while visiting Frankfort, Wise observed the second of the three famous rabbinic conferences held in Germany in the period 1844–46. Leaders of the German Reform movement, men such as Abraham Geiger, Samuel Holdheim, Leopold Stein, Samuel Adler, and David Einhorn, debated a wide variety of reforms in Jewish liturgy. Filled with great ideas, Wise must have felt constrained in the little town of Radnitz. Looking back, almost fifty years later, Wise claimed that

I was well satisfied with my condition materially and yet I was morbidly dissatisfied with everything; the country, the city, Judaism and Christianity, everything in any State appeared to me a disappointment; my ideals were far above the realities, and I could see no prospect of improvement. I felt sick of home. The irresistible longing for other conditions; another state of things generally became to me finally the message to Abraham—"Get thee out of my country, and far from thy kindred, and from thy father's house unto the land which I shall show thee." All my considerations as to such a venturous step were silenced by the charge to Eliezer—"He will send his angels before thee." "You must emigrate" became to me a divine commandment which I could not overcome in spite of myself.[8]

While in Bohemia, Wise had begun to learn about the United States. He had learned to read English and had obtained a variety of works concerning the United States, including Richard Henry Lee's *Letters from the Federal Farmer*, written in opposition to the adoption of the Constitution. Though Lee's tracts did not prevent the adoption of the Constitution, they no doubt provided the Bohemian rabbi who read them with a vision of a democracy where momentous questions were meaningfully and freely discussed.[9] In addition to Lee, Wise read many of James Fenimore Cooper's novels and an English Bible.[10] Wise read a large number of works about America, later observing that he read with "the heart more perhaps than with the reason. That literature made of me a naturalized American in the interior of Bohemia."[11]

It was not long before this "naturalized American" sought to become a full-fledged American. Wise had difficulty in getting the proper passports and papers for himself and his family.[12] Nevertheless, in late May of 1846, Wise and his wife and daughter took passage to the United States on the ship *Marie*. On July 23, 1846, after an often stormy voyage of sixty-three days, they arrived in New York City.

Shortly after arriving in the United States, Wise met with Rabbi Max Lilienthal, a German immigrant who had preceded him to New York. Lilienthal, who was subsequently to follow Wise to Cincinnati, quickly introduced Wise to the New York Jewish community, where ordained rabbis were very rare. More importantly, Lilienthal arranged for Wise to conduct services and deliver sermons at a variety of synagogues in New Haven, Syracuse, and Albany. In each instance, Wise was well received.

The Beth El Congregation in Albany was particularly impressed with Wise, and members of that congregation suggested that he apply for the position of preacher and religious school director, but not rabbi. The synagogue evidently feared that it could not afford to hire a learned and cultured rabbi. Wise responded by stating that

if you wish to elect me, you must elect me as rabbi. That is my province. I will preach and open a school. I leave you the determination of the amount of salary, because I do not know how much is needed here. . . . I have never sought a position and will never do so.[13]

Wise returned home, and the next day he received word of his election as rabbi. By the end of the summer of 1846, he and his family were well established in Albany.

Albany was a fortunate choice for Wise. Here in the state capital, Wise had the opportunity to be exposed to the resources of the state library and other fine libraries, as well as the speaking that took place in the legislature. In his *Reminiscences* Wise recounts how he made several friends while studying English in the library. His friends, who included Amos Dean, professor of medical jurisprudence at the Albany Law School and a pupil of Daniel Webster, helped him with English rhetoric and criticism.[14] Evidently, Wise devoted about two hours a day to improving his mastery of English during his first years in Albany.[15]

In February of 1850, Wise fell ill, and his doctors advised him to leave the harsh Albany winter and go south for a few weeks. With the permission of his congregation, he took a leave of absence and traveled for several weeks down the East Coast. On his way to points farther south, Wise spent eight days in Washington listening to the Senate debates on the Compromise of 1850. During this time he heard virtually every major speaker in the Senate, and through Senator William Seward of New York and through his Albany congressman, Wise met many of the nation's leaders. He visited John C. Calhoun while the South Carolinian lay on his death bed in a Washington hotel, preparing his speech on the Compromise of 1850, which Wise later heard read for him in the Senate. He was also introduced to President Zachary Taylor.

Nevertheless, it was the speaking of men such as William Seward, Henry Clay, Daniel Webster, Lewis Cass, and Stephen Douglas that made the biggest impression on Wise. "I felt," he recalled,

the truth of the doctrine of the immortality of the soul while I listened to the powerful and eloquent words of these aged, gray-headed intellectual giants many of whom stood with one foot in the grave. Sickness, cough, and hypochondria had disappeared; the past was forgotten. I lived a new life, or rather, I dreamed a new dream, and my imagination soared to other heights, and disported itself in new fields.[16]

In 1854, after serving for eight years in Albany, Wise accepted the call of Congregation Bene Yeshurun in Cincinnati, serving as rabbi of that congregation until 1900. During this forty-six-year period, Wise became the guiding genius of Reform Judaism. As an editor and writer, Wise founded the German-language *Deborah* and the English-language *American Israelite* newspapers. The *Israelite*, as it is generally called, became the chief voice of Reform Judaism, and through its pages Wise became the outstanding advocate of the movement. As an organizer, Wise founded the Union of American Hebrew Congregations and the Central Conference of American Rabbis. These two bodies helped to unify the work of American Reform Judaism, providing an institutional framework that united Reform Jews throughout the country. As an educator, Wise founded and served for thirty years as president of Hebrew Union College.

Wise's principal tool in all of his major endeavors was the English language. His ability to persuade and inspire, in the language of his new homeland, distinguished him from virtually all of his countrymen, particularly the vast body of his fellow Jews, who, like himself, had immigrated. Wise's mastery of English, particularly as a speaker, was no accident. We have seen how he first worked at mastering the language of his new nation while in Europe and how he continued to work diligently at improving his ability to speak throughout his stay in Albany.

Wise went one step beyond virtually every other American Jewish preacher who had preceded him. Unlike Isaac Leeser, who claimed that he had scarcely studied speechmaking and had no models, Wise openly acknowledged that he studied rhetoric and homiletics, counseled others, particularly aspiring rabbis, to do the same, and acknowledged the rhetorician whom he most admired and emulated.

The Blair-Wise Connection

Wise had worked to master English while he was in Europe, but as he prepared to immigrate, he recognized that his mastery was far from complete. Recalling his aspiration at the time he immigrated, Wise claimed, in my dreams aboard ship I had decided to conquer America, but since no weapons save the living word were at my command, I had to acquire the means of gaining some skill in the language, at least in its style and form.[17]

To that end, one of his shipmates, a Boston schoolteacher, recommended that Wise obtain a copy of Hugh Blair's *Lectures on Rhetoric and Belles Lettres*. Wise followed that advice, calling his purchases of Blair's *Lectures* and Joseph Addison's *Spectator* his "first important purchases in the United States."[18]

Blair's *Lectures* were not mere fillers on Wise's bookshelf. He used them frequently and greatly admired Blair. In the 1860s, when Wise described his hopes for the ill-fated Zion College, he hoped that students would study both Hugh Blair and Quintilian to improve their speaking.[19] Why, of all the classical rhetoricians, did Wise select Quintilian? Perhaps because he is the one classical rhetorician whom Blair endorses almost without reservation.

In 1888, Wise instructed Julius Mayerberg that to be a "competent Jewish preacher," Mayerberg should do four things. First, he should diligently read the Bible. Second, he should regularly and carefully read Jewish history. Third, Wise suggested three of his own works for Mayerberg to read. Finally, Wise advised Mayerberg, "as regards to form, read Blair's lectures on rhetoric."[20] In 1896, fully fifty years after he had first been exposed to Blair, Wise was still recommending the Scottish rhetorician. "Blair was the only master of the form of speech," commented Wise in that year, adding that Blair "had developed rhetoric into a science."[21]

From 1783 to the outset of the twentieth century, Hugh Blair was arguably the most influential rhetorical theorist in the English-speaking world. His *Lectures on Rhetoric and Belles Lettres*, first published in 1783, were the texts of lectures he had been delivering as regius professor of rhetoric and belles lettres at the University of Edinburgh for the past twenty-four years. Between 1783 and 1911, Blair's lectures were in continuous demand, going through at least 130 editions.[22] When Isaac Mayer Wise first turned to Blair in the late 1840s, the rhetorician was at the peak of his popularity.

Hugh Blair came to his regius professorship by way of the pulpit. Born in Edinburgh, on April 7, 1718, he matriculated at the University of Edinburgh at the age of thirteen. Here he studied humanities, classical language, logic, and rhetoric for nine years, receiving a master of arts degree in 1739.[23] The presbytery of Edinburgh licensed him to preach in 1741, and the next year he was ordained. In 1759, at the age of forty, he was called to the most influential pulpit in Edinburgh, the High Church of St. Giles. The popularity he had won as a pulpit speaker and the fact that he had for over a decade been studying and writing about rhetoric and criticism quickly caused the University of Edinburgh to invite him to lecture. Thus, it was the rhetorical theory of a distinguished Scottish man of letters and of the cloth that Isaac Mayer Wise discovered shortly after arriving in the United States.

Though Isaac Mayer Wise never expressly wrote a homiletic text or a fully developed rhetorical theory such as that of Blair, he nevertheless wrote extensively about homiletics, preaching, public speaking, speech education, and related topics. His many observations about these topics can be found throughout the pages of *The American Israelite* and in his essays, personal letters, and other works. Moreover, his sermons and lectures offer evidence of his attempts to apply his ideas. From this body of material Wise's rhetorical theory can be accurately constructed.

Wise's rhetorical theory was strikingly foreshadowed and no doubt influenced by the work of Hugh Blair. When Blair lectured and published, rhetorical theory was in a state of great ferment. Four broad schools of thought were current in Blair's day.[24] They remained largely current when Wise became concerned with rhetoric, approximately fifty years after Blair wrote.

The Blair-Wise Response to Classical Theory

The first major school of rhetorical theory prevalent in Blair's day was the classical tradition of ancient Greece and Rome. Blair accepted major ideas from the work of Aristotle, Longinus, Demetrius, Cicero, and Quintilian. Wise did also.

Blair accepts the classical communication model: that communication involves the speaker, the speech, and the audience, and that the skilled speaker must adapt himself and his speech to his audience. Clearly, Wise also accepts this notion. Wise frequently urges aspiring rabbis to adapt themselves and their messages to their congregations. We find him, for example, cautioning young rabbis not to chastise their audiences, but if they must, to do so by always including themselves in the criticism, by using such terms as *we* and *our*.[25] Wise notes that sermons differ from other speeches and that certain practices he recommends for the sermon are not appropriate to other types of speeches because of audience expectations.[26] Hence, Wise clearly evidences Blair and the classical rhetoricians' concerns about adapting to audiences.

Blair also endorses the classical concept that there are three types of proof—ethical, logical, and emotional—and that all three are important. Wise's writing illustrates his agreement with this concept. He is particularly concerned with the ethical proof, or the ethos, of the rabbi.[27] He is concerned with logical reasoning[28] and seems to feel that emotional proof can best be attained through the use of emotionally appealing images and language.[29]

The third aspect of classical rhetorical theory that Blair stresses deals with organization. Blair feels that "there should be some one main point to which the whole strain of the sermon shall refer. . . . one object must predominate throughout. This rule," he continues, "is founded on what we all experience, that the mind can attend fully only to one capital object at a time."[30] Echoing Blair, Wise finds that "the simple ideas developed from the theme and text of the sermon must be connected logically and accurately . . . to present clearly to the audience the central idea of the discourse—and a sermon must have one central idea only."[31]

An additional aspect of classical rhetoric that Blair accepts is the stress on a simple style. As we will see, Blair is exceptionally concerned with style; it is central to his rhetorical theory. "With respect to style," he writes, "that which the pulpit requires, must certainly in the first place be very perspicuous."[32] Plainness and simplicity "should reign" in the pulpit, according to Blair.[33] Wise agrees, even using the same language to describe a desirable pulpit style.[34] Like Blair, Wise also stresses that the speaker should seek brevity and simplicity in his language.[35]

Hugh Blair was firmly convinced that natural talent could only take a public speaker so far. Indeed, the whole point of his lectures was to help improve upon natural talent. Training and practice, felt Blair and the classical rhetoricians, were essential for the successful speaker.[36] Wise, like Blair, clearly accepts this fifth key classical idea. His personal advice to associates about their preaching,[37] his own diligent efforts to improve as a speaker,[38] and his suggestions for homiletics courses at Hebrew Union College all evidence his acceptance of the classical dictum that speakers need more than natural talent.

Hugh Blair rejected one central aspect of classical rhetorical theory. The classical theorists advised the use of commonplaces, or topoi, as a means of developing ideas for a speech. Blair rejects the use of a commonplace or topoi system for invention.[39] Wise also rejects the use of such systems to help generate ideas for sermons and speeches. Wise advises the preacher to "beware of commonplaces and Aunt Jemimah nursery tales."[40] For Wise, as for Blair, such systems no doubt resulted in the excessive use of clichéd sermon subjects and reasoning. Commonplace systems were just that, common. Their usage would not provide novel and challenging ideas for the pulpit.

The Blair-Wise Response to Elocution

The second major school of rhetorical theory current when Blair wrote was the elocutionary school. Elocutionary theory singled out the classical canon of delivery from the other four canons, claiming that delivery was the most vital. Although Hugh Blair did admire the work of Thomas Sheridan, the most moderate of the British elocutionists, by and large Blair totally rejected the elocutionary approach. He felt that the speaker should simply deliver the speech in what he referred to as "tones of sensible and animated conversation."[41]

Like Blair, Isaac Mayer Wise totally rejects the elocutionary approach to speechmaking. In an editorial titled "Scholastic Education," Wise heaps scorn upon what he considers to be the foolish use of elocutionary training on young children. He concludes by observing that great orators spoke "without any gesticulation, and with no more emphasis than a natural swell of the voice when their theme inspired them."[42] For Wise, as Blair, elocutionary training was largely useless and, indeed, probably counterproductive.

The Blair-Wise Response to Belletristic Rhetoric

The third major school of rhetorical theory current in Blair's day was the French belletristic school of rhetoric, based on the concept that rhetoric was related to poetry, literature, drama, art, and music, since all had major interests in taste, style, and criticism. Belletristic rhetoricians felt that one gained insight into public speaking by also studying a variety of related disciplines, and they united this work under the rubric "rhetoric and belles lettres."

Hugh Blair was the most outstanding practitioner of this school of rhetoric in England. In his *Lectures on Rhetoric and Belles Lettres*, his principal emphasis is on the development of good oral style, to which he devotes almost half of his forty-seven lectures. In contrast, he dispenses with delivery, the heart of the elocutionary movement, in one lecture.

Isaac Mayer Wise, like Hugh Blair, accepts the essence of the belletristic movement, that is, its combined study of rhetorical theory with that of belles lettres and its stress on the importance of style.

But the men differ with regard to the study of rhetoric and belles lettres in two respects. First, because Wise never actually wrote a fully developed rhetorical theory, we cannot say for certain that he would stress style to the extent that Blair does. Clearly, Wise shared Blair's desire for perspicuous and simple style. But the degree of emphasis on style that is evident in Blair's work, particularly at the expense of delivery, may not have been shared by Wise. This is a question of degree, and Wise has simply not left us sufficient materials to judge whether he shares Blair's degree of emphasis on style. Additionally, there seems to be a difference in the motives Blair and Wise bring to their acceptance of the unity of rhetoric and belles lettres. Blair accepts the belletristic movement as the best means for producing outstanding speakers and writers. It must be remembered, his lectures were originally prepared for teenage schoolboys. He was attempting to illustrate how they might become articulate, cultured, learned adults.

Blair's rhetorical theory was meant for students who might use it in the future, as they took their places in the pulpits, in the classrooms, and in the courts. Wise's writing about preaching and speaking—found in the pages of *The American Israelite*, his letters, and his advice to others—was meant for all of American Jewry. Importantly, his audience included large numbers of immigrants. Wise's desire to unify the study of rhetorical theory, which was important for the rabbi, with other disciplines, which perhaps on the surface was not so important for the rabbi, may have been a means of producing an Americanized Jewish leadership. His motive in accepting the belletristic notions of uniting the study of speaking with a wide variety of other disciplines may have been to produce a well-rounded, cultured rabbinate and, through them, an Americanized Jewry. He writes that a rabbinic seminary should be located "at the side of an existing free college or university, as is the case now in Berlin.[43] He favors this idea because the rabbinic student could utilize the resources of the university to study poetry, literature, drama, and music. Wise finds that "at the University he may learn everything he needs except Judaism, Jewish literature, theology, philosphy, and the history thereof."[44] Once he has acquired knowledge of not only rhetorical theory but also poetry, literature, drama, music, and related disciplines, as well as knowledge of Judaism, the rabbi can satisfy a congregation. For, "the smallest as well as the largest congregations in this country of eloquence," claimed Wise, "wants an eloquent preacher, the fluent eloquent and correct speaker."[45] They want, he continued, men of literacy and social culture in the pulpit."[46] Because, Wise says,

A community with a corrupt style of language becomes ridiculous, contemptible and estranged to the better class at least. The proofs are before us in our immigration. The neglect of language made them strangers at home, strangers everywhere. The instinct of our co-religionists here is correct. . . . They know fully well the influence of the pulpit upon themselves, the rising generation and their neighbors. The language of the pulpit becomes the language of the community. They justly and wisely want eloquence, genuine and pleasing eloquence, beauty of form, correctness and exactness of language, the right words in the right place, no brogues, no jargon, no lingual poverty, no crude and angular forms, and they are right. The rabbi must be a scholar, a reasoner, an eloquent speaker, and an honest man.[47]

With large numbers of immigrants among the American Jewish population, Wise's unifying the study of rhetoric with the study of belles lettres might well have been motivated in part by a desire to produce a class of Americanized rabbis. Such a rabbinate, conversant and comfortable with the poetry, literature, drama, and music of America, could serve as models for their coreligionists.

The Blair-Wise Response to Faculty Psychology

The final school of rhetoric prevalent during Blair's day was the faculty psychology school, which based rhetorical theory on the knowledge of human nature or psychology, and which used the beginnings of empirical methodologies. Blair accepted one key concept from this school and otherwise largely ignored it. Like the psychological school, Blair accepted the conviction-persuasion, or reason-emotion, dichotomy. That is, he claimed that, to persuade, the speaker must secure conviction, which is done by the use of logic, argument, and reason. But the use of reason by itself, though sufficient to secure conviction, will not secure the real end of persuasion, that is, action. To be truly persuasive, to secure action, Blair and the faculty psychologist school argued, one must also appeal to the emotions and feelings of listeners.[48]

Like Blair, Wise also accepted the reason-emotion dichotomy. Essentially, somewhat like Blair again, he seems to have felt that the content of the message would provide the appeal to reason. For Wise, speakers should appeal to the emotions primarily through their style: the use of apt metaphors, figures of speech, appropriate word choice, and similar stylistic concerns. He writes:

suasion is one of the objects of the sermon and nothing is more suasive than eloquence and poetic beauty. Argument convinces, eloquence actuates the will to grasp the conviction and enliven it to an active principle. In the school room the mere argument suffices, in the pulpit it must appear in the artistic garb of eloquence.[49]

Hence, Blair's reaction to the faculty psychology of his day, to largely ignore it except for the reason-emotion dichotomy, is reflected in Wise's writing.

In general, Hugh Blair's reaction to the rhetorical theory of his day seems to have been largely shared by Isaac Mayer Wise. But, of course, Blair was also a clergyman, and that too influenced his rhetoric. Much of Blair's writing deals with pulpit speaking and is no doubt based not only on his own studies but also on his vast experience. Blair's experience in the pulpit led him to several conclusions with which Wise concurred.

Blair firmly believed that the sermonist should sharply limit his topic: "Never study to say all that can be said upon a subject, no error is greater than this." Rather, he continued, "select the most useful, the most striking and persuasive topics which the text suggests, and rest the discourse upon these."[50] Wise agreed. He sharply distinguished between the sermon, which should take no more than a half hour to present, and the lecture, which might take much longer and provide much fuller development of the topic.[51]

Blair finds that "the practice of reading sermons is one of the greatest obstacles to the Eloquence of the Pulpit in Great Britain." He is highly critical of preachers who read their sermons, claiming that "no discourse which is designed to be persuasive, can have the same force when read, as when spoken."[52] Wise agreed. In a letter to Max Heller he wrote, "It is killing among our people to speak from a manuscript or even notes."[53] Recalling his own early preaching, Wise described the first sermons he delivered without manuscripts and the realization that he did not have to read a sermon as "a victory" and "a conquest."[54]

Blair firmly believed that a sermon must open with a text.[55] Similarly, Wise advises, "Never preach a sermon without a text from the Bible, a text containing the theme which you can elaborate. The text is the best proof in support of your argument. A sermon without a text is an argument without a proof."[56] On another occasion, Wise refers to "textless preachers of headless sermons," claiming that they do not preach, they merely lecture.[57]

Isaac Mayer Wise seems to have thought, written, and spoken about homiletics, preaching, public speaking, speech education, and related topics to a greater extent than any American Jewish leader who preceded him. He avidly listened to great speakers, read rhetorics and related works, and conscientiously attempted to improve his speaking and that of his students. He was particularly impressed with the rhetorical theory of Hugh Blair, and his own advice on homiletics and public speaking duplicates Blair's work in numerous instances. But, Wise was not only a rhetorical theorist and teacher, he was also a practitioner.

Isaac Mayer Wise: Preacher

Isaac Mayer Wise was, by all accounts, an excellent preacher. From the very outset of his career he gave sermons in the vernacular. His appointment to his position in Albany, as well as many of the other successes of his life, can be attributed at least in part to his skill in oral discourse. His speaking evidences the basic characteristics of his theory.

Wise clearly attempted to adapt to his audiences, for throughout his career he spoke to a wide variety of groups. Typically, his sermons involved relatively short introductions with no attempt on his part to establish or enhance his credibility. As a rabbi speaking to his own congregation, or as a guest conducting services at another congregation, he had no real need to build credibility. However, when Wise lectured, his introductions were much longer than the introductions to his sermons, and typically included attempts on his part to build his ethos or credibility. Even when he was sensitive to limits on the time he had to lecture, as in his 1869 presentation before the Convention of the Free Religious Association in Boston, he found time to note that

I represent this cause here on my own responsibility, and am delegated by none. Twenty-five years in the pulpit and twenty years connection with the Jewish press, are my credentials, the diffusion of truth the purpose of my presence on this platform.[58]

Working to enhance his credibility by illustrating his character, competence, and goodwill toward the audience, as he does in this introduction, was typical of Wise's approach to audiences who were relatively unfamiliar with him.

Wise's sermons illustrate his concern for proof, and he offers some evidence to support virtually all of his major points. His primary forms of proof are statements from authority, such as the Bible, the Talmud, and the works of prominent rabbis and Jewish leaders of the past, and he makes frequent use of examples, biblical, historical, and literary. As one samples his sermons and lectures, it is easy to understand why Wise advised, as he did in a Hanukkah sermon, that the most useful reading anyone can do for the purpose of self-culture is to read history and biography.[59]

Wise's sermons offer evidence of his concern for organization. Wise, whose own sermons are models of clarity, constantly advocated that a sermon develop "one central idea only,"[60] and he himself rarely deviated from this rule. His normal sermon opened with a text, on which he then elaborated to develop his thesis. For example, in "Hebrew Monotheism," a sermon he delivered at the dedication of the new sanctuary of Congregation Anshe Chesed, he takes as his text the most famous passage in Judaism, the Shema, "Hear O Israel, God is our Lord, God is One."[61] He suggests that these words contain the essence of Hebrew monotheism. He then presents his thesis, that these words "contain the mystery of all mysteries, the sole contents of absolute truth, reason's grandest theme, ethic's primeval rock, and man's most sacred hope in heaven and on earth."[62]

Once Wise had presented his text and expanded it into his thesis, he typically presented a sermon that followed topical organization.[63] Most of his sermons contained three major points, though the number did vary. "Hebrew Monotheism" illustrates his approach. Wise's thesis statement serves as a preview that indicates each of the three principal topics he will discuss: "reason's grandest theme, ethic's primeval rock, and man's most sacred hope." Wise devotes approximately equal time to each of his major points.[64] He keeps them clearly independent of one another by making good use of repetition, signposts, internal summaries, and transition devices. He is consistent in the way he words his main points. The conclusion of this sermon, like that of many others, serves to summarize and reinforce his thesis. In this instance he concludes by summarizing and repeating the Shema.[65]

Wise's sermon organization is one of the major strengths of his preaching. As one rhetorical critic has observed, his organization is "quite clear" and "easy to follow."[66] His sermons are models of sound topical organization: they include a clear preview statement of the major points; each major point is worded in a similar fashion; he signposts major points and summarizes them in his conclusion, thereby offering his listeners at least three opportunities to hear his key ideas. The overall effect of his sermon organization is to produce a work that no doubt struck his listeners as unified and coherent.

Just as he advised others, Wise delivered his sermons and other speeches extemporaneously. He felt that sermons should not be read. After delivering several poorly received sermons and speeches that he read from manuscripts when he first arrived in the United States, Wise changed his approach, delivering his next two sermons "from pencil notes written upon the backs of calling cards while traveling."[67] The reception these sermons received was much better, and Wise recalled that "after this victory I never again wrote a sermon"[68] (he did write out his sermons for publication after they were delivered).[69] Wise evidently felt that his early experiences were typical of those that most rabbis would encounter, for he repeatedly advised against reading from a manuscript, as when he wrote Rabbi Max Heller that "it is killing among our people to speak from a manuscript or even from notes."[70]

Wise's own delivery style varied, evidently based on his subject. Letters about his speaking, written by Wise's former students, describe him as having a pleasing baritone voice and speaking softly, forcefully, or even fierily, depending upon the subject.[71] Evidently, he also gestured as he spoke. His most characteristic gesture is reported to have been to bring his right hand to his temple or brow and then extend it, as though drawing a thought out.[72]

Finally, Wise used an effective oral style to present his ideas. As suggested earlier, Wise was exceptionally concerned that American rabbis become adept at using the English language well, in large part so that they might serve as role models for the large immigrant Jewish community. Not only did he seek to encourage good oral style among his students and associates, but he even used the pages of the *Israelite* to reprint articles on English style, presumably hoping that his readers would put them to good use.[73]

Any evaluation of Wise's oral style must be tempered by an awareness that his sermons and speeches were written for publication after delivery. The written versions, which evidence excellent oral style, probably did not differ appreciably from what he actually said. He often did use notes, so that he had a basis from which to reconstruct his speeches. There are several relatively consistent stylistic traits in his printed sermons that are characteristic of good oral style but are not necessarily desirable in written work. These facts at least suggest the likelihood of his written sermons being accurate records of what he actually said.

Wise's oral style was, as he advised, perspicuous. The simple and clear organizational structure, the sentence structure and length, and the choice of words all contribute to a concise, understandable style. Wise made frequent use of parallel sentence structure and avoided excessively flowery language. He did, however, recognize the occasional need for ornate language.[74] In addition to parallel sentence structure and appropriate word choice, Wise made frequent use of metaphors and brief analogies.

Wise was also sensitive to rhythm and cadence. Rhetorical critic Robert Kully claims that "it was in phrasing his words in rhythmical patterns that he achieved his greatest success in being eloquent.

Through the use of rhythm and the repetition of short phrases Wise was often able to build climaxes."[75] Kully's observation seems entirely correct. Wise was sensitive to the way a speaker literally sounded,[76] and his own speaking reflects that sensitivity. He seems to have utilized language to enable himself not only to express his ideas but also to express them in a manner that literally sounded good.

In sum, virtually all of the major points that Wise expressed over the years about preaching and speaking are exemplified in his own speaking. His rhetorical theory, influenced in part by Hugh Blair, stressed the importance of adapting to an audience, building and maintaining ethos, utilizing proof, and employing clear organization. Moreover, Wise favored extemporaneous delivery and placed great stress on good oral style. All of these characteristics are evident in his own speaking.

Isaac Mayer Wise was not the only outstanding Jewish preacher of his day. In 1855, one year after Wise moved to Cincinnati, his old friend from New York City, Rabbi Max Lilienthal, accepted the call of Congregation Bene Israel and also moved to Cincinnati. At that time the Queen City of the West was truly that. By the Civil War, Cincinnati had become the largest city west of the Allegheny Mountains, the sixth largest city in the nation, and a major center of culture and education. Affording its residents an abundance of opportunities in commerce and business, Cincinnati soon became a major center of American Judaism. At the time of the Civil War, Cincinnati's Jewish population had reached approximately ten thousand, and the city was home to four congregations, including two very large ones, Bene Yeshurun, which Wise served, and Bene Israel, which Lilienthal served. Both men no doubt felt comfortable in Cincinnati, a city that gave evidence of a promising future, a city with a growing Jewish population, and a city with a heavy influx of German immigrants, in both the Jewish and Christian communities. In Cincinnati, Lilienthal became a precedent-setting figure in the history of American Jewish preaching.

Max Lilienthal: Background

Rabbi Max Lilienthal arrived in Cincinnati, at the age of forty, by one of the most circuitous routes imaginable. Lilienthal was born in Munich on October 16, 1815.[77] His mother died when he was nine, and family tradition has it that while she was on her deathbed, Lilienthal promised her that he would become a rabbi. Lilienthal's family was among the more affluent Jewish families of Munich, and

Max Lilienthal (1815–1882). Courtesy, American Jewish Archives, Cincinnati, Ohio

they provided their son with an excellent education at some of the finest secular schools and yeshivas in Europe. At the age of twenty-two, he finished at the University of Munich by writing such a brilliant set of examinations that he was offered the opportunity to join the diplomatic service if he would convert to Catholicism. A graduate of the Wolf Hamburger Yeshiva, which produced many of the leaders of the early German Reform movement, Lilienthal rejected this offer to instead pursue a rabbinic career.

But Lilienthal was never to officiate in Germany. By 1838, the German authorities passed highly restrictive legislation against the Jews. Rather than seek a pulpit, Lilienthal soon began to write. His work brought him into contact with Dr. Ludwig Philippson, perhaps the best-known German Jew of the day. Philippson and others recommended Lilienthal to Count S. S. Uvarov, minister of Russian education, who was seeking a leader to establish for Russian Jews schools that would combine religious and secular education, as many German Jewish institutions did.[78] Russian diplomats, familiar with Lilienthal in Munich, also recommended him.

Uvarov's goal, at least at the outset when he hired Lilienthal, was to transform Russia's Jews into educated citizens who, like their German counterparts, might be productive members of the larger society.[79] Lilienthal departed for Russia in 1839, believing that the czar, who had approved his minister of education's plans, and Uvarov himself were both sincere in their desire to improve the education of Russia's Jews. The few schools open to them at this time were primarily yeshivas, which, from the government's perspective, tended to separate them from other Russians, doing little toward making them productive citizens. Though the evidence suggests that in the beginning the Russian authorities may have been sincere, Lilienthal gradually became disenchanted with his task. The extent of Jewish education to be provided in the new schools was steadily reduced. Uvarov was replaced, and the new authorities were not sympathetic to Jewish education. In 1844 and 1845, repressive edicts were passed, which, among other things, sharply limited the areas in which Jews could reside. After five years in Russia, attempting to work with government authorities and with often skeptical Russian Jewish communities, Lilienthal asked for and received a vacation, enabling him to return to Germany. Once back in Germany, he evidently met strong family resistance toward his returning to Russia. Both his own family, and that of his bride, felt that a return to Russia would be a mistake. Evidently, Lilienthal agreed, or at least his initial optimism and enthusiasm for improving the education of Russian Jewry had been so sufficiently diminished that he never returned.[80]

Lilienthal felt that the prospects for German Jews were also bleak. His brother and sister, feeling the same, had already immigrated to the United States. They praised the freedoms they enjoyed in their new nation and boasted of the opportunities it presented. Hence, in November of 1845, shortly after his thirtieth birthday, Max Lilienthal and his family immigrated to the United States. Lilienthal's disillusionment with the lack of religious freedom and secular opportunities he found to exist for Jews in Europe colored the remainder of his life. His ardent enthusiasm for the American principle of separation of church and state traces at least in part to his European experiences.

The situation Lilienthal had found to exist for Jews in Europe contrasted dramatically with what he found in the United States. Shortly after arriving in New York he wrote his old mentor Ludwig Philippson:

My fraternal and friendly greetings from New York, from the blessed land of freedom, the beautiful soil of civic equality! Old Europe with its restrictions lies behind me like a dream; the memory of the repellent Judaeophobia of Russia is like a distant mirage; the frightful images of oppression and persecution are distant from the harried soul—I breathe freely once more, my spirit unfolds its pinions and I would waft exultingly the heartiest kiss of brotherhood to all men who find here the bond of union! . . . you must have shaken off the centuried dust of the old Jewish oppression in order to appreciate to the full the feeling "I am a man like every other"; you must see here our Jewish brethern, the persecuted emigrants of persecuting Europe, in order to become convinced how worthily the Jew cooperated with his Christian brethern here. . . . here nothing is known of the puppet play of nationalism which divides men and confines them. . . . here nothing is known of the idea of a Christian state which after creating pariahs, brands them as pariahs; here men are known only as men who respect one another in liberty and equality and work together for the common weal.[81]

Lilienthal's love for his adopted country, based primarily on the spirit of toleration that he found there, affected his work and preaching throughout the rest of his life.

Lilienthal's attempts to aid Russia's Jews had won him a substantial reputation. His arrival in New York as a well-respected rabbi made it relatively easy for him to find employment in a land where rabbis were scarce. He was quickly employed on a rotating basis by three synagogues in New York City. After his inaugural sermon, preached on January 10, 1846, he continued to preach regularly in German, for the sake of his three German Jewish congregations. He quickly became a leading figure in American Jewish life, initiating a number of reforms.[82] He developed a new prayer for the government, which became a standard part of his services and subsequently evolved into the prayers for the government that are so common in American Jewish services today. Like other German Reformers of his day, he organized a choir and began to introduce music to the service. He also formed the first confirmation class in American Judaism.

Lilienthal was a leader in forming the first association of rabbis in the United States. In 1846, he was elected president of the Beis Din, the first rabbinic association. Isaac M. Wise served as secretary. The Beis Din lasted only a brief time, but it was the forerunner of all the rabbinic associations in the United States. Lilienthal soon founded the Hebrew Union School, a day school that, like the schools he had hoped to establish in Russia, provided both an excellent secular and religious education. Hebrew Union School, which soon took up more of his time than his pulpit, became so highly thought of in American Jewish circles that it began to attract students from throughout the nation.

In 1855, when Congregation Bene Israel of Cincinnati began to search for a rabbi, several members recommended the director of the Hebrew Union School, where their sons attended. Lilienthal, perhaps attracted by the opportunity to assume one of the most prominent Jewish pulpits in the nation, located in the highly German city to which his friend and associate Isaac M. Wise had moved the previous year, accepted the offer. In July of 1855, he assumed the leadership of Bene Israel, where he served for the remaining twenty-seven years of his life.

Lilienthal Preaches from a Christian Pulpit: An Interfaith Landmark

Lilienthal quickly became a prominent figure in Cincinnati's religious, cultural, and educational communities. A leader of the Jewish community, he was elected to the city Board of Education, to the Board of Directors of the University of Cincinnati, and to the Board of Directors of the Relief Union, a citywide charitable fund.[83] In these and a wide variety of other capacities, Lilienthal became friendly with a number of Christian clergymen.

In March of 1867, one of those clergymen, Thomas Vickers, invited Lilienthal to preach to the Unitarian First Congregational Society, while he, Vickers, was out of town. Vickers was himself noted as an ecumenically oriented leader. He had become a good friend of both Lilienthal and Wise and he was frequently involved in community-wide efforts with the city's two most prominent rabbis, often representing the Christian religious and educational establishments at Jewish ceremonial occasions, such as the dedication of

Hebrew Union College's first building. Vickers subsequently became both the head librarian of Cincinnati and president of the University of Cincinnati.[84] Vickers extended his invitation to Lilienthal with the support of his congregation.[85]

Although he was aware that his acceptance might draw considerable criticism from more Orthodox Jews, Lilienthal readily accepted. On March 2, 1867, the *Cincinnati Daily Gazette* reported that, at the Unitarian First Congregational Society, services would be held the next day and that, in the absence of Pastor Thomas Vickers, the Reverend Max Lilienthal would preach.[86] The two men were breaking barriers.

Lilienthal subsequently preached frequently in Christian churches. He later commented that he began and continued his practice for two reasons. First, he claimed,

I always cheerfully seize the opportunity of stating before a Christian audience the sublime doctrines of our religion. To Christians they are a "terra incognita." They read our religious papers as little as we read theirs. . . . It is true that "we kept our light too long under the bushel," and when in past times we found a proper excuse in the fact that we did not dare to speak without being persecuted, this excuse is no longer valid in our age of free inquiry and religious liberty.[87]

Second, Lilienthal felt that by explaining Judaism to Christian audiences he was improving relations between the two groups.[88]

The sermon that Lilienthal delivered to the Unitarian First Congregational Society on March 3, 1867, which was titled "Free State—Free Church," followed the basic sermon structure that most Jewish preachers were adopting by this time. It opened with a text that was amplified into the thesis.[89] The thesis was then explicated through the development of three major points. Lilienthal did add several embellishments that he did not normally utilize.[90]

The sermon began with one of those embellishments, an extensive opening prayer. Lilienthal rarely used an opening prayer, normally starting immediately with his text. On those few other occasions when he did make use of one, it was typically quite brief. But on this occasion he used a long opening prayer to stress that all men are equal before God. "Thy paternal kindness," said Lilienthal, "knows of no distinction of either race, or creed: with all-loving heart Thou art dispensing Thy blessings and Thy mercies to all of them. Thou hast created us all in Thy image."[91] Lilienthal, highly aware of the precedent-setting nature of this situation,[92] suggests the equality of all mankind in God's eyes no less than twelve times in his opening prayer.

Following his opening prayer, Lilienthal read from the Book of Isaiah, read a hymn, and then presented his text for the morning's sermon.[93] The opening prayer, the biblical reading prior to the text, in this case from Isaiah, and the reading of a hymn were all embellishments that Lilienthal evidently utilized as means of adapting to this unique rhetorical situation. Since Lilienthal clearly recognized this sermon's uniqueness and potential significance, we must conclude that these deviations from his normal practice of opening immediately with his text were deliberate attempts on his part to adapt to the rhetorical situation. Why he chose these tactics is not altogether clear. He may well have attended services that Vickers conducted and thus observed some of his friend's techniques and practices.

Max Lilienthal's ostensible text for this precedent-setting sermon was the thirteenth verse of the fourteenth chapter of Exodus, "Fear ye not; stand still and see the salvation of the Lord." Lilienthal read this text and then explained the circumstances in which Moses spoke these words to the Hebrews, who in their flight from Pharaoh's army had reached the Red Sea. From this text and his explanation of the circumstances of its utterance, Lilienthal, instead of moving into the traditional threefold analysis, then uses two paragraphs for transitional purposes to move from this text to a topic that he must have felt was particularly appropriate for this sermon. He notes that he is concerned with audience expectations.[94] Evidently, it was this concern that caused Lilienthal to read a biblical text and then use two transitional paragraphs to get to a more acceptable text for this sermon. In these two paragraphs he observes that we live in a modern age, and since the laying of the Atlantic cable we were able to learn rapidly of events in Europe. Recently, we learned, Lilienthal continues, of "the old man Count Cavour, the good man who was called away in the midst of his activity, proclaiming 'chiesa libera in-libero statu'—A Free Church in a free state."[95] In effect, this motto, a free church in a free state, becomes the real text of Lilienthal's sermon. From this point forward, he utilizes a traditional threefold analysis.

Transitional passages that subordinate the biblical text to a contemporary motto that serves as the text are not typical of Lilienthal's sermons. Rather, they were clearly used here to facilitate his speaking on a favorite, and in this case highly appropriate theme: the glory of America's separation of church and state. That such a topic was appropriate, given the unique rhetorical situation that Lilienthal confronted, is evident. This theme provides a common belief that both the rabbi and his Christian audience held in high esteem. Moreover, the very service of which his sermon was part evidenced his theme. Lilienthal's early experiences, particularly in Russia, had made him value America's separation of church and state perhaps above all other characteristics of his adopted land. It was a theme to which he continually returned in much of his writing and preaching.[96] It was only natural that he preach on it in this sermon, a precedent-setting sermon that Lilienthal recognized as potentially one of the most significant sermons he would ever deliver.

Lilienthal used "a free church in a free state" as the text of his sermon and developed three points. First, he explains the status of this idea in Europe and in America. He finds that Europeans are "astonished" at the concept and do not practice it.[97] Americans, on the other hand, "wonder what is their astonishment, what is their surprise. We have been reared in the principles of religious liberty; but they cannot understand it."[98] Whether any of Lilienthal's audience knew of his experiences in Europe, which might have heightened his ethos and credibility when he spoke on this first point, cannot be accurately determined. It would seem likely that Vickers might have been aware of Lilienthal's background and perhaps mentioned it to others. Certainly, under these circumstances, it seems wise that he opened by developing a point that he was uniquely qualified to discuss: the lack of religious freedom in Europe and its presence in the United States.

Second, Lilienthal attempts to examine what religious freedom means for the relationships of our nation's churches. He finds that it means that each church must be free in relation to its sister churches. While the state can enforce such freedom, preventing any one church from dominating its sisters, Lilienthal is more concerned that every church develop a spirit of toleration toward its sisters. He develops this idea extensively, again primarily by contrasting the wars and bloodshed caused by religious intolerance in Europe with the tolerance evident in the United States.[99]

Third, Lilienthal attempts to explain what religious freedom means for the teachings churches must provide to their members. No church can preach love and then practice bigotry, hatred, and fanaticism, claims Lilienthal. "There is no freedom," he argues, "in such a church."[100] Churches cannot teach love toward one's fellow man, claims Lilienthal, "and then say those who do not believe like you are to be damned to hell."[101] To do so, he claims, "is an absurdity."[102]

Rabbi Max Lilienthal's message of tolerance was altogether fitting for the rhetorical situation he confronted. He spoke as a man who had experienced religious intolerance, fleeing it to find a home in a land that practiced separation of church and state. Now well established in his new homeland, he had received the ultimate compliment from the minister and members of the Unitarian First

Congregational Society. The tolerance they displayed in asking Lilienthal to preach from their pulpit during a Sunday morning service had never before been extended to any American rabbi by any Christian church. By their actions, the Unitarian First Congregational Society of Cincinnati had evidenced religious tolerance. Through his words, Max Lilienthal attempted to respond.

Reactions to Lilienthal's Preaching in a Christian Pulpit

Lilienthal's sermon was considered newsworthy by only one secular news organization in Cincinnati.[103] However, it did receive attention in the Jewish presses. Predictably, the Orthodox Jewish press was critical of Lilienthal, while the Reform press praised him.[104] Wise's *Israelite* described Lilienthal's precedent-setting sermon by observing:

By fine tact, solid piety and a happily chosen subject, the Jew touches the hearts of his Christian audience, and like the eolian harp at the soft current of rosy morning's breeze, he makes them thrill with devine emotion at the grand accords of liberty, humanity, brotherly love, on God, on right, justice to all.[105]

On the Sunday following Lilienthal's sermon, the Reverend Thomas Vickers reclaimed his pulpit. Following Lilienthal's lead, he delivered a sermon on religious toleration. One Jewish member of the audience observed that

the Christian minister was not behind the Jewish rabbi, neither in broadness of principle, nor in depth of sentiment, nor in loftiness of intentions. He accepted humanity as the grand basis of the future. He accepted one God as the benign father of all, without distinction of sect, country, race, or color. There was no mentioning of the Son, or the Holy Spirit. . . . But Mr. Vickers did not stop at these general theories of humanity and tolerance. He entered more particularly into the sad history of Christian fanaticism and Jewish sufferings. He seemed to be well versed in our melancholy annals. He did not spare any prejudice and told his audience plainly and boldly how often, how unjustly, how cruelly their parents wronged ours, under the pretense of a false, often a mercenary piety. He boldly spoke out that Christianity is but a transformed Judaism, the religion of Moses put into a hellenistic form and that the persecution with which the Church visited the Jews during the Middle Ages was but out of fear the Christians might recognize that they are but Jews without circumcision and without fringes.[106]

Vicker's response was made from his own pulpit, to his own congregants. It is unclear whether Lilienthal ever discussed inviting him to Bene Israel with the leaders of that congregation. Certainly the invitation to Lilienthal, his acceptance of that invitation, and the subsequent sermon by Vickers, in which he reaffirmed his often-demonstrated goodwill toward the Jews, might have given rise to some discussion of a true pulpit exchange. That such an exchange did not take place may suggest that Lilienthal was somewhat ahead of his congregants in this matter.

In the decades following the Civil War the Americanization of the Jewish sermon took place. By the 1860s, the vast preponderance of Jewish sermons delivered in America were delivered in English. American Jewish leaders were conscious of the need to master English. They were equally conscious of the need to master skill in oral delivery. Such rabbis as Isaac M. Wise and Max Lilienthal became models, delivering sermons that were artistically sound and providing messages that, as in Lilienthal's precedent-setting interfaith sermon, often reflected the unique American environment.

5

American Jewish Preaching and Zionism

During the late nineteenth century, foreign policy issues grew increasingly important to Americans. By 1900, a foreign policy issue dominated the presidential campaign.[1] During the same period, a foreign issue surfaced for American Jews. It too grew to dominate much of the thought, time, and effort of the American Jewish community. For in August of 1897, under the leadership of Theodor Herzl, the First World Zionist Congress was held. Zionism grew to play an increasingly prominent role in America Jewish life. Initially, Zionism divided American Jews, creating animosity and tension, but gradually, those divisions were healed. The impact of Zionism on American Jewry is evident in American Jewish preaching, as Zionism became perhaps the major pulpit concern of the first half of the twentieth century.

Zionism: A Brief Background

Zionism was the movement or effort to reestablish a Jewish homeland. Prior to 1948, Zionists sought to establish a Jewish state in Palestine, but with the founding of Israel in 1948, the Zionist impulse turned to support of the state of Israel. The movement itself originated in the destruction of Judaea by the Romans. The fall of Judaea caused the dispersion of Jews throughout the rest of the world.

Many Jews soon desired to return to their Palestinian homeland, where a Jewish nation had existed for approximately twelve hundred years prior to the Roman victory. The Jewish desire to return to Palestine was, from the outset, intimately interwoven with religious belief, as well as the social, economic, and political conditions in which most of the world's Jews found themselves during the centuries following the fall of Judaea.

Religiously, Jews based their faith upon God's promise to Abraham that the holy land would belong to his seed. The Messiah would not only bring everlasting peace to the world, but he would also gather Jews together from throughout the Diaspora, leading them back to their ancestral homeland. Jewish liturgy was full of prayers for the return to Israel. As one historian of the Zionist movement observed of European Jewry:

physically they might live within the walls of a European Ghetto, but spiritually they were encircled by the hills of ancient Judaea. Their religious festivals commemorated momentous events in their early history; their fasts, which were real days of mourning, recalled the disasters that had befallen their State. Their Scriptures, upon which they were bidden to meditate day and night, filled their minds with scenes of the land in which their kings had ruled, their prophets had taught, and their Psalmists had sung. The Talmud and other religious works which they studied, often at the peril of their lives, gave them comforting glimpses of the land that their fathers had tilled and of the Temple in which they had worshipped. . . . Twice a year, at the domestic celebration of the Passover and at the termination of the Day of Atonement, they declared with sincere emotion: "Next year in Jerusalem!"[2]

Such was the religious faith that animated the Jewish people for centuries.

Moreover, that faith was strengthened by the social, economic, and political conditions in which most Jews found themselves. Traditionally perceived as strangers and outsiders, Jews were the object of countless persecutions, pogroms, inquisitions, and discriminations throughout the Middle Ages and into modern times. These conditions also gave rise to the desire for a homeland, a land where persecution and discrimination would not exist, a land where the Jewish religion could be practiced without fear of reprisals. Thus, the Zionist movement was an outgrowth of a wide variety of factors, all of which contributed to Jews' maintaining an unswerving desire, over centuries of time, for a state of their own in Palestine.

In 1896, Theodor Herzl published his book *Der Judenstaat*. Its publication almost single-handedly transformed religious, philanthropic, and cultural Zionism into a political question.[3] Herzl claimed that "the Jewish question is a national question which can only be solved by making it a political world question to be discussed and controlled by the civilized nations of the world in council."[4] The following year, Herzl called the First World Zionist Congress in Basle. The congress adopted what became known as the Basle Programme. That program summarized the goals of Zionists as follows:

The aim of Zionism is to create for the Jewish people a home in Palestine secured by public law. In order to attain this object the Congress adopts the following means:
1. The systematic promotion of the settlement of Palestine with Jewish agriculturists, artisans, and craftsmen.
2. The organization and federation of all Jewry by means of local and general institutions in conformity with the local laws.
3. The strengthening of Jewish sentiment and national consciousness.
4. Preparatory steps for the procuring of such Government assents as are necessary for achieving the object of Zionism.[5]

Herzl and the First World Zionist Congress had transformed an age-old Jewish dream, woven deeply into the fabric of Jewish religious beliefs, into a political movement that called upon Jews throughout the Diaspora to unite in establishing a new national homeland in Palestine. As the twentieth century opened, few Jewish communities in the Diaspora were better equipped to aid the Zionist movement than the one found in the United States. By 1900, the Jewish population of the United States, swollen by massive emigration from eastern Europe in the 1880s and 1890s, had grown to about one million.[6] Though many recent emigrants were poor, many of those whose families had emigrated prior to the Civil War, free to worship and work as they wished, had prospered in their new nation. How would the American Jewish pulpit respond to Zionism? Upon the answer to that question might well rest the movement's fate.

There was no single response to political Zionism on the part of the American Jewish pulpit. Just as no one voice could speak for American Jewry on the issue of slavery a generation earlier, at the turn of the century, no one voice could speak for American Jewry on the issue of Zionism. Indeed, by that time, three distinct branches of Judaism existed in America: Orthodox, Conservative, and Reform. The remainder of this chapter will first examine the rhetorical problems and opportunities political Zionism presented to each branch of American Judaism. Second, this chapter will examine the speaking of the two preeminent American Zionist rabbis, Stephen S. Wise and Abba Hillel Silver.

Orthodox Judaism and Zionism

Prior to 1881–82, most American Jews traced their heritage back to western or central Europe. In the year 1880, America was home to approximately 250,000 Jews, the majority of whom were Reform and in many cases second-, third-, or fourth-generation Americans. However, a wave of pogroms and a series of new anti-Jewish decrees in Russia and Romania started a substantial wave of Jewish immigration to the United States in the early 1880s. Although there had been eastern European immigration prior to 1881, and indeed there was an Eastern European synagogue in New York City as early as 1852, the 1880s marked the opening of large-scale eastern European Jewish immigration to the United States. It continued until the restrictive immigration laws of the 1920s. From 1880 to 1900, over five hundred thousand eastern European Jews immigrated to the United States.[7] From 1900 to the outset of World War I, another 1,250,000 eastern European Jews had immigrated to the United States.[8]

In 1880, prior to the massive European immigration, 270 synagogues existed in the United States. Within ten years, the number had risen to 533, and almost all of the new synagogues were traditionally oriented synagogues established by eastern European Jews.[9] Throughout the next twenty-five years, until the outset of World War I, continued immigration of massive numbers of eastern European Jews gave rise to more and more traditional Orthodox synagogues. By 1916, Reform Judaism, which dominated the American Jewish community in 1880, had been "reduced statistically to the position of high social level representing only a fraction of the American Jews."[10]

The first organized American response to Herzl was made in early 1896, more than a year prior to the First World Zionist Congress in Basle. A group of eastern European Orthodox Jews founded the Chicago Zionist Organization, No. 1.[11] There was one conspicuous addition to the eastern European Orthodox Jews who founded America's first Zionist organization. Rabbi Bernard Felsenthal, who, along with David Einhorn, had been perhaps the outstanding anti-slavery speaker in the Jewish pulpit, now in the twilight of his career, lent his support. According to one participant in those early meetings, Felsenthal claimed that "though he was an old man and would not live to see the fruits of the vast undertaking, he would do everything he could, until his last day on earth, and in the world to come, to further the cause of Zionism."[12]

The founding of the first American Zionist organization typified the subsequent movement in several ways. The founders were primarily eastern European Orthodox or Conservative Jews, just as the movement was to be supported initially almost exclusively by these communities. But perhaps the most eloquent spokesman was a Reform rabbi. For just as Felsenthal is perhaps the best-known and assuredly the most outstanding speaker amongst the Chicago founders, later Reform rabbis, such as Judah L. Magnes, Max Heller, James Heller, and, most notably, Stephen S. Wise and Abba Hillel Silver, would prove to be the most eloquent spokesmen enlisted in the Zionist cause.

The fact that Zionism initially presented rhetorical opportunities to eastern European Jews, who in the United States turned primarily to Orthodox and Conservative Judaism, was a function of at least three distinctions between eastern European Jews and those of central and western Europe. First, "Eastern European Jewish life was remarkable, even in Jewish History, for the singlemindedness with which it pursued the study of the Jewish law and banned every other form of education as heretical."[13] This strong emphasis on traditional Judaism included support of a Jewish homeland. Reform Judaism, which had accommodated itself to many customs of host cultures, did not stress the importance of a Jewish homeland but, rather, suggested that Jews should serve as moral lights in all lands. Hence, Zionism presented rhetorical problems to Reform rabbis.

Second, western and central European Jews, from nations such as Germany, "lived in an ethnically homogeneous society which was attempting to become a modern national state. They could envisage themselves becoming a religion, like the Lutherans or Roman Catholics, and enjoying all the benefits of full citizenship and perhaps even social equality."[14]

Eastern European nations, on the other hand, were not ethnically homogeneous and religiously diverse. Rather, religion was interwoven with nationality. The Poles were Catholic; the Russians were Greek Orthodox; German communities of eastern Europe were Protestant. In eastern Europe religions were identified with nationality. Jews thought themselves unique in national terms as well as religious terms. Their eastern European neighbors perceived them similarly. But Reform Jews from Germany and western Europe did not perceive themselves in uniquely national terms. They were Germans, or Englishmen, who happened to be Jewish. Thus, Zionism again presented rhetorical opportunities to eastern European Conservative and Orthodox Jews who thought of themselves in much more national terms than did Reform Jews.

Finally, in western Europe Jews had a reasonable opportunity to become part of the middle class. But the strong anti-Semitism of eastern Europe, often directly encouraged and sanctioned by the government, made it impossible for Jews to think realistically of becoming integrated into the middle class. German Reform Jews had, as we have seen, modified their practices, introducing such features of Christian services as the use of music and sermons, partly to make Jewish services more like those of the German middle class that Jews realistically aspired to enter. But such aspirations were unreasonable in eastern Europe.[15] Hence, again Zionism presented rhetorical opportunities to eastern European Conservative and Orthodox Jews who were not as prone to think of integration into the mainstream of society as were western European Reform Jews.

These distinctions between eastern, western, and central European Jews were continued in the United States. The wave of eastern European immigration, which started in the early 1880s, transformed the face of American Judaism, which had, until then, been largely western European and German-style Reform Judaism. In city after city, full-blown eastern European Orthodox and Conservative Jewish communities grew rapidly in the period 1880–1916. It was in these Orthodox and Conservative communities that Zionism received its strongest support.[16]

Conservative Judaism and Zionism

Like Reform Judaism, Conservative Judaism had its origins in Germany, where it was first known as Positive Historical Judaism.[17] Conservative Judaism was a response to the perceived excesses of both Orthodox Judaism and the newly developing Reform Judaism, which preceded it by several decades in Germany. Conservative Jews perceived Reformers as too willing to change Jewish tradition and, concomitantly, too willing to deny the authority of halakah. Yet, they perceived Orthodox Judaism as unwilling to acknowledge that Judaism ever had to change and that change could be accomplished legitimately.[18] In contrast, Conservative Jews perceived themselves as maintaining that Jewish law has authority in the lives of Jews, that Jews are bound to halakah, and that the teachings of the past have a vital role to play in current life. But Conservative Jews also perceived themselves as recognizing that Jewish traditions have always grown, always been modified, and always changed.

By the decade following the Civil War, all three religious tendencies existed in the United States. As we have seen, the Reform movement was the first to become well institutionalized, by successfully founding the Hebrew Union College in 1875 and by developing, under the leadership of Isaac Mayer Wise and others, a host of various institutions, such as the Central Conference of American Rabbis, which solidified the movement.

Conservative Judaism was institutionalized in the late 1880s, with the successful founding of the Jewish Theological Seminary, which began to instruct its first class of ten students on January 3, 1887.[19] However, it was not until 1902 that the floundering seminary, under the direction of Solomon Schechter, was finally put on a firm foundation. Schechter's background as a historian and student of Jewish literature made it likely that he would be favorably disposed toward Zionism. In 1906, he firmly declared himself a Zionist.

Schechter and those he assembled around him on the faculty at the seminary viewed the reestablishment of a Jewish homeland in Palestine as more than a political program. As one historian of Zionism observed, "For them, the Jewish Torah, the God-ideal of Israel, the Jewish people and the land of Palestine constituted an indissoluble partnership, the well being of all being necessary to the health of any single element."[20] Schechter's commitment to Zionism made the Jewish Theological Seminary and the Conservative rabbis it produced pillars of Zionism. Graduates of the seminary spread Zionism throughout the nation until, as Samuel Halperin has observed, "one could safely say that where stood a Conservative synagogue there stood a Zionist base."[21]

The Conservative support of Zionism was not due simply to the ardor of Solomon Schechter. Rather, as Simon Greenberg, vice chancellor of the Jewish Theological Seminary, points out,

it is no mere accident that our Movement was at all times completely and unwavering devoted to Zionism, to the effort to reestablish an autonomous Jewish community upon the soil of Israel. We were loyal to Zionism not only in days of distress but also in days of comparative ease, because Zionism to us was always more than another typical nationalistic movement of the nineteenth century, more than a philanthropic movement concerned merely with the rescue of the persecuted, more than merely an answer to anti-Semitism. . . . Our interests . . . were first and foremost spiritual and cultural.[22]

Although Schechter's Zionism antagonized some of his anti-Zionist Board of Directors, it was highly consistent with the outlook of America's conservative Jews. Most conservative synagogues were frequented by Jews who had recently emigrated from eastern Europe or were the offspring of such emigrants. Just as with the eastern European Orthodox Jews, so too did Conservative Jews retain the age-old hope of rebuilding Zion. Though Conservative Jews were more committed to reconciling Jewish tradition with contemporary America, on the question of Zionism their attitudes were ages old. From the ranks of both the seminary faculty and its graduates, the Zionist movement found many of its most eloquent spokesmen.

Reform Judaism and Zionism

The First World Zionist Congress of 1897 met in Basle, Switzerland, though it was originally planned for Munich, Germany. The shift in location was caused by the protest of Munich's Reform rabbis.[23] This incident typifies the precarious relationship between Reform Judaism and Zionism, which existed throughout the world, particularly in America. While America's Orthodox and Conservative Jewish communities strongly supported the Zionist movement, it was not until June 25, 1943, when the Central Conference of American Rabbis passed a resolution stating that

The Conference declares that it discerns no essential incompatibility between Reform Judaism and Zionism, no reason why those of its members who give allegiance to Zionism should not have the right to regard themselves as fully within the spirit and purpose of Reform Judaism.[24]

The fifty-year history of "incompatibility" to which this resolution alludes was concluded by a firm, though often difficult, reconciliation between Reform Judaism and Zionism. Though the history of this conflict and its resolution has been well detailed elsewhere,[25] a brief review is necessary to understand the problem that Zionism presented for America's Reform rabbis.

As early as 1841, leaders of America's Reform movement, such as Gustav Pozanski, had claimed that "this country is our Palestine, this city our Jerusalem, this house of God, our Temple."[26] Isaac Mayer Wise and the leadership of the American Reform movement maintained their antipathy toward Zionism throughout the 1890s, as Herzl and others gave impetus to the movement's growth. In 1897, prompted by Herzl's First World Zionist Congress, the Central Conference of American Rabbis reaffirmed its earlier positions, resolving

that we totally disapprove of any attempt for the establishment of a Jewish state. Such attempts show a misunderstanding of Israel's mission which from the narrow political and national field has been expanded to the promotion among the whole human race of the broad and universalistic religion first proclaimed by the Jewish prophets. . . . We affirm that the object of Judaism is not political nor national, but spiritual, and addresses itself to the continuous growth of peace, justice, and love in the human race, to a messianic time when all men will recognize that they form "one great brotherhood" for the establishment of God's Kingdom on earth.[27]

This resolution well reflects the attitudes of American Reform Jewish leaders toward the birth of the Zionist movement.[28] The western European orientation of Reform Jews provided them with beliefs in liberty, equality, fraternity, and democracy. They were firm believers in the political messianism, which proclaimed the imminent brotherhood of all men. Far better able than their eastern European counterparts to assimilate in the nations of western Europe and the United States, Reformers tended to reject the need for a national homeland. Reform prayer books eliminated references to Galuth, or exile from Palestine, as well as the restoration of world Jewry to Israel and the rebuilding of the Temple in Jerusalem. Prayers calling for a return to Zion were also eliminated. The Reform movement rejected the belief that Jews were homeless or in need of a homeland. As Pozanski had proclaimed, "this country is our Palestine." Jews, the Reform movement suggested, were more at home in the dynamic young democracy that was America than they could be anywhere else in the world. As Wise wrote in the *Hebrew Union College Journal* of 1899, "no normal man can believe that we Jews would leave the great nations of culture, power, and abundant prosperity in which we form an integral element, to form a ridiculous miniature State in driedup Palestine."[29]

The spiritual and practical divisions that were evident between Reform Judaism and early Zionism have caused one historian of these two movements to characterize Reform's initial response to political Zionism "as virtually an anti-Zionist monolith."[30] The reconciliation of Reform beliefs and Zionism posed a major rhetorical problem for Reform preachers. Gradually, some Reform preachers began to resolve the problem, helped by changing exigencies of the rhetorical situations in which they preached. After considerable controversy, on May 29, 1915, student rabbi James G. Heller delivered the first Zionist sermon preached in the Hebrew Union College chapel.[31] In the first decades of the twentieth century, events quickly altered the rhetorical situation confronting American rabbis. The onset of World War I, the British mandate over Palestine, and the growth of worldwide Zionism, including its growth in the Orthodox and Conservative American Jewish communities, all altered the rhetorical situations faced by Reform rabbis. As Reform opposition to Zionism abated, evidence of rampant and virulent anti-Semitism in eastern Europe, particularly Germany, grew.

In 1930, a mere fifteen years after Heller's pro-Zionist sermon created a major controversy on campus, fully sixty-nine percent of the Hebrew Union College students indicated that they were in favor of Zionism, twenty-two percent were neutral, and only nine percent were opposed. This was a dramatic change from a generation earlier, when only seventeen percent of the student body and virtually none of the administration had been sympathetic.[32] As the situation turned grave in Europe, Hebrew Union College gradually added European rabbinic students to its enrollment and European scholars to its staff, further weakening the anti-Zionist position within the movement itself. Ultimately, as indicated at the outset of this section, by 1943, Reform Judaism had embraced the Zionist movement.

American Zionist Preachers

Since Zionism grew to become a major topic of Jewish preaching, it would be impossible to indicate all of the American rabbis who spoke on this subject. Nevertheless, two men stand out. Few, if any, American rabbis have ever spoken with the artistic ability and evident audience effect of the two dominant spokesmen of the American Zionist movement, Rabbi Stephen S. Wise and Rabbi Abba Hillel Silver.

Ironically, in light of the rhetorical problems and opportunities Zionism posed to the various denominations of American Jewry, both Wise and Silver were Reform rabbis. While outstanding preachers on behalf of Zionism were to be found speaking from the pulpits of Orthodox, Conservative, and Reform synagogues, the dominance of these two men so transcends their peers that they warrant our special attention. The speaking and preaching practices that they engaged in influenced their contemporaries, for whom they often served as models, and, through them, the entire movement.

At least three reasons may account for the fact that two Reform rabbis became the preeminent Zionist speakers in twentieth-century America. First, the stress placed by the Reform rabbinate on preaching may have made it particularly attractive to men such as Wise and Silver, who had strong secular educations and natural propensities toward preaching. Second, the training provided Reform rabbinic students, a legacy from Isaac Mayer Wise, had always been unusually strong in homiletics and preaching. Finally, perhaps the very fact that, unlike their more Orthodox and Conservative peers, the early champions of Zionism among the Reform movement were not speaking to the already converted forced them to refine their arguments and hone their persuasive skills on this issue to a greater extent than many of their more Orthodox and Conservative colleagues had. For whatever reasons, Wise and Silver became the commanding speakers of the American Zionist movement.

Stephen S. Wise

Stephen S. Wise was born in Budapest on March 17, 1874.[33] His family immigrated to the United States when Wise was an infant. His father, Aaron, sixth in a family line of rabbis, became rabbi of Congregation Rodeph Sholom in New York City, where he remained for twenty-one years. Aaron Wise was involved in the founding of the Jewish Theological Seminary and was among the most respected leaders of the New York Jewish community.

Aaron Wise was one of two major childhood influences that helped shape his son's early Zionist feelings. The other was a family friend, Simon Joseph Stampfer, who told young Stephen and other family members what Wise later recalled as "wonderful tales" of Palestine.[34]

Wise pursued his education in private rabbinic studies and at Columbia University, where he was graduated with honors in 1892. Following his graduation, he traveled to Europe, where he continued his rabbinic studies under Rabbi Adolf Jellinek, chief rabbi of Vienna. Jellinek, one of Europe's foremost Jewish scholars ordained Wise in 1893. Wise's decision to seek his ordination through study with an outstanding European scholar was caused, in part, by his reservations concerning both the Jewish Theological Seminary and the Hebrew Union College. Wise was already moving toward liberal Jewish beliefs, and the seminary struck him as unsympathetic to this view of Judaism. By the same token, Hebrew Union College, though more liberal in its outlook, was perceived by Wise, who had majored in classics at Columbia, to lack the breadth of education he was seeking.[35]

Wise had begun his college studies at City College of New York and then transferred to Columbia at the age of fourteen. By the age of nineteen he was an honors graduate of Columbia and had been ordained by one of Europe's foremost scholars. Thus, at age nineteen he received his first position, as an assistant to Rabbi Henry Jacobs at Congregation B'nai Jeshurun in New York. Jacobs died within months of Wise's joining B'nai Jeshurun. Although there were some

Stephen S. Wise (1874–1949). Courtesy, American Jewish Archives, Cincinnati, Ohio

congregants who had reservations about his youth, Wise was offered the position of senior rabbi.

Wise remained at B'nai Jeshurun until 1900. During this period, he began his formal Zionist work. In 1897, he helped to found the New York Federation of Zionists Society. In 1898, he helped in the formation of the National Federation of Zionists. In that same year, at the age of twenty-four, he attended the Second World Zionist Congress and began to work with Theodor Herzl. From the late 1890s forward, Wise was continuously involved in Zionist activities, normally serving in leadership roles. As Myles Martel has observed, Wise was the only American of prominence "whose career spanned the years from the founding of the world Zionist movement in 1897 to the establishment of the State of Israel in 1948."[36]

Wise was one of the fifty-three founders of the National Association for the Advancement of Colored People and a founder of the American Civil Liberties Union. He worked ardently on behalf of a variety of social reforms, often associating himself with Christian leaders, such as John Haynes Holmes, Walter Rauschenbusch, Josiah Strong, and Washington Gladden, in the pursuit of social justice. He founded the Free Synagogue, ensuring that he would always have a pulpit from which he could preach without restraint.[37] He founded the Jewish Institute of Religion. Nevertheless, the Zionist cause was always uppermost in Wise's mind. His speaking on Zionism made him "the foremost Zionist spokesman in America," according to no less an authority than Theodor Herzl.[38]

Characteristics of Wise's Zionist Preaching

Though speaking as a Reform rabbi, from the very outset of his ministry Wise delivered Zionist sermons. In his excellent study of Wise's major nonsermonic addresses on Zionism, Martel claims that the late 1920s marked the division of Wise's career into two phases:

From 1898 to the late 1920's, he stressed the necessity for a Jewish homeland in Palestine by emphasizing the Jews historic homelessness and by conveying his optimism in Palestine development. From the late 1920's until the birth of the State of Israel in 1948, he criticized the British Government for its mandatory policies regarding Palestine, particularly for its refusal to increase immigration during and following the gruesome Hitler years; attacked Nazism; and reaffirmed the increasing necessity of a Jewish homeland.[39]

An analogous pattern can be seen in the themes Wise developed in his Zionist sermons.

Numerous other similarities between Wise's nonsermonic addresses on Zionism and his sermons on Zionism exist.[40] Indeed, with the exception of the nature of the proof he used, Wise's sermons on

Zionism were strikingly similar to his major public addresses on the topic.

Wise tended to rely "almost entirely on personal experience and intuition as opposed to external proof," Martel claims, after examining Wise's key public addresses.[41] While Wise's sermons evidence a greater reliance on personal experience and intuition than any other form of proof, he typically utilized external proof, particularly statements from authority, in his sermons on Zionism. Enormously well-read in the classics and literature, Wise quoted such diverse authorities as Homer, Theodore Parker, Theodor Herzl, John Morley, and Jane Addams in his sermons.[42] Frequently, he would not provide specific identification of the person he quoted but, rather, referred to "a friendly observer of affairs in another land," or an "unimpeachable and most distinguished authority."[43] Given that Wise was a highly credible speaker in the eyes of his congregation, it is unlikely that his occasional failure to identify specifically the individuals he was quoting diminished the acceptability of his message to his audiences. Additionally, though not as often as might be expected, Wise also cited scripture in his Zionist sermons.[44] In sum, while Wise relied heavily on personal experience and intuition in his sermons, he did make use of external proofs, particularly statements from authority.

The other major characteristics of Wise's nonsermonic Zionist addresses seem to be well reflected in his sermons. His sermons typically have a clear introduction, body, and conclusion, but the organization of the body frequently seems to lack unity or coherence. Stylistically, Wise utilizes considerable sentence variety and a wide variety of stylistic devices. Additionally, he often incorporates poetry into his sermons. These organizational and stylistic characteristics of Wise's nonsermonic speaking[45] are clearly evident in his Zionist sermons.

Wise's organizational shortcomings, which Martel attributes largely to an absence of a rhetorically defensible method of ordering ideas in his secular speeches,[46] seem to be caused by a different problem in Wise's sermons. Wise's Zionist sermons were often organized in topical order.[47] Because the major points of the body are not presented in chronological, spatial, causal, problem-solution, or virtually any other readily recognizable organizational pattern, it is exceedingly important that the speaker who uses topical organization explicitly states at the very outset of his speech what the major points will be and the order in which they will be presented. In effect, the speaker using topical organization is imposing his own organizational pattern upon a body of material. For the audience to understand that pattern, the speaker must present it early in the speech. Wise often fails to do this. In some sermons he totally fails to acquaint the audience with his organizational pattern.[48] In others, he does so midway through the sermon, not at the outset, and often in an understated way that fails to call attention to itself.[49] In all these instances it is probable that the audience missed his organizational pattern. Lacking an overall guiding organizational pattern because of his failure to identify clearly the pattern he is imposing on his material, Wise's Zionist sermons, like many of his public speeches, often seem to lack an overall sense of unity.

Stylistically, Wise's sermons are excellent. He utilizes a wide variety of sentence structures. He also varies his sentence length, though he does have a propensity for longer sentences. The last paragraph of his sermon "Zion and Zionism" illustrates these two characteristics:

The rest of the picture it is for us to fill out, for after all the future of the Jewish Palestine will not be a matter of Conference and of Charter. The Balfour Declaration did not restore Palestine to the Jews. The League of Nations cannot re-establish the Jews in Palestine. What may be hoped for is that under the League of Nations and with the furthering help of British trusteeship there will be such a re-occupation of Palestine as will in itself constitute the foundations of that Jewish commonwealth which under God is once again to arise in the land of Israel.[50]

In this one paragraph of four sentences, Wise utilizes compound, complex, and simple sentences. Moreover, his sentence lengths range from ten to fifty-two words.[51] This paragraph is typical of the variety in sentence structure and length that Wise employs.

Wise makes use of a wide variety of stylistic devices, which tend to make his sermons more memorable. Alliteration, repetition, and metaphors are all utilized frequently in his Zionist sermons. He also makes especially frequent use of balanced sentences as a stylistic device to prove a point.[52] The use of balanced sentences, which also involve repetition, can be seen in the following passage:

It may be true that not all things are ready if our minds be so, but surely nothing is ready unless our minds and hearts be so. Whether we shall effectively further Jewish interests will largely depend not on what we do after peace has been concluded but upon what we are now preparing to do before peace has been attained.[53]

Though this passage may be a bit unusual insofar as Wise uses two balanced sentences in a row, the use of this type of construction is highly characteristic of Wise's Zionist sermons.

A final stylistic trait of Wise's Zionist sermons is his tendency to utilize brief passages of poetry. This technique is not uncommon in sermons. Poetry provides a sense of eloquence and splendor that prose often cannot duplicate, and hence it is utilized by many clergymen of all faiths. However, Wise utilized poetry frequently in his nonsermonic addresses on Zionism, as well as his sermons.[54] Wise's use of poetry in his sermons was typically confined to quoting no more than a two- or four-line verse. However, on at least one occasion, he quotes three stanzas to end a sermon.[55]

Wise's platform and pulpit delivery have been commented on by many of those who heard him. Invariably, they note that he was a vigorous and active speaker, who exuded energy and an exceptional platform personality.[56] He was a large man, over six feet tall, with a broad chest and shoulders. He knew how to use his resonant voice, at times soothing his audiences with its richness and at other times moving them with its striking power. In sum, his striking physical appearance, his energetic delivery, and his remarkable voice all contributed positively to his preaching.

Like Isaac Mayer Wise, in 1922, Stephen S. Wise founded a rabbinic seminary, the Jewish Institute of Religion. Both men were Reform rabbis, and though Stephen Wise founded the Jewish Institute of Religion in part to offer potential rabbis a seminary that was not "avowedly Orthodox or Reform,"[57] the Jewish Institute of Religion ultimately, in 1950, merged with the Hebrew Union College. Stephen Wise, like Isaac Mayer Wise before him, placed exceptionally high value on the ability to speak and preach. Unlike Isaac Mayer Wise, Stephen Wise spoke and wrote comparatively little about public speaking. However, in his autobiography he does include a brief chapter titled "The Art of Speaking."

Wise offers three rules for preachers and speakers, claiming that they are rules that he has always tried to follow. First, he suggests, "have something to say"; second, "believe in what you are going to say"; third, "say it clearly and without fear."[58] These three rules, trite as they may seem, exemplify Wise's Zionist preaching. For the strength of Wise's Zionist preaching was not necessarily in the specific message, use of proof, organization, stylistic traits, or delivery, as strong as many of those characteristics of his speaking were.

Rather, Wise's ultimate impact as a speaker seems to have stemmed primarily from the intensity of his sincere belief in Zionism and his credibility or ethos. As illustrated earlier, he had labored on behalf of Zionism virtually his entire life. His knowledge of issues and personalities was virtually unmatched.

Moreover, repeatedly throughout his life he had illustrated a willingness to battle fearlessly for what he perceived to be just. He was a Zionist rabbi years before that position was a popular one among

Reform Jews. He rejected the most prestigious pulpit in America when he perceived that to accept it might put constraints upon what he could say. He battled political corruption in New York when others were silent. He was a founder of both the National Association for the Advancement of Colored People in 1908 and the American Civil Liberties Union twelve years later. He spoke to ease the plight of child laborers in Oregon and subsequently on behalf of social justice for all American workingmen. In each of these instances, his was among both the first and the most influential voices to be raised. And of course, he perceived the horror of Hitler's Germany, attempting to alert his countrymen, at a time when most American leaders remained ignorant and silent.

The intensity of Wise's Zionist beliefs, his manifest accomplishments and labor on behalf of the Zionist movement, his fearless social activism, and his abilities as a speaker all contributed to the total effect that Wise had on his audiences.

Abba Hillel Silver

Abba Hillel Silver was born in a small Lithuanian town in 1893.[59] His father, Moses, was the third in succession of a line of rabbis, though he earned his living as a soap manufacturer. In June of 1902, the Silver family immigrated to the United States, joining Moses who had preceded them to find a residence and establish himself. The family settled on the lower East Side of New York. Exposed to Zionism by his father, Silver became a founder of the Dr. Herzl Zionist Club, the first Hebrew-speaking youth group committed to Zionism in the United States.[60] Silver was especially active in the plays and debates of the club.

He soon decided to make the rabbinate his profession. In 1915, he was graduated simultaneously from the University of Cincinnati and Hebrew Union College, winning awards for his oratorical ability at the university and graduating as valedictorian from the seminary.[61] Silver had shown great promise as an orator while in high school, and his simultaneous graduation from the university and the seminary was a remarkable achievement. He had accomplished the equivalent of nine years' work in but four.[62]

In light of Silver's eastern European Orthodox background and his Zionist sympathies, his decision to become a Reform rabbi is somewhat surprising. However, Silver was struck by the appropriateness of Reform Judaism for life in the United States. Moreover, he saw no real contradiction between Zionism and Reform. Additionally, his father supported his decision, and he was joined at Hebrew Union

Abba Hillel Silver (1893–1963). Courtesy, American Jewish Archives, Cincinnati, Ohio

College by friends from the Dr. Herzl Zionist Club.[63] The presence of these friends meant that Silver would not be the lone Zionist at Hebrew Union College. For a time Silver did not advocate Zionism from the pulpit. This fact seems to be a function of the clear delineation he drew between his responsibilities to the temples he served and the Zionist movement.

Silver believed, as did Wise, that Reform and Zionism were compatible. He perceived Zionism as an addition to Reform Judaism, which in no fashion replaced or nullified the doctrines of Reform. "The upbuilding of a strong Jewish commonwealth in Palestine," he claimed, "however much desirable, will not achieve the miracle of preservation for the Jews of the United States."[64] For the American Jew, Silver believed, religion must be the focus of his life, for he cannot realistically practice a secular Jewish life, as can the Palestinian Jew. For Silver, an American Jew could be both Zionist and Reform.[65]

Silver's first pulpit was the Eoff Street Temple, in Wheeling, West Virginia, where he served for three years. In 1917, at the age of twenty-four, he accepted the pulpit of Cleveland's Congregation Tifereth Israel, better known as The Temple, in Cleveland. Silver remained spiritual leader of The Temple, one of the largest and most prominent in the United States, for the rest of his life. Silver, like Wise and many Reform rabbis, was a strong supporter of organized labor and other liberal causes. Though sometimes his other interests varied, he consistently remained a political Zionist.

Silver's rise in the Zionist movement was remarkably fast. The central work of his life was that of rabbi. But his constant advocacy of Zionism brought him, in 1943, to the head of the American Zionist Emergency Council. The council had been formed to mobilize American public opinion, both Jewish and non-Jewish, on behalf of Zionism and the creation of the state of Israel. Silver recognized that only if America intervened in favor of a pro-Zionist solution of the Palestine problem, would the Zionist dream be recognized after the War.[66] To this end, he worked to mobilize American public opinion and hence to force the hand of an often reluctant State Department and White House. Silver felt that Great Britain would not act favorably in Palestine unless she felt pressured to do so by the United States. He reached the summit of his leadership in May of 1948, when, as chairman of the American Section of the Jewish Agency, he argued the case for an independent Jewish state before the United Nations General Assembly.

Silver's work as a rabbi was never diminished by his role on behalf of Zionism. He remained constantly loyal to the basic philosophies of Reform Judaism and consistently took leadership positions within

Reform groups. While Wise's pulpit was unabashedly Zionist, Silver was more restrained in utilizing his position as rabbi of an exceptionally prestigious Reform temple to further Zionism.

Unlike Wise, who had been privately ordained, Silver had been graduated as valedictorian of the Reform seminary, Hebrew Union College. He consistently remained loyal to the institutions of Reform Judaism, though he differed sharply, of course, with respect to Zionism. Ultimately, in 1945, by which time Reform Judaism had been reconciled with Zionism, Abba Hillel Silver was elected president of the Central Conference of American Rabbis.[67] His election as president of the Reform rabbinate's chief professional association evidences his success in maintaining his profile as a leading Reform rabbi, while speaking on behalf of Zionism.

Characteristics of Silver's Zionist Preaching

Silver did not always advocate Zionism from his pulpit. He preached on Zionism less frequently than did Wise. Hence, any serious examination of Silver's speaking on Zionism must also include an examination of his nonsermonic addresses, such as those that he made to the United Nations and various Zionist organizations. An examination of key secular speeches and sermons indicates that, with minor exceptions, Silver used the same basic arguments, whether he spoke about Zionism from the pulpit or elsewhere.[68]

Frances Wolpaw discerns eight lines of argument in Silver's speaking. None of them seems unique to Silver, many being used by Wise and other Zionists. They include:

1. Solidarity with other Jews does not imply that American Jews are not also loyal Americans.
2. Zionism should not be sacrificed for increased Jewish immigration or other expedient measures.
3. The reconstruction of the Jewish national homeland is a worldwide policy.
4. Arabs and Jews can live peacefully together if they are given the opportunity to do so.
5. Palestine is indispensable to Jewish life.
6. Zionism is wholly distinct from the question of Jewish immigration.
7. The promises of diplomats and statesmen must be backed by action.
8. The terms of the Mandate must be affirmed.[69]

At different times, in front of different audiences, Silver gave emphasis to different arguments. His arguments were often well publicized and may have served as models for other Zionists. However, his arguments are not unique. For example, many Zionists, most notably Louis Brandeis years earlier, had to deal with the issue of dual or conflicting loyalty. Similarly, many of these eight arguments are echoed in the sermons and speeches of other Zionist leaders. However, few men were as eloquent as Silver in presenting the Zionist position.

Unlike Wise, Silver often used evidence based on something beyond his own experience. He frequently quoted or paraphrased Presidents Abraham Lincoln, Franklin Roosevelt, and Harry Truman. He often cited Senator Robert Taft, with whom he was especially close, Prime Ministers Clement Attlee and Winston Churchill, and a wide variety of other historical and contemporary figures. He made very rare reference to the Bible.[70] He often read from official documents and/or cited various contemporary meetings and events to support his positions. Moreover, he also used statistics or other appropriate forms of evidence.[71]

Silver's speeches were clearly organized, with a distinct introduction, body, and conclusion. Silver was clearer than Wise in the body of his speeches, for he tended to state each argument to which he was responding and then to respond. In effect, this was often a form of topical organization similar to what Wise used. But because he clearly stated the argument to which he was responding, it may have been somewhat easier for Silver's audiences to follow his topical organization than for Wise's.

Wolpaw found that Silver's conclusions "synthesized the meaning of his thesis and main points. They were climactic in quality and often contained the only impassioned rhetoric in the speech."[72] Silver tended to argue his case in a rational fashion in the body of his speeches and then often used more emotional appeals in his conclusions.

Like Wise, Silver was a master stylist. He was exceptionally concerned with style, once advising one of his assistant rabbis at The Temple to write a complete manuscript for each of his sermons during the first five years he preached. Significantly, Silver recommended this course of action because "the vocabulary thus acquired would provide the flexibility that would enable one to become emancipated from the written manuscript and speak from notes or outline."[73] Though Silver may have recommended using manuscripts for only five years, he continued to write out most of his addresses, rarely deviating from his final manuscripts.[74] Once he had dictated a rough copy of his sermon or speech, Silver then rewrote it, making corrections, he claimed, for "style and color—is the word or phrase strong enough, colorful enough, does it say what it means?"[75]

Silver's physical appearance and voice also contributed to his success as a speaker. He was tall, with a striking appearance. He spoke slowly, pronouncing words clearly and giving clear emphasis to key words and concepts.[76]

Zionism Alters the Nature of American Jewish Preaching

The advocacy of Zionism from American Jewish pulpits opened the way for the advocacy of a wide variety of social and political issues from the Jewish pulpit. As we have seen, Jewish preachers from the earliest days did, on occasion, deal with social and political issues from the pulpit. However, though those occasions grew more frequent with the passage of time, they still remained comparatively rare. Even such a momentous issue as slavery, with its moral implications, gave rise to relatively few Jewish sermons.

In the first decades of the twentieth century, the American Jewish pulpit still shied away from treating social and political issues. But to preach on Zionism, a well-informed rabbi had to examine and discuss a wide variety of secular topics, including the history and development of the foreign policy of various nations, including the United States. Moreover, Zionist sermons often resulted in conclusions and suggestions for both individual congregants and for government officials.

From treating the topics necessary to intelligently discuss Zionism, it was but a short jump for most rabbis to preach on other important issues of the day. The trials of Nazi war criminals, restitution to the victims of Nazi persecution, the establishment of the state of Israel, and American relations with Israel were simply a few of the many issues that American Jewish preachers addressed in the months immediately following the war. Though American Jewish preaching had first started to treat social and political issues extensively by preaching on Zionism and the many concerns related to that issue, doing so paved the way to treat other concerns. So, for example, in contrast to the abolitionist movement a century earlier, the civil rights movement of the 1950s and 1960s was heavily supported by the Jewish pulpit. By mid-twentieth century, Jewish preachers, like their Christian counterparts, were frequently dealing with the nation's concerns.

6

American Jewish Preaching 1945–70:
Representative Voices

In the twenty-five years following World War II, preaching was central to American Judaism. The principal reason for this goes back to the days of Isaac Leeser. Preaching, during the postwar decades, was the primary means of adult education. It was the best means the rabbi had of educating his congregation on Jewish law and tradition. It was the medium that enabled the rabbi to place current problems and events in a Jewish context.

Moreover, in the post–World War II era, rabbis spoke to congregations that desired such an education. Since American Jews suffered from the normal problems of daily living, compounded by the unique circumstances of being a small minority in an essentially Christian nation, they desired guidance from their religion. The sermon was the principal tool the rabbi had to provide that guidance.

The educational level of American Jews in the twenty-five years following the war, as well as the nature of that often-specialized secular education, also enhanced the role of preaching among the rabbinic functions. Many American Jews felt uncomfortable with the level of their Jewish knowledge. Extensive secular educations that well prepared them to earn a living often left them feeling ill prepared to cope with the complexities of everyday life. Their participation in religious services and congregational life provided American Jews an opportunity to learn about the fundamental ideas that had enabled their ancestors to endure for thousands of years.

In the period 1945–70, that opportunity was often best fulfilled by the sermon.

In this chapter we will examine the preaching of five rabbis representative of that period. These men have been selected for examination for a variety of reasons. Each has been recognized by all denominations of American Judaism, not just their own, as an outstanding preacher. Each has, through publication, teaching, and professional activities, had an impact far beyond his local community. This is in no way to suggest that these are the five outstanding Jewish preachers of the last four decades. Such a list would at best be highly subjective and serve no useful purpose. Rather, it is to suggest that in discussions of the outstanding American Jewish preachers of the postwar period these men, among many others, are consistently mentioned as representative of the best that the American Jewish pulpit has had to offer.

Not only were these men selected on their individual merit and reputation, but it is hoped that collectively they reflect the totality of the American congregational rabbinate of their day. All three major branches of Judaism are represented in their number. Like the distribution of American Jews, these men are concentrated in urban areas, with a slightly heavier proportion of easterners. Though several of these men remain active today, collectively their preaching reached its zenith during the twenty-five years between 1945 and 1970.

Following a brief biography of each man, an examination of his rhetorical theory and an examination of the characteristics of his sermons will be presented. Concluding this chapter will be a synthesis of American Jewish preaching during the period 1945–70. In sum, it is hoped that these rhetorical biographies will serve both as models for those interested in the beliefs and practices of a highly successful group of preachers and as illustration of the broad patterns evident in the evolution of American Jewish preaching during that period.

Rabbi Morris Adler

Biography

In 1913, Rabbi Joseph Adler and his family emigrated from Russia to the United States. Seven-year-old Morris grew to manhood in New York City. His father taught Talmud at a variety of yeshivas in both Russia and the United States, helping instill Morris with his love of Judaism and his early background in his faith. Additionally, Morris attended the New York City public schools.[1]

Morris was an exceptional student, eventually graduating from both the City College of New York and the Jewish Theological Seminary. At the seminary, his strong background in Judaism, as well as his unique personal abilities, caused him to make an immediate impression. Louis Finkelstein, for years a friend and collaborator of Adler in a wide variety of endeavors, and chancellor of the Jewish Theological Seminary at the time of Adler's death, recalled that when Adler first entered "he was quickly recognized by the faculty as a student-colleague, a status he retained throughout his life."[2] Finkelstein observed that Adler's memory "was fantastic. It seemed to the rest of us that he had total recall, never forgetting anything that he read."[3]

After his 1935 ordination, Adler took pulpits for brief periods in St. Joseph, Missouri, and Buffalo, New York, until 1938, when he was offered the pulpit that he would make famous, Detroit's Congregation Shaarey Zedek. Under Adler, Shaarey Zedek became one of the largest congregations in the world. Adler became a major public figure both in Detroit and in the Conservative movement, while simultaneously serving the needs of his congregation. Within the Conservative Jewish movement he may have been best known as the author of *The World of the Talmud*, as well as other volumes. He served as adjunct professor of Agodda at the Jewish Theological Seminary and chairman of the Law Committee of the Rabbinical Assembly of America. Within his own community he served on the Cultural Commission of Michigan, was a charter member and subsequently chairman of the Public Review Board of the United Auto Workers. He held a variety of positions within the Detroit Jewish community, as well as positions within the city's interfaith and interracial movements. In March of 1966, having just finished speaking from his pulpit, with seven hundred members of his congregation looking on in disbelief, Morris Adler was shot to death by a mentally ill young man whom he had been counseling. Michigan Governor George Romney declared March 13, 1966, the day of his funeral, a day of mourning in the state. Estimates place the number of mourners who attended his funeral at about fifteen thousand.

Rhetorical Theory

Unlike some of the individuals who will be discussed in this chapter, Adler did not write or speak extensively about public speaking, preaching, or rhetoric. However, based on remarks scattered through his conversations and writings, a skeleton outline of his beliefs concerning preaching becomes apparent.

Adler felt that the major function of the sermon was to educate. He was concerned to make Judaism function as a source of strength and guidance. He was disturbed by what he called "the Jewish lag,"[4] the discrepancy between modern intelligent Jews and their Jewish "illiteracy." He perceived the sermon as a major tool for overcoming "the Jewish lag." Hence, though he frequently gave messages on current events and though he lectured widely on a variety of subjects, his weekly sermons focused primarily on the Torah and Midrash.

Adler was enormously widely read. His sermons are replete with examples from a variety of fields to illustrate the points that he makes. One of his closest associates noted: "once, when I questioned his interest in a certain journal that did not seem to be related to any aspect of his work, he replied that all printed matter was of interest to him; he did not believe in censorship or specialization."[5] While the heart of his sermon content was, of course, based on his studies of Judaism, the breadth of Adler's knowledge also contributed to his success.

Adler was particularly sensitive to the use of the English language. "I have a feeling," he once claimed, "of love and tenderness for words. . . . They are among the greatest gifts the past has given us."[6] Until the last seven years of his life, Adler routinely wrote and rewrote many of his sermons, attempting to polish their language. For Adler, the medium was, if not the message, vital in successfully conveying the message.

Adler's concern for word choice is all the more striking when we realize that he did not like to deliver his sermons from a manuscript. He would write out a manuscript and then read and reread it about six times. At that point, he reports, he felt ready to preach, not read, from it.[7] On many occasions he simply preached from notes. During the last seven years of his life, though, he entirely stopped writing out sermons in advance. "He claimed that if the idea is clear in the mind of the preacher, he should be able to deliver the message without any notes."[8] Fortunately his sermons from this period were taped and transcribed.

Adler's methods of preparation and delivery clearly depend on an enormous amount of background and learning, considerable thought about his sermon, and the self-confidence and poise necessary to deliver sermons week after week in an extemporaneous manner. Clearly his maturing intellectual abilities no doubt facilitated his eventually giving up manuscripts and notes altogether during the last years he preached.

Characteristics of Adler's Sermons

A large number of Adler's sermons are available.[9] An examination of those sermons indicates some of the techniques that help to account for his pulpit success.

Adler's introductions are abnormally long, often accounting for twenty-five to thirty percent of the length of his typical sermon. Rhetoricians suggest that an introduction should usually be ten to twenty percent of the total length of a speech.[10] This is all the more noteworthy when one considers that one of the common functions of an introduction, to build the credibility and ethos of the speaker, is largely unnecessary in the case of Adler. Instead, Adler uses his long introductions to arouse audience interest in his topic in one of several ways.

On occasion, as in his sermon "The Sanctuary: Dimensions and Limitations," he presents two apparently contradictory attitudes expressed by the Torah.[11] He explores each in detail, citing the appropriate section of the Torah and explicating it. The contradiction invites the listener's interest in its resolution, which Adler then provides in the body.

Often Adler arouses interest by utilizing the introduction to indicate why a contemporary audience should be concerned with the question addressed in the weekly Torah portion. He does not do this in a cursory fashion but, rather, goes to far more effort than typically found in speech introductions. For example, in the introduction to "The Battle Within," which deals with the life of Jacob, Adler uses the Torah passage for the week to point to his thesis, that what happens within a person is "more crucial, is more profoundly decisive, than anything that happens outside of him."[12] But rather than just indicate the truth of this passage for a contemporary audience, he attempts to prove the truth of his statement with references to Shakespeare, Freud, and contemporary psychology. These are references to which modern intelligent Jews, suffering from "Jewish lag," might well respond.

Consistently, Adler presents exceptionally lengthy introductions designed to focus audience interest and attention on his topic. Often, his introductions include or end with one or more questions.[13] These questions serve as transitions into the body of his sermon.

The majority of Adler's sermons are organized topically,[14] but he also makes use of problem-solution organization and chronological organization.[15] Adler's heavy reliance on topical organization is, perhaps, a function of at least three aspects of his speaking. First, since he spoke extemporaneously, he may have found that topical organization would give him the opportunity to add ideas and material as he was speaking. Second, topical organization is the least structured of any common organizational pattern and consequently seems to lend itself to the nature of his speech preparation and delivery. Finally, of course, many of the topics he developed simply lend themselves to topical organization.

The conclusions of Adler's sermons typically summarize or restate his thesis, making little use of the rhetorical devices commonly suggested for ending a speech. Those of his conclusions that seem especially effective seldom derive their strength from any of the rhetorical techniques commonly recommended for providing a definite sense of closure at the conclusion of a speech, that is, references back to the introduction, use of dramatic statements, quotations and examples that emphasize the thesis, or similar techniques.[16] Rather, they derive their strength from his use of language.

Adler uses language exceptionally well for several reasons. First, his word choice seems highly appropriate. Highly emotional issues, for example, are discussed in language that is rich with emotional connotation, as in his sermon of May 23, 1964, on Soviet Jewry.[17] Second, he creates vivid images with concrete language. Third, he frequently employs both repetition and alliteration. He particularly uses repetition to stress major ideas, as in his first sermon in Congregation Shaarey Zedek's new sanctuary, where he signposted and stressed each major idea by introducing it with the phrase "We here affirm."

Adler draws on the breadth of his knowledge to provide evidence for his sermons. Though the vast majority of this evidence comes from Jewish sources such as the Torah, Talmud, and Midrash, he also draws heavily upon literature, history, and current events. His sermons also contain numerous assertions. However, his credibility and ethos as rabbi no doubt compensated for those situations where more evidence might have been desired to illustrate a point conclusively.

Rabbi Solomn B. Freehof

Biography

Solomn B. Freehof was born in Russia on August 8, 1892. His family immigrated to London briefly and then, when Solomn was eleven, to Baltimore, Maryland. Here, Freehof received the bulk of his early education. In preparation for the rabbinate, Freehof received a bachelor of arts degree from the University of Cincinnati in 1914 and was ordained by Hebrew Union College in 1915.[18]

Upon graduation, Freehof was immediately invited to join the faculty of Hebrew Union College. He did so but shortly left to serve as a chaplain with the American Expeditionary Force in Europe. At the conclusion of World War I, he resumed teaching as professor of liturgy at Hebrew Union College, while simultaneously earning a doctor of divinity degree. However, in 1924, he chose to leave academia, accepting a position as rabbi of Congregation Kehillah Anshe Maariv in Chicago. In 1934, he was called to the pulpit of Rodef Shalom Congregation in Pittsburgh, where he remained for the rest of his professional career. Revealingly, Freehof's associates claim that "his eagerness to preach was one of the main reasons he left the faculty at Hebrew Union College."[19] Freehof perceives the pulpit as the rabbi's "grandest opportunity" for service.[20]

Freehof has been a key figure in the development of Reform Judaism during the second half of the twentieth century. As chairman of the Liturgy Committee of the Central Conference of American Rabbis, he was a major figure in the revision of the prayer books used in Reform temples. As a member of the Board of Governors of Hebrew Union College, he helped give direction to that institution. As president of the Central Conference of American Rabbis and also as president of the World Union for Progressive Judaism, he provided direction and leadership to those major organizations. As a scholar, his extensive publications, primarily in the areas of liturgy and biblical interpretation and response, have made his influence far-reaching and contributed to his receiving honorary degrees from Dropsie College, the University of Pittsburgh, and Hebrew Union College. Nevertheless, it is as a sermonist and speaker that Freehof remains best known throughout the American Jewish community.

Rhetorical Theory

Freehof has written and spoken extensively about public speaking and preaching.[21] Our knowledge of his rhetorical theory is based on his writing, often aimed at rabbinic students, on accounts of conversations he has had with students and colleagues,[22] and on observation of his practices.

Freehof's sermon preparation is based on wide reading and discussion of his ideas with others.[23] As he reads and talks through his ideas with others, he develops the body of his sermons and lectures. Then he spends generous time and effort developing an appropriate title and introduction. Freehof believes that the title is "of considerable importance."[24] Moreover, he feels that the introduction "is crucial,"[25] since it must clearly present the topic while simultaneously gaining and holding audience interest.[26]

In critiquing the work of others, Freehof indicates his major concerns for the body of a sermon. First, was it well organized; was there continuity to the development of a single theme throughout the sermon? Second, was the theme made relevant and meaningful to the audience? Third, was the theme presented in concrete language and images? Finally, was there something new in the conclusion?"[27]

Though Freehof planned his sermons thoroughly, he never wrote them down. He delivered his sermons extemporaneously.[28] Freehof advocated this type of delivery, as opposed to delivery from a manuscript, for two reasons: he felt that it provided for "better contact with the congregation" and that it forced the speaker, "of necessity, to be more logical in his approach to his subject."[29] Because of the crucial importance he attached to introductions, Freehof evidently did memorize the first few sentences of his introductions. Otherwise, the entire sermon was delivered extemporaneously.[30]

Characteristics of Freehof's Sermons

Freehof's sermons are widely available.[31] Analysis of them indicates that he clearly followed the advice that he offered to others. His introductions are excellent. Like Adler's introductions, Freehof's run considerably longer than the standard ten to twenty percent of a speech. Most of his introductions comprise three or more pages in sermons that typically run thirteen to fifteen pages long. Freehof's introductions invariably account for twenty percent or more of the total length of his sermons.

Moreover, his introductions fulfill the functions he sets forth for an introduction. They gain and hold interest while simultaneously introducing the topic. For example, in a sermon on religious prejudice,[32] Freehof opens by discussing the novel *Great Expectations*, illustrating how the great expectations of Charles Dickens's central character ultimately become great disappointments. From the Dickens novel he concludes that hope must be tempered with caution. He then illustrates this point again by discussing how people often have their hopes aroused by the announcement of potential medical discoveries, only to find that the discovery is tentative and needs years of work. Having now twice illustrated that great expectations must be tempered with caution, in ways with which the congregation can readily identify, Freehof moves to his topic, religious prejudice. He observes that in America we have done much to foster great expectations but that our expectations must be tempered. Freehof concludes his introduction by observing that we have not met great expectations for curing religious prejudice in the United States but that we do have medicine to help alleviate it.

This introduction is also typical of the way Freehof treats each of the major points in his longer sermons. He introduces each major point with an abstract concept, "great expectations." He then develops the concept, making it more concrete and meaningful, as in this case by relating it to medical advances. Finally, he utilizes the concept by relating it to the religious, moral, or ethical topic that he wishes to discuss, religious prejudice.[33]

The overall organization of the body of Freehof's sermons is consistent. Typically, the body is composed of three major points. Invariably, the first two points build to and are drawn together in a climactic final point. For example, in his sermon titled "Jewish Missionaries," Freehof opens the body of his presentation by observing that the phrase "Jewish missionaries" is, for Jews, disturbing.[34] He develops this by illustrating all the negative connotations that Jews might associate with missionary work, based on the Jewish experience with the Crusades, the Inquisition, and other "missions." The second major point Freehof makes is that Judaism sees itself as a true religion, but not the only true religion. Hence, he claims Judaism had a "missionary mood" when the world was pagan, but when it became monotheistic, "in the Christian form indeed, but still monotheistic, we saw no need for missionizing anybody."[35] These two points clearly build to support Freehof's final point.

We do not propagate Judaism. We demonstrate faith in God. We mean to intensify everyone's faith in his own faith by, if God helps us, being worthy examples of what religion should mean in the lives of men. Stating it plainly, it is our function to be such worthy Jews that those who see us become nobler Christians.[36]

Freehof advocated adding new material to the sermon in the conclusion. Typically, he does so, but the material is new only insofar as it is a new example, or illustration, used to support the climactic third point of the body. It is not a new idea. In the sermon just discussed, for example, Freehof's conclusion revolves around hypothetical comparisons of how Christians and Jews might react if it were first reported that a group of Shintoists had decided to convert to Christianity or Judaism and then later this report proved to be false. Such a report would initially spread joy in the Christian world and, when proved false, would result in disappointment, claimed

Freehof. But a report of such a conversion would result in bewilderment in the Jewish world and, when proved false, would result in relief.[37]

The strength of Freehof's language lies not in its eloquence or in his use of figures of speech. Rather, Freehof's strength is his use of concrete language to create meaningful images in the minds of his audience. Indeed, Freehof uses the word "pictorial" occasionally to introduce a comparison or example that he feels will simplify an abstract concept by making it vivid and concrete. His ability to paint word pictures is the strength of his language.

Freehof relies unusually heavily on literature for support materials in his sermons. Exceptionally well read, he routinely delivered a series of Wednesday "literary lectures" on best-sellers for many years. Not only did they attract members of his congregation, but they also attracted thousands of community members, particularly students and teachers. Freehof clearly distinguished between his function as a rabbi and that of the literary critic. Freehof's purpose was to assess "the social and moral impact of those writers who are already recognized and read."[38] His familiarity with best-sellers and his exceptional knowledge of Shakespeare[39] frequently manifested themselves in his sermons. His use of literature is secondary to his use of Jewish sources, but his reliance on literature distinguishes his sermons from those of his colleagues.

Freehof's delivery reminded some listeners of Lowell Thomas.[40] He spoke rather slowly but with considerable forcefulness and vocal variety.[41] His conversational manner is easy to listen to and no doubt contributed to the success of his public speaking endeavors.

Rabbi Robert Gordis

Biography

One of the most distinguished leaders of the Conservative branch of American Judaism in the post–World War II era has been Rabbi Robert Gordis. Variously described as "one of the leading theologians in American Jewish life,"[42] "a noted religious thinker and Biblical scholar,"[43] and "one of America's outstanding Rabbis,"[44] Gordis was born in New York City in 1908.[45]

He served as Rabbi of Temple Beth El of Rockaway Park, New York, from shortly before his ordination by the Jewish Theological Seminary in 1932 until his retirement in 1968. Gordis is an enormously productive scholar, having written or edited over fifteen books. He is editor of *Judaism* and has served on the editorial boards of several publications, including *Conservative Judaism*. He has been a contributor to virtually every major Jewish publication.

A professor of Bible at the Jewish Theological Seminary since 1940, Gordis has also been a faculty member at Columbia and Temple universities and Union Theological Seminary. Though perhaps best known as a distinguished scholar and congregational rabbi, Gordis has been highly active in a variety of professional organizations. At the age of thirty-six, within twelve years of his ordination, Gordis became one of the youngest men ever elected to the presidency of the Rabbinical Assembly of America. Additionally, he has served the Synagogue Council of America in a variety of capacities, including president, and the Zionist Organization of America. Having played a crucial role in the establishment of the first Conservative day school in the country at Temple Beth El, Gordis has been a major figure in the growth of the day school movement.

Though he retired in 1968, after thirty-seven years as spiritual leader of Temple Beth El, Gordis's active schedule of writing, editing, lecturing, and preaching causes him to remain a major influence in the Conservative movement, two decades since his official "retirement."

Rhetorical Theory

Gordis has not written extensively about homiletics, preaching, or public speaking. His observations focus primarily on the functions and goals of preaching, rather than on technique. In the introduction to a collection of a decade's worth of his high holiday sermons, Gordis indicates the three basic areas of concern that must be addressed from the contemporary Jewish pulpit. First, that pulpit must function to present congregants with "a vital and meaningful faith for twentieth-century man that will draw upon the wisdom of the past and be responsive to the call of the present."[46] Second, the contemporary Jewish pulpit must function to help resolve the problems of the Jewish people in the United States, in the state of Israel, and throughout the world.[47] Gordis feels that these problems must be approached "within the framework of the values that are to be found, and are all too often ignored, in the Jewish heritage."[48] Finally, the contemporary Jewish pulpit must function to help individuals achieve their "personal well-being in a new and chaotic world."[49] The Jewish pulpit must, Gordis indicates, deal with "the abiding issues of sin and forgiveness, of tragedy and joy. . . . the perennial and agonizing question of man's suffering in a world created by a good God."[50]

If his high holiday sermons are indicative, the last of these three functions, which accounts for almost half of the sermons he delivers, is of paramount importance to Gordis.[51] While a survey of the topics Gordis treats in his sermons is not available, the emphasis his high holiday sermons place on helping individuals achieve personal well-being is certainly consistent with the fact that he targets sermons heavily at young people,[52] who are so often seeking such help.

Gordis is a firm believer in the value of sermons. Acknowledging that sermons have frequently been attacked as "artificial and useless," he responds that "where the preacher approaches his task with a high sense of responsibility and devotes adequate preparation, the sermon can prove both inspiring and enlightening in the future as it has been in the past."[53]

The Jewish sermon can prove enlightening, Gordis claims, without abandoning its traditional function, "the exposition of Judaism, based upon its classical sources in general, and the scriptural reading of the day in particular."[54] Gordis is somewhat critical of preaching that utilizes current social, economic, and political issues or books and plays of current interest, because he feels that the treatment of such topics "was generally that of the lecture or secular address, with relatively little reference to Bible, Talmud, or Midrash."[55] He observes that television and radio preachers now satisfy much of the appetite for this type of presentation, and he is pleased that the 1970s have seen "a distinct diminution" in this type of "rabbinic preachment."[56]

Characteristics of Gordis's Sermons

Many of Gordis's high holiday sermons are readily accessible.[57] Gordis opens his sermons with introductions that comprise about ten to fifteen percent of the overall length of the sermon. Typically, he utilizes a startling statement or a historical occurrence to gain audience attention. The statement or historical example is used to lead into a Hebrew quotation from the Torah, Talmud, Midrash, or other rabbinic work. The explanation of the Hebrew quotation concludes the introduction and sets the stage for the body of the sermon. While this pattern is not always used, it is frequently evident. For example, Gordis's sermon preached on Kol Nidre in 1964 opens with an explanation of how the high priest of Israel prepared for Kol Nidre in ancient days.[58] Gordis details the robes the priest would have worn, the place where he would have worked, the books he would have studied, and similar information. He points out that in ancient days the high priest would have pleaded to God for the people of Israel on Yom Kippur, and hence these details were important to all. However, today "the Jewish people itself must plead for its life in the future, for in the words of the Torah, *Ve'attem tiheyu li mamlekheth kohanim vegoy kadosh*, 'You shall be for Me a kingdom of priests and a holy nation' (Exodus 19:6)."[59] This explanation is briefly amplified at the end of the introduction and leads directly to the body of the sermon, which treats the ways in which each individual Jew should prepare for the future.

The overall organizational pattern that Gordis follows in his sermons varies. However, the two predominant patterns are topical and problem-solution organization. For example, in a Passover sermon preached in 1960, Gordis effectively utilizes topic organization to illuminate the meaning of Passover.[60] He has three major points. First, Passover is the most beloved of all Jewish holidays. Second, Passover exemplifies the struggle for liberty that men have had in countless places throughout history. He illustrates this point by likening the struggle of the Israelites against the Egyptians to those of the colonists with Great Britain, the blacks against slavery, the current civil rights movement against racial discrimination, and the fight of South African blacks against their oppressors. Finally, he presents the "four great truths" regarding liberty that are evident from the Passover story and that apply to virtually all struggles for liberty.

The second predominant pattern of organization Gordis makes use of in his sermons is problem-solution. For example, in his Rosh Hashanah sermon "The Revolution in Man," Gordis opens the body of the sermon by asking "What has happened to modern man?"[61] He then discusses a variety of problems plaguing modern man: dehumanization of man, mechanization of man, depersonalization of man, manipulation of man, and the breakdown of communication among men. Moreover, he points out that if current trends continue, these problems will dominate our future. However, Gordis finds that Rosh Hashanah is the world's birthday, the beginning of the year, the first ray of light that ends the night. If we have true faith, remembering "that God rules His world, which He created not for chaos but for human habitation," our problems will not appear so insurmountable. After all, he continues, "the evils that man has made he can unmake."[62] The problems are great, but they are man-made. The solution is faith in God and our own resolution at this new year that the world is not dying of problems, but rather that, fashioned in the image of God, we can overcome them.

The conclusions of Gordis's sermons are brief, rarely accounting for more than ten percent of their total length. Frequently, Gordis concludes his sermons by utilizing a quotation from Jewish sources to exemplify the major idea he is presenting. His interest in biblical poetry is reflected in the fact that he often utilizes poetry for this purpose.

Perhaps also reflecting his interests in poetry, Gordis uses a full range of figures of speech in his sermons. His figures of speech serve not only as "decorative devices," making his sermons pleasant to hear, but also serve to provide clarity and vividness to his message. For example, in his sermon "Leave a Little to God," Gordis draws an analogy between the history of man's progress and a pendulum. In both instances, "we do not go forward in a straight line, but fluctuate from one extreme to the other."[63] Gordis employs this analogy to characterize the balance between science and man's progress on one hand and faith in God on the other. In addition to analogies, Gordis makes frequent use of metaphors, similes, parallel structure, alliteration, and rhetorical questions.

Gordis refers heavily to Jewish sources in his sermons. Secondarily, he relies on great literature and popular periodicals. His use of a variety of material serves not only to strengthen his arguments but also to hold interest. Indeed, most often when literature or current sources are cited it seems that they serve more to hold interest and attention than to really advance an argument.

Rabbi Robert I. Kahn

Biography

Robert Kahn was born in Des Moines, Iowa, in 1910. His family was active in the Reform community, and Kahn became interested in the rabbinate as a career while in high school.[64] Entering Hebrew Union College at age sixteen, he was ordained in 1935 and then moved to Houston, Texas, to serve as assistant rabbi at Congregation Beth Israel. With the outbreak of World War II, Kahn enlisted in the chaplaincy corps, serving in the South Pacific. In 1944, he was invited to serve as the founding rabbi of a new Houston congregation, Temple Emanu El. He assumed that position upon returning from the service in 1945 and remained there until his retirement in 1978. Under his leadership Temple Emanu El grew from two hundred families to over fifteen hundred.

Kahn received a doctorate of Hebrew letters from Hebrew Union College in 1950, and his dissertation was a study of liberal thought in nineteenth-century Jewish preaching.[65] More so than most rabbis, Kahn has studied, lectured, and written about preaching. In addition to his dissertation, which focuses more on liberal thought than on homiletic practices but which demanded his exposure to a large sample of sermons preached by a wide variety of rabbis, Kahn has lectured on preaching at Hebrew Union College-Jewish Institute of Religion.[66] His lectures form the basis of several publications on preaching.[67]

Kahn has been a major figure in both the Reform movement and in the Houston community. He served as chairman of the Central Conference of American Rabbis' Liturgy Committee, which helped prepare several new Reform prayer books, including a new Haggadah for the Passover service. Ultimately, he was elected president of the Central Conference of American Rabbis. He has also served as chairman of the United Jewish Appeal's Rabbinic Advisory Committee.

Within Houston he may be best known as the author, for twenty-five years, of a weekly column in the *Houston Chronicle*, "Lessons for Life." He has also been president of the Houston Rotary Club (the largest in the world), district governor of the Rotary, chaplain of the Grand Masonic Lodge of Texas, and national chaplain of the American Legion. Though officially retiring from the pulpit in 1978, he remains highly active as an author and speaker.

Rhetorical Theory

Kahn sees himself standing in the tradition of many of the early Reform preachers he studied in his dissertation, those who preached for social justice.[68] Moreover, he perceives this to be the current and future direction of at least the Reform pulpit, if not the entire Jewish pulpit, claiming that "probably the outstanding character of the Reform Jewish pulpit sermon has been its concern for social justice. Traditional Judaism emphasized the Torah. Reform moved the focus of attention to the *Nev'im*, the prophets. And so with Reform preaching."[69] Although he was taught to read the upcoming weekly Torah portion and study the commentaries "until a portion of the text, in effect, says, 'Preach me!'," Kahn finds that this is not his common practice. Rather, he finds that both he and most rabbis of his acquaintance "have an idea for a sermon first and then seek a text." If he is unable to find a text in the weekly portion, then he may preach a sermon not tied to text.[70]

Kahn is well aware of the fact that, when composing a sermon, the speaker must be sensitive to the needs of the audience, which mandate that "a sermon requires careful outlining, outlining which is apparent to the listener."[71] Similarly, the needs of the audience mandate that the sermonist "frequently restate ideas" and use "short and simple sentences" and "a largely Anglo-Saxon vocabulary."[72]

Kahn advises sermonists to spend hours and hours of hard work preparing.[73] He recommends preparing the sermon carefully in writing and then reviewing and practicing it so thoroughly that "you can preach not only without a manuscript, but without any notes."[74] After delivering the sermon, the preacher, Kahn feels, should rely on an honest critic. He cautions young rabbis not to be flattered when someone compliments their sermons, because "someone will always be kind enough to flatter you."[75] Rather, the rabbi should seek out the comments of an honest, candid, and discerning critic. He suggests the speech departments at local universities as a possible source for a reliable critic.[76]

Kahn has written about wedding sermons, funeral sermons, and special occasion sermons.[77] The essence of his advice for each of these situations is to anticipate audience expectations and then attempt to meet those expectations in an artistically sound fashion. For example, Kahn feels that audiences at funerals expect the rabbi to attempt to provide comfort to the family and friends, highlight the meritorious qualities of the deceased, and treat the ultimate values of life.[78] Hence, he offers advice on how to meet these three audience expectations and thus how to conform to the demands inherent in the rhetorical situations created by funeral services.

Characteristics of Kahn's Sermons

Perhaps the most conspicuous characteristic of Kahn's sermons is his language. It is spare, concise, unadorned, direct, and readily understandable. Kahn makes little use of figures of speech but utilizes concrete language to create images with which the audience can readily identify. He relies heavily on simple sentence structures. Clearly, he is making every effort to follow his own advice and make the language easy for the audience to follow.

A sermon preached the day after Thanksgiving, "Leftover Turkey," well illustrates many characteristics of Kahn's style.[79] The very title creates a clear, concrete image and serves as an appropriate metaphor for the low points, depressions, and anticlimaxes that often follow big events in our lives.

Notice the many vivid concrete everyday images that Kahn creates, the unadorned language, and the simple sentence structure, when he first advances his thesis:

Now the real test of a good housewife is not what she serves on Thanksgiving, but rather how she handles leftover turkey. It is no trick to please a family with fresh turkey, or broiled steak, or standing rib roast every night and just throw away the leftovers. All that takes is money. But the test of a housewife is to take the leftovers and turn them into some appetizing, attractive and tasty dish.[80]

A second characteristic of Kahn's language is his reliance, precisely as he advises, on Anglo-Saxon vocabulary. Kahn rarely uses any foreign language, including Hebrew. This is not to say that Hebrew is never used, but it is to say that his sermons are conspicuous by its absence, when contrasted with most of his colleagues in the Jewish pulpit. This may be partly a function of Kahn's audience analysis. His Reform audiences may not be as familiar with Hebrew as those in Orthodox and Conservative synagogues.

A third characteristic of Kahn's sermons no doubt contributes to the comparative paucity of Hebrew in his sermons. Kahn relies less on the Torah, Talmud, Midrash, and other Jewish sources for evidence than most of his colleagues. To utilize this material as heavily as others might cause Kahn to violate some of his own rhetorical beliefs about making the sermon understandable.

Kahn's reliance on secular rather than traditionally Jewish sources of evidence is particularly evident in his sermon "The Need for Reasonable Dialogue," preached immediately after the Kent State incident in which four students were killed by the Ohio National Guard during a demonstration against the Vietnam War.[81] One might well expect a rabbi to preach a sermon drawing heavily on Jewish tradition and teaching to help guide his congregants in this emotionally charged situation. Kahn's sermon does not cite a single Jewish source. Rather, his support materials include references to current events, to his own experience at a recent Rice University commencement, to a report issued by Dr. Martin Luther King, to a letter written to *Time* magazine by a nineteen-year-old college student, to a conversation between Kahn and one of his congregants, to William Shirer's writing about Nazi Germany. While this sermon represents the extreme, insofar as Kahn makes no references to things Jewish, certainly his reliance on rabbinic literature is markedly less than most of his contemporaries in the Jewish pulpit. Kahn's comparatively limited use of figures of speech, Hebrew, and Jewish sources, all seem to be deliberate choices on his part, designed to foster clear and immediate understanding by his audiences.

These characteristics of his sermons, coupled with their clear organization, make them exceptionally easy for an audience to understand. Kahn most often uses topical organization, with some reliance on problem-solution organization. His introductions and conclusions are of typical length. One of the strengths of his organization is his ability to, in a variety of ways, repeat his major ideas. For example, in the passage quoted above from "Leftover Turkey," notice that he makes the major point twice, both in the first and last sentences. Subsequently, in the following paragraph he uses two brief illustrations with which his audience could readily identify to make the point. This passage is then followed with two extensive examples about the lives of Jewish leaders to make the same point. He then moves from illustrating that the challenge of our individual lives is in what we do when we are depressed, saddened, and afflicted to illustrating that the challenge to nations is similar. Here he reviews both American and Jewish history. Kahn's ability to amplify an idea is exceptional and contributes appreciably both to audience interest and audience understanding.

Rabbi Joseph H. Lookstein

Biography

Norman Lamm, president of Yeshiva University, appointed Rabbi Joseph H. Lookstein University Professor of Homiletics and has called him "probably the greatest orator of his generation of rabbis, certainly of the Orthodox rabbinate."[82] Joseph Lookstein had a profound influence on Orthodox preaching. His influence was a result of both his teaching and the example he set, from 1923 until his death in 1979, at Congregation Kahilath Jeshurun, in New York City.

Born in Russia in 1903, Lookstein was brought to the United States as a child.[83] Lookstein had actually begun to serve as an assistant rabbi at Kahilath Jeshurun several years prior to his ordination by the Rabbi Isaac Elchanan Theological Seminary of Yeshiva University in 1926. In 1929, he helped to found the Hebrew Teachers Training School and served for ten years as its principal. In 1931, he joined the Yeshiva faculty, becoming professor of sociology, homiletics, and practical rabbinics.

In 1936, he became rabbi at Kahilath Jeshurun and also that year founded the Ramaz School. The Ramaz School pioneered in the development of curriculums that provided students with an excellent secular education, focusing on the best elements of Western civilization and the American democratic heritage, as well as the study of Judaism. For thirty years, Lookstein served as principal of this school and was a major figure in the growth of the Jewish day school movement in the United States.

In the mid 1950s, Lookstein was heavily involved in the founding of Bar-Ilan University in Israel. In 1958, upon the premature death of its president, Lookstein was urged to assume the role of acting president. He did so with distinction, inheriting a fledgling school of several hundred students and moving it dramatically toward its present position as an outstanding university of approximately ten thousand students, who study a wide variety of disciplines, including a full complement of graduate and professional programs.

Yet for all of his work in the field of Jewish education, Lookstein is perhaps best known as a congregational rabbi. Under his leadership Kahilath Jeshurun became a model for many Orthodox synagogues. As his successor and son has written, Lookstein "strove to combine warmth with dignity, the enthusiasm of Orthodoxy with the aesthetics of Reform, the tradition of four thousand years of Jewish practice with the modern, active tempo of young men and women who were born and bred in the New World."[84] To that end, Kahilath Jeshurun was among the early Orthodox synagogues to develop a men's club, a sisterhood, a young people's club, the use of English prayers, and sermons on relevant and timely themes.

Lookstein was active in a wide variety of professional groups. At various times in his career he served as president of the Rabbinical Council of America, the Synagogue Council of America, and the New York Board of Rabbis. At the time of his death he was serving as chairman of the Rabbinical Advisory Council of the United Jewish Appeal.

Rhetorical Theory

Although he taught homiletics for a number of years, Lookstein did not publish extensively about preaching. Nevertheless, his writings do reveal some basic thoughts about the nature of preaching. A sermon, according to Lookstein, is "first and foremost a religious homily—the word of God that comes from a divinely inspired emissary. And second, it must register some effect upon a listener."[85] Both of these requirements of a sermon are crucial to Lookstein's perception of the modern sermon. The preacher who preaches without reference to the word of God or without exhorting or inspiring the listener has not preached a sermon. For Lookstein, the sermon "teaches what is right, and inspires audiences to do what is right."[86]

According to Lookstein, these twin goals of the sermon can be attained in three ways,[87] the first of which is through use of the classical sermon. By "classical," Lookstein means a sermon in which the preacher opens by quoting a biblical or rabbinic text and then proceeds to analyze and interpret it in a manner that is both informative and inspirational. The second type of sermon Lookstein utilizes is the "topical sermon." He believes that many topics, such as hunger, freedom, and other contemporary questions, can be discussed from the pulpit as long as the rabbi presents "the religious view" of these topics. Finally, Lookstein believes that the preacher might fulfill his goals by use of the "project sermon." Lookstein draws the designation "project sermon" from the work of Harry Emerson Fosdick and utilizes it to describe a sermon dealing with personality and the problems that assail us as we try to make our way in life. While all people face many problems, Jews may have unique problems because of the threats of assimilation, acculturation, hostility, persecution, memories of the holocaust, and the like. The "project sermon" addresses these concerns.

Lookstein is firmly convinced that the sermon must make use of classical Jewish sources. Though he notes that sermons often deal with contemporary life, he observes that a sermon's "spirit and substance" should be "drawn from the classic sources of Judaism, Biblical and rabbinic texts."[88]

Finally, Lookstein feels that one becomes an effective preacher through imitation and practice. Calling the sermon an art form, Lookstein claims that "artists begin by imitating others whom they admire."[89] Eventually, he continues, the preacher will develop his own style of preaching based both on those whom he admires and imitates and on his own abilities and limitations.

Characteristics of Lookstein's Sermons

Lookstein's sermons typically open with comparatively brief introductions. He most frequently makes a brief, startling statement to gain initial audience attention and then moves quickly into the body of his sermon. Similarly, the conclusions to his sermons tend to be brief. His conclusions often utilize a biblical or other quotation that exemplifies the major point of the sermon.

Lookstein's organization is quite clear. He relies almost exclusively on problem-solution organization or topical organization. His unusually heavy reliance on problem-solution organization is no doubt an outgrowth of his perception that sermons are of three types. Both the topical sermon and the project sermon clearly lend themselves to problem-solution organization.

In his topical sermons, Lookstein first develops the dimensions of a contemporary social issue. For example, in his Rosh Hashanah sermon "The Erosion of Authority," he examines the loss of respect and authority that such social institutions as the legal system, the family, and organized religion suffered in the 1960s and 1970s.[90] He presents this erosion of authority as a serious social problem. In the last portion of the sermon he offers a solution, observing that "Rosh Hashanah is the one festival which more than any other stresses the principle of authority."[91] He continues, illustrating that on Rosh Hashanah we acknowledge God as a higher authority who commands our respect. In doing so, we acknowledge the appropriateness of obedience to just authorities.

In his project sermons, Lookstein first develops the dimensions of a personal problem that many members of his audience might share. For example, in "Gloom and Doom: Are There No Other Alternatives?" he observes that many people suffer from an overwhelming feeling of apprehension and fear.[92] He develops three reasons why this mood is so pervasive, claiming that ours is an "unhappy generation."[93] Having thus described the problem and some of its principal causes, Lookstein then turns to the solution. For Lookstein, the solution is a return to the principles from which many of us have strayed. Quoting a Watergate conspirator, Lookstein notes that we lack an "ethical compass." Judaism can provide us with that ethical compass.[94]

The major strength of Lookstein's sermons is his ability to simultaneously harness traditional biblical and rabbinic literature and contemporary events and literature. Invariably, his sermons included five to ten, and occasionally as many as twenty, references to traditional Jewish sources. Yet he also supports his points by citing contemporary events, personalities, and literature. Norman Lamm has observed that Lookstein was one of those very rare individuals who lived in two cultures: the traditional rabbinic culture and the culture of contemporary America.[95] Perhaps nowhere is this more evident than in the blend of materials Lookstein drew upon for his sermons.

Lookstein's language is generally unadorned. He uses vivid concrete language, simple sentence structure, and comparatively few figures of speech. He does frequently use rhetorical questions, often for transitional purposes.

Characteristics of American Jewish Preaching: 1945–1970

An assessment of the characteristics of American Jewish preaching in the decades following World War II helps to indicate how far that preaching has progressed since it first began. Moreover, based in part on an examination of five of the outstanding Jewish preachers of the period, it also provides insight into the rhetorical practices of the period. At least six major characteristics of American Jewish preaching during the twenty-five years following the war warrant attention.

1. *American Judaism provided an environment where preaching could and did flourish.*

Perhaps at no time in its long history had America's Jewish community been more sensitive to the fact that they were Jewish than in the decades immediately following World War II. While their faith had always distinguished American Jews from their countrymen, the years after the war, which saw the full revelation of the scope of the holocaust and the establishment of the state of Israel, heightened self-awareness on the part of American Jews. This increasing awareness of their faith contributed to providing an environment where preaching could flourish. Interest in Jewish beliefs, customs, and traditions could all be satisfied, at least in part, by effective preaching. Moreover, seminaries, as we will see more fully in the epilogue, improved their homiletic offerings, responding to the demand for preaching by placing greater stress on the study of communication and preaching skills than ever before.

Additionally, the reward system for rabbis placed great emphasis on preaching during these decades. Preaching became, as Robert Kahn wrote, the "show window" of a rabbi's life.[96] Through preaching, the rabbi could counsel, educate, affect human lives, and affect society. Preaching could provide the rabbi with enormous personal satisfaction. Additionally, the effectiveness of a rabbi's preaching became a major criterion utilized by synagogues and temples in selecting their rabbis. Preaching became a key to rabbinic advancement. Larger and better-paying congregations, particularly in the Conservative and Reform branches of American Judaism, weighed preaching heavily when they searched for new rabbis.

2. *American rabbis sought to provide distinctive sermons.*

Jewish sermons are distinctive from all other forms of speaking because of their fundamental reliance upon Jewish sources. The degree of that reliance differs from rabbi to rabbi. But the fact that the Torah, Talmud, Midrash, and other rabbinic literature, as well as Jewish history and tradition, serve as the underpinnings of the sermon has never been in doubt. It is this fact that originally distinguished the Jewish sermon from all other forms of speaking, and which continued to distinguish it in the period 1945–70.

Joseph Lookstein calls the sermon "first and foremost a religious homily," and he frequently cited religious sources fifteen to twenty times a sermon. Robert Gordis frowned upon preaching that relied heavily on current books, plays, or social issues and had little reference to Jewish sources. Even such Reform rabbis as Freehof and Kahn, who utilized secular sources to a greater degree than many of their colleagues in Conservative and Orthodox pulpits, claimed that the ultimate purpose of the sermon was, as Kahn expressed it, "to make our religious principles relevant to life today. . . . The pulpit sermon is the tool by which the eternal becomes timely, and the universal becomes local."[97] Timely and local references and support materials always serve to illustrate distinctively Jewish principles.

3. *American rabbis sought to provide sermons that treated matters of both private faith and public concern.*

In post–World War II America, Jewish sermons dealt with matters of both private faith and public concern. On the private or individual level, sermons were often designed to educate, to overcome what Morris Adler called "the Jewish lag." As Robert Gordis observed, sermons were often designed to help congregants achieve "personal well-being in a new and chaotic world." They did so, Lookstein hoped, by teaching "what is right" and by inspiring audiences "to do what is right."

But sermons were designed to provide congregants not only with guidance in conducting their own private lives but also with guidance in reacting to the public issues of the day. From the days of Gershom Seixas's holiday and fast sermons, Jewish sermons had, on occasion, dealt with contemporary affairs. However, in the postwar period these occasions became so numerous as to become virtually the norm. The Orthodox Joseph Lookstein defined one of his three sermon types, the topical sermon, by pointing out that it presents a "religious view" of a "contemporary question," such as hunger or freedom. Robert Kahn claimed that the distinctive feature of the Jewish pulpit was its concern for social justice, and he repeatedly addressed that concern from his own pulpit, particularly during the civil rights movement of the 1960s.

The prevalence of problem-solution organization among the sermons of the rabbis of this period reflects their twin interests in matters of private faith and public concern, for the problem-solution organizational pattern lends itself to dealing both with private or individual questions of faith and with questions or problems of public concern.

4. *American rabbis sought to provide sermons that both informed and persuaded through personal involvement.*

The effectiveness of any speech is at least in part, and often in very great part, dependent upon the credibility of the speaker. To the extent that the speaker seems personally involved with the ideas being expressed and totally conversant and fluent with them, he will be perceived as credible. During the latter half of the twentieth century, many American rabbis sought personal involvement with the ideas they preached. Many of the outstanding speakers of this period, including Adler (during the last portion of his life), Freehof, and Kahn, sought to preach from few notes and without manuscripts.

Their methods of preparation, which included wide reading, thorough study, repeated and detailed outlining, and long practice, enabled many of the leading rabbis of this period to deliver their speeches in an extemporaneous fashion. These methods of preparation and delivery, as Freehof expressed it, "created better contact with the audience." While many rabbis of this period continued to rely on manuscripts, a large number of those who were recognized for their excellence as preachers prepared and delivered their sermons in ways that minimized their reliance on a manuscript. By doing so, they clearly increased their personal involvement with both the topics of their sermons and their audiences.

5. *American rabbis sought to provide sermons that captured audience attention.*

By 1945, sermons were no longer a novelty, and audience attention was not something that the rabbi could simply assume. Rather, it was something that he had to earn. American rabbis of this period often worked diligently to secure audience attention. Some, such as Adler and Freehof, often devoted as much as twenty-five percent of their entire sermon to gaining audience attention in the introduction.

The classical sermon, which opened with a text, was certainly still used. But more and more, rabbis were opening their speeches with a wide variety of other attention-gaining rhetorical devices. Startling statements, rhetorical questions, personalized examples, and similar material served to introduce the sermon. The usage of these techniques reflects a growing awareness of the need to gain attention. Moreover, American rabbis of this period also seem to evidence a clear awareness of the need to hold attention throughout the speech. The increased use of secular sources—references to current events, popular literature, and other nonrabbinic support materials—points to the rabbis' concern that their sermons both gain initial attention and then hold the congregation's attention throughout.

6. *American rabbis sought to provide sermons that clearly reflected the needs of a listening audience.*

Listeners, unlike readers, have unique needs that must be satisfied by the speaker if that speaker hopes to meet with success. Because of the transient and impermanent nature of speech, language is of particular importance. The speaker's word choice and use of language are the principal means available to him to ensure that he is able to present his ideas clearly, understandably, and memorably. It is no accident then that each of the sermonists examined in this chapter use language exceptionally well. Adler talks of his love of language and words. Freehof stresses the need for concrete language and imagery. Gordis's interest in biblical poetry seems to translate into his excellent use of metaphors, alliteration, and similar rhetorical devices to give clarity and vividness to his message. Kahn stresses clarity as perhaps the chief goal of the sermonist, and he seeks it through the use of simple sentence structure, repetition, and word choice. Lookstein too keeps his language simple and concrete.

Additionally, audiences have clear expectations about sermon content. Each of the principal Jewish holidays has certain messages that Jewish audiences have traditionally come to associate with it. Rosh Hashana and Yom Kippur, for example, are traditionally times for introspection and self-evaluation; they are times to think about one's personal relationships. Passover is a time of rejoicing, a time to think not quite so much about one's self but, rather, about the entire Jewish people. Similarly, each of the holidays, to a lesser extent each of the weekly Torah portions, and, of course, each of the special services where audiences have grown to expect a sermon, such as funerals or weddings, all generate clear audience expectations about the content of the rabbi's message.

American rabbis have conscientiously sought to reflect those audience needs and expectations in their sermons. In so doing, they have continued to perpetuate those same audience needs and expectations throughout the years. Obviously, individual rabbis take individual approaches and attempt to vary their approaches. Nevertheless, in the twenty-five years between 1945 and 1970, American rabbis sought to provide sermons that reflected the needs of their audiences in terms of both language and thematic content.

Epilogue

![line]

Current Homiletic Training in American Rabbinic Seminaries and the Future of American Jewish Preaching

In the previous chapters a history of American Jewish preaching from the inception of the American Jewish community in 1654 through the year 1970 has been presented. This epilogue attempts to anticipate what we might expect from the American Jewish pulpit in the next few decades. As a means of anticipating the future, this epilogue examines current pedagogical practices in American rabbinic seminaries. The homiletic training received by recent graduates and current students in American rabbinic seminaries may well be the most important single factor in the ongoing evolution of American Jewish preaching. Current seminary practices are likely to have an impact on American Jewish preaching for years to come. They serve as a reasonable point of departure from which to anticipate the nature of American Jewish preaching in the remainder of the twentieth century and beyond.

Current Homiletic Education

Hebrew Union College-Jewish Institute of Religion and the Jewish Theological Seminary of America both have well-developed homiletic programs. Yeshiva University and the Reconstructionist Rabbinical College offer students less work in homiletics. The comparatively slight offerings at Yeshiva, like that at other Orthodox seminaries, is an accurate reflection of the Orthodox movement's perception of the rabbinic functions. Clearly, Orthodox Judaism does not place the preaching function on quite the same level as the Conservative and Reform movements. The Reconstructionist movement, a comparatively recent outgrowth of Conservative Judaism, whose seminary was first chartered in 1968, takes a substantially different approach to rabbinic training from any of the other three major American rabbinic seminaries. It offers students only one course in homiletics.

Hebrew Union College-Jewish Institute of Religion (HUC-JIR) requires students to complete an extensive two-semester course in homiletics and three courses of one semester each in speech.[1] The two-semester core homiletics course covers three major units: textual sermons, life cycle and special occasion preaching, and high holiday and other sermons.[2] Required readings focus on the homiletic work of Jewish scholars but also include works by and about non-Jews such as Harry Emerson Fosdick.[3] The course requires of each student a minimum of seven sermons, as well as many text analyses, sermon outlines, and readings.

Each of the three required courses in speech is designed to focus on a different aspect of the rabbi's communication functions. By design, they are meant to avoid treating sermons extensively, since sermons are treated in the two-semester homiletics core course. One of the speech courses focuses on the oral interpretation of religious literature. The second focuses on nonsermonic public address functions of the rabbinate: informative speaking, persuasive speaking, speeches of presentation, introduction, dedication, and panel and symposium presentations. This course acquaints students with basic concepts of rhetorical theory drawn from the works of Aristotle, Cicero, Blair, Campbell, Whately, and other seminal figures in rhetorical theory. Additionally, the thoughts of outstanding Jewish preachers, such as Isaac M. Wise, Stephen Wise, and Abba Hillel Silver, on basic concepts of rhetorical theory are also presented. Student assignments involve each type of speech.[4] The third course focuses on oral style. Typically, it is the last communications course taken and is an attempt to help students polish their oral style.[5]

Those involved in providing homiletic training at HUC-JIR perceive three strengths to their program. First, the overall stress that the school places on preaching and communication skills is perceived as a major strength. Students take a homiletics or speech course every year of their program, excepting the first year, which is spent in Israel. Additionally, they must prepare sermons for services in the school's chapel and for the congregations that many of them serve for one or more years during their schooling. Each student is also responsible for a senior sermon, delivered in the college chapel and critiqued by potentially the entire college community. As one faculty member expressed it, "communication skills are emphasized throughout four years of the five year program. This gives students time to mature—to practice—and to become effective self-critics."[6]

A second strength of the program, alluded to in the statement above, is that it provides students with a basis for critiquing their own work. Faculty members perceive this as exceptionally important, since many students may have difficulty getting informed critiques of their preaching once they leave the institution. Through practice in joint critiquing by faculty and students and through exposure to the basic rubrics of homiletic thought and rhetorical theory, the students, it is hoped, will be able to accurately evaluate their own efforts.

A final strength of the HUC-JIR program is thought to be the extensive experience in preaching that is provided each student. While the number will vary depending on such factors as the demands of the congregation in which the student may serve as student rabbi and the length of time of that service, virtually every HUC-JIR student will have preached, according to their faculty, at least thirty or more sermons, many in circumstances that have allowed for feedback about their preaching, prior to assuming a pulpit.[7]

The homiletic faculty of HUC-JIR identifies three weaknessess in the current program. First, virtually every faculty member laments the lack of time devoted to homiletics. Faculty members feel that more time would be highly desirable. Second, and no doubt related to the time problem, virtually every faculty member lamented the overall writing/speaking level of current students. As one faculty member stated, "it is difficult to compensate for weaknesses of prior training."[8] Clearly, the lack of time to work with students on homiletic and other communication-related matters and the perception that current students do not come to this graduate institution with the language skills that they had as recently as ten years ago constitute the major weaknesses of the program as the faculty sees them. This second problem may well reflect growing national concerns about communication skills. Students at HUC-JIR are often among the most outstanding students at their undergraduate institutions. Nevertheless, as another faculty member expressed it:

the greatest weakness, which plagues our entire effort, is our inability to demand *eloquence* from the students. Some of our students simply cannot write well. Even if they master the fundamentals, however, they do not necessarily achieve or even strive for a level of rhetoric or a depth of thought that we normally associate with "fine homiletics." Our students dare to be adequate.[9]

The third weakness of their program, as expressed by the HUC-JIR faculty was that students often were not exposed to a great deal of highly effective preaching. Their schedules as students, and often simultaneously as rabbis serving smaller and more isolated temples, make it difficult for typical HUC-JIR students to hear outstanding preachers week after week. Several faculty members regretted this situation but saw little possibility of remedying it.[10]

While each of these three weaknesses is understandable, all do have obvious remedies. A faculty uniformly concerned about providing more time for homiletics certainly ought to be able to devise some methods for doing so. Training out of class, using audio and video tapes, might be one way of overcoming the time problem. Asking students to consistently practice critiquing speakers, such as those who visit the campus, and then informally discussing those critiques with faculty members might be another.

Though one does not expect a graduate institution to provide remedial work, certainly if dissatisfaction with the speaking and writing abilities of the student body is widespread, solutions might be devised. Perhaps greater emphasis should be placed on these skills by the admissions office when recruiting. Perhaps oral and written style might be treated earlier and more extensively in the curriculum. Perhaps style might be a component of work evaluated by all instructors, in all departments, in all written and spoken assignments. Certainly, such a procedure would telegraph a message to students signaling the importance of communication skills.

Finally, the fact that students are not exposed to as much effective preaching as the faculty would wish might also be remedied. A library of video tapes of effective preachers would be one way to expose students to a variety of techniques. There are no doubt others. In sum, the problems that the HUC-JIR homiletic faculty perceives are amenable to change, though doing so will require commitments of additional time, effort, equipment, and money.

The homiletic program at the Jewish Theological Seminary (JTS) requires students seeking ordination as Conservative rabbis to take three one-semester courses,[11] a requirement introduced in the late 1970s. The first class focuses on developing student abilities to interpret texts and use good oral style.[12] The two subsequent courses focus on other aspects of preaching and speaking, including delivery. The senior course requires the student to preach, both in class and in the seminary synagogue, a sermon that is to be "written out in full before delivery in class"; however, the "sermon would be delivered in class and in synagogue preferably from notes only."[13]

A survey of the faculty involved with the homiletic program at JTS in academic year 1984–85 indicates a pattern of strengths and weaknesses very analogous to those found at HUC-JIR.[14] The seminary perceives its students as learning well how to interpret texts. This facet of homiletic education is stressed in each of the seminary courses, particularly the first and third. Second, the seminary faculty feels that students are at least made aware of the importance of language. Like their counterparts at HUC-JIR, the faculty at JTS are concerned about the ability of students to use language well. However, they do feel that since revising their program in the late 1970s, they are now making students aware of the importance of language in virtually every aspect of a rabbi's job, particularly preaching.

Students at the seminary will have preached a minimum of fifteen, and in many cases more than twice that number, sermons prior to ordination.[15] The number will vary depending on what the student does to supplement his seminary courses. Some will hold pulpits on a part-time basis while students, often for several years, thereby dramatically increasing the number of sermons preached. In sum, it would appear that the faculties at both HUC-JIR and JTS have somewhat similar perceptions of the strengths of their programs.

Virtually every faculty member at the seminary expressed concern about the lack of time they had to work on the preaching skills of their students. The fact that this was also true at HUC-JIR, which does require more classroom time of its students to be spent on homiletics and speaking, probably reflects the fact that training in the use of a language is not something that can be provided quickly. Like their counterparts at HUC-JIR, faculty members at JTS are also concerned about the mastery of English exhibited by their students. One noted that his homiletics course was to be a course in homiletics not English composition, but that he was disappointed to find how often that skill (English) had not been mastered in high school or undergraduate work.[16]

No systematic surveys of student or alumni opinion about the homiletic programs at HUC-JIR or JTS are available. However, a 1968 study by Charles Lieberman provides at least one measure of student opinion.[17] As part of a larger study, Lieberman asked students at HUC-JIR and JTS to evaluate the degree of emphasis their institutions placed on "homiletics and practical rabbinics." Students attending the New York branch and the Cincinnati branch of HUC-JIR had somewhat different ideas. While only fifteen percent of the New York students claimed that the institution placed "too little emphasis" on homiletics and practical rabbinics, fully forty-eight percent of those in Cincinnati reached that conclusion. Among the future rabbis attending JTS in 1968, thirty-two percent felt that "too little emphasis" was placed on homiletics and practical rabbinics. This study is somewhat dated. It also links homiletics with practical rabbinics. Nevertheless, it does suggest that the current homiletics faculty concern about the lack of stress placed on their discipline has been shared by significant numbers of students for a considerable period.

While both JTS and HUC-JIR have well-developed programs to provide for the homiletic education of their students, the remaining rabbinic seminaries do not have as fully developed programs.

The principal Orthodox seminary, the Rabbi Isaac Elchanan Theological Seminary (RIETS) of Yeshiva University, requires students to take "six semesters of courses" in the Department of Supplementary Rabbinic Training. After a required survey course, students may elect one of three tracks: pulpit, education, or chaplaincy. Those who elect the pulpit or chaplaincy track are required to take one semester of homiletics.[18]

The approach to homiletics at RIETS seems highly consistent with that of Orthodox Jewry, which has traditionally tended to minimize the preaching and pastoral functions of the rabbi and to maximize the scholarly function. As of 1984–85, RIETS was the only school among the three major rabbinic seminaries in the country where it was possible to be ordained without any work in homiletics. The fact that most students might take but one course, and that course offered by a department of "supplementary rabbinic training," signifies the lack of emphasis placed on homiletic and speech education at RIETS. This lack of emphasis may be changing. As of 1985, RIETS noted that the program in supplementary rabbinics "as it exists now, is being re-examined" in light of other program changes.[19] The RIETS program is consistent with that offered by the remaining Orthodox seminaries, none of which stress study in homiletics, speaking, and other communication-related skills to the degree that the Conservative and Reform seminaries do.

While the practices at RIETS are consistent with the Orthodox perception of the rabbinic role, the Lieberman study suggests that students would be appreciative of greater emphasis on training in homiletics and practical rabbinics. He found, in 1968, that fully fifty-nine percent of the future rabbis at RIETS felt that their institution placed "too little emphasis" on homiletics and practical rabbinics.[20] The current consideration of program revisions at RIETS may reflect this as an ongoing problem, dating back at least to 1968.

The Future Of American Jewish Preaching

Based largely, though not exclusively, on an examination of the current homiletic practices of American Jewish seminaries, at least five observations concerning the future of American Jewish preaching seem warranted.

1. *Preaching will remain a vital part of American Jewish religious services, though new sermon forms may gain popularity.*

Every sign points to the fact that preaching will remain a vital part of the Jewish service. When asked to evaluate the importance of preaching to a congregation hiring a new rabbi, administrators and faculty at America's Jewish seminaries uniformly spoke of the desire of most congregations to have outstanding preachers.[21] Recent growth in the homiletic offerings of American seminaries gives clear evidence of the continued importance of preaching. The establishment of a homiletic service by the Rabbinical Assembly of America, as an outgrowth of its members' wishes, is yet further evidence of the continued importance that preaching will play in the future of American Judaism.[22]

Though the sermon will, no doubt for the foreseeable future, remain primarily the traditional one-way presentation with the rabbi addressing the congregation, some changes in that format can be anticipated. Already many Conservative rabbis are using "Torah Dialogues" with their congregants for Sabbath morning services. This practice is also growing among Reform rabbis.

2. *Reform and Conservative Judaism will continue to place greater emphasis on preaching than Orthodox Judaism, though the gap may narrow.*

The more extensive homiletic programs available and required of students at the Reform and Conservative seminaries suggest that these branches of American Judaism will continue to place greater emphasis on preaching than Orthodox Judaism. However, Orthodox seminaries such as RIETS are evidencing greater receptivity to homiletic training, perhaps reflecting a reassessment of the importance of the preaching function of the Orthodox rabbi. To the extent that such reassessment takes place, it is liable to narrow the gap between the emphasis placed on preaching by Orthodox Jewish leaders and their Reform and Conservative counterparts.

3. *The eloquence that marked the language of the outstanding Jew-ish preachers of the mid-twentieth century is not likely to be as conspicuous a feature of the American Jewish pulpit of the late twentieth and early twenty-first centuries.*

The decline of eloquent language seems to be a characteristic that has affected virtually all of American society. Indeed, as high school and college test scores decline, our society worries not simply about the decline of eloquence but about a pervasive decline in basic language skills. Whatever the causes, and they are numerous, the decline in language skills that seems to mark contemporary American youth is evident, according to their instructors, in current rabbinic students, who are not perceived by seminary faculty as having the language skills of their predecessors. This is not to suggest that eloquence will disappear from the American Jewish pulpit, anymore than it will disappear from our entire society. But it is to suggest that it may not be as conspicuous among the next few generations of American rabbis as it has been in mid-twentieth century American Jewish pulpits.

4. *The skillful organization of ideas will be a strength of American Jewish sermons in future years.*

The faculties of both HUC-JIR and JTS consider the ability to organize ideas as the single most important trait of a skilled preacher.[23] Hence, sermon organization receives extensive treatment in the course work of both institutions. To the extent that current faculty and courses may influence future preachers, we must surmise that well-organized sermons will be a characteristic of American Jewish preaching in the late twentieth and early twenty-first centuries.

5. *The ordination of women will have a subtle, not dramatic, effect on American Jewish preaching.*

The presence of over seventy women rabbis, ordained since the mid-1970s, has not dramatically altered the nature of Reform Jewish preaching. However, women, according to most observers, have had subtle effects on Reform preaching. They often tend to preach on topics that men would not select. When they do preach on topics that men also use, they occasionally present slightly different approaches, based at least in part on their life experiences as women.[24] Currently about forty percent of the students at HUC-JIR are women. Additionally, JTS has recently begun to ordain women. Though the number of women in the Jewish pulpit will be increasing, it seems fair to say that, based on the experience that the Reform movement has had with women rabbis for over a decade, women preachers will have subtle, not dramatic, effects on the future of American Jewish preaching.

●

Perhaps the most significant prayer in Judaism, the Shema, begins with the phrase, "Hear O Israel." American Jews have heard their preachers from the earliest period of Jewish settlement in the United States. Since that time, American Jewish preaching has undergone many changes, as this work has attempted to illustrate. No doubt American Jewish preaching will continue to change as American Jews continue to listen to the preaching of their rabbis, seeking leadership and guidance for the twenty-first century.

Notes

Chapter 1: Jewish Preaching in Colonial
and Revolutionary America

1. Quoted in Lawrence A. Cremin, *American Education: The Colonial Experience 1607–1783* (New York: Harper and Row, 1970), 210.

2. Michael A. Meyer, "A Centennial History," in *Hebrew Union College-Jewish Institute of Religion at One Hundred Years*, ed. Samuel E. Karff (Cincinnati: Hebrew Union College Press, 1976), 7–8.

3. Sigmund Maybaum, "Jewish Homiletics," trans. Oswald Haberman (unpublished M. A. thesis, Hebrew Union College-Jewish Institute of Religion, 1960), 2; Israel Bettan, *Studies in Jewish Preaching* (Cincinnati: Hebrew Union College Press, 1939), 4–6.

4. See Bettan, *Studies in Jewish Preaching*, for studies of a variety of outstanding European Jewish preachers from the thirteenth century to the eighteenth century. Also see Abraham Cohen, *Jewish Homiletics* (London: M. L. Cailingold, 1937), 2–5, for background on early Jewish preaching.

5. Bettan, *Studies in Jewish Preaching*, 8–9.

6. Information on the Jewish population and settlement in the colonies can be found in any standard history of American Judaism. Two particularly informative sources that have been relied upon in this paragraph and the following paragraphs are Stanley Feldstein, *The Land That I Show You: Three Centuries of Jewish Life in America* (New York: Anchor Press/Doubleday, 1978), 1–34, and Rufus Learsi, *The Jews in America: A History* (New York: Katv Publishing, 1972), 26–38.

The definitive study of American colonial Jewry is Jacob R. Marcus, *The*

Colonial American Jew: 1492–1776 (Detroit: Wayne State University Press, 1970). On early religious practices and synagogue development see chap. 47–49. Also see Jacob R. Marcus, "The Colonial American Jew," in *Jews and the Founding of the Republic*, ed. Jonathan Sarna, Benny Kraut, and Samuel Joseph (New York: Markus Weiner Publishers, 1985).

7. Marcus, *The Colonial American Jew* 2:860.

8. See Marcus, *The Colonial American Jew*, chap. 53, for a full discussion of the leadership of the colonial synagogues.

9. Most colonial hazzans had to supplement their incomes. They did so in a variety of ways, including serving as shohet, mohel, or teacher. Many also earned income with jobs that had nothing to do with any aspect of their religion, such as merchants and businessmen. See Marcus, *The Colonial American Jew* 2:934–37.

10. Jacob R. Marcus, *The Handsome Young Priest in the Black Gown: The Personal World of Gershom Seixas* (Cincinnati: American Jewish Archives, 1970), 5.

11. Marcus, *The Colonial American Jew* 2:972–73.

12. Nathan Kagnoff in "The Traditional Jewish Sermon in the United States from Its Beginnings to the First World War" (unpublished Ph.D. dissertation, American University, 1960), 25, suggests that this may be the first Jewish sermon in the United States.

13. See Kagnoff, "The Traditional Jewish Sermon in the United States," 24–26, and Marcus, *The Colonial American Jew*, 973, for background on Pinto and this sermon.

14. This and all future biblical references are cited as given by the speaker himself. A widely used contemporary version of the Torah following the same notation system used by the speakers cited throughout this volume, is *The Holy Scriptures* (Philadelphia: Jewish Publication Society of America, 1955).

15. Kagnoff, "The Traditional Jewish Sermon in the United States," 24.

16. Details of Seixas's biography can be found in any standard Jewish Encyclopedia or history of American Jewry. An exceptionally fine monograph is Marcus, *The Handsome Young Priest*. Also see Learsi, *The Jews in America*, 30–36.

17. Learsi, *The Jews in America*, 36.

18. See Marcus, *The Handsome Young Priest*, 7–9, for a description of this facet of Seixas's work.

19. Gershom Seixas, "Prayer for Peace" (New York: undated), 2. Photocopy of the original in Seixas Manuscript Collection, American Jewish Archives, Box 1. Original in the Lyons Collection, American Jewish Historical Society. Hereafter cited as Seixas, "Prayer for Peace."

20. Ibid.

21. Ibid.

22. On May 17, 1776, Shearith Israel observed a colony-wide day of prayer, and Seixas prayed for peace. By implication, he suggested remaining in the British Empire. This would have been consistent with prevailing thought in New York, if the New York delegation to the Continental Congress can

be considered an accurate measure of the colony. The New York delegation refused to vote for independence on July 4, instead abstaining. However, certainly by August, if not earlier, Seixas was publicly supportive of the revolutionary cause.

23. Marcus, *The Handsome Young Priest*, 14.

24. Details on Seixas's life during the eight years he spent outside of New York (1776–1884) are discussed in Marcus, *The Colonial American Jew* 2:1272–73, and Marcus, *The Handsome Young Priest*, 10–15.

25. For concise explanations of why most American Jews, including Seixas, supported the Revolution and were optimistic about the new nation see Feldstein, *The Land That I Show You*, 21–32 and Learsi, *The Jews in America*, 39–53.

26. See the title page of Gershom Seixas, "Religious Discourse—Thursday 26th of November, 1789" (New York: Archibald McClean, 1789). Photocopy of the original in the Seixas Manuscript Collection, American Jewish Archives, Box 1. Original in the Lyons Collection, American Jewish Historical Society. Hereafter cited as Seixas, "Discourse, November 26, 1789."

27. Seixas, "Discourse, November 26, 1789," 2.

28. Many rhetorical theorists claim that similar rhetorical situations tend to produce similar rhetorical responses. This "genre" school of rhetorical theory and criticism would readily account for the similarities in Seixas's civilly inspired sermons by the analogous situations that gave rise to them. The classic short exposition of generic theory is Lloyd Bitzer, "The Rhetorical Situation," *Philosophy and Rhetoric* 1 (January 1968): 1–14. Also see Karlyn Kohrs Campbell and Kathleen Hall Jamieson, "Form and Genre in Rhetorical Criticism: An Introduction," in *Form and Genre: Shaping Rhetorical Action*, ed. Karlyn Kohrs Campbell and Kathleen Hall Jamieson (Falls Church, Va.: Speech Communication Association, 1977).

29. Seixas, "Discourse, November 26, 1789," 3.

30. Ibid., 6.

31. Ibid., 13.

32. Ibid.

33. Ibid., 13–14.

34. Ibid., 14.

35. Ibid., 15.

36. Kagnoff, "The Traditional Jewish Sermon in the United States," 29–31.

37. Gershom Seixas, "Sermon of December 20, 1804" (no place or date of publication), 2. Photocopy of the original in the Seixas Manuscript Collection, American Jewish Archives, Box 1. Original in the Lyons Collection, American Jewish Historical Society. Hereafter cited as Seixas, "Sermon of December 20, 1804."

38. Seixas, "Sermon of December 20, 1804," 2–5.

39. Ibid., 5.

40. Ibid., 11.

41. Ibid., 11–14.

42. Thomas A. Bailey, *A Diplomatic History of the American People* (New York: Appleton-Century-Crofts, 1964), 93–94.

43. John C. Miller, *Alexander Hamilton and the Growth of the New Nation* (New York: Harper and Row, 1959), 466–68.

44. Gershom Seixas, "A Discourse Delivered in the Synagogue in New York on the Ninth of May, 1798, Observed as a Day of Humiliation Conformably to a Recommendation of the President of the United States of America" (New York: Naphtali Judah, 1798), 5. Hereafter cited as Seixas, "Discourse of May 9, 1798."

45. Seixas, "Discourse of May 9, 1798," 5.

46. Ibid.

47. Ibid., 6–7.

48. Ibid., 8–9.

49. Ibid., 11–13.

50. Ibid., 14–15

51. Ibid., 15–23.

52. Ibid., 23.

53. Ibid.

54. Ibid., 26–27.

55. Raphael Mahler, "American Jewry and the Idea of the Return to Zion in the Period of the American Revolution," *Zion* 16 (1951): 105–34. I wish to thank Rabbi Marla Subeck for her help in translating this article.

56. Seixas, "Discourse of May 9, 1798," 23–27.

57. Gershom Seixas, "A Charity Sermon, January 11 1807" (no place or date of publication), 1. Photocopy of the original in the Seixas Manuscript Collection, American Jewish Archives, Box 1. Original in the Lyons Collection, American Jewish Historical Society. Hereafter cited as Seixas, "Charity Sermon, January 11, 1807."

58. Seixas, "Charity Sermon, January 11, 1807," 2.

59. Ibid., 3–4.

60. Ibid., 4.

61. Ibid., 5.

62. Ibid., 8.

63. Ibid.

64. Ibid., 12–14.

65. Ibid., 19–20.

66. Ibid., 20–21.

67. This fact is made manifestly apparent in the growing stature that he was accorded within the congregation and in the tributes paid to him at his death in 1816.

68. We know that on occasion he received extra payment for delivering a sermon. Additionally, at least two of his sermons were published, presumably at the expense of his congregation or at least some of its members. Moreover, their very novelty, and the fact that they were delivered in English to an audience that was more fluent in English than in Hebrew, the language of the rest of the service, would also make it likely that Seixas's sermons were well received. Certainly, there is no evidence to the contrary.

Chapter 2: Jewish Preaching in Jacksonian America

1. The changes introduced by German Reformers are treated in a wide variety of sources, including any good history of German Jewry. Additionally, see Harry Simonhoff, *Jewish Notables in America 1776–1885* (New York: Greenberg Publishers, 1956), 345–55. The sources cited in nn. 2 and 3 below also detail many of the changes introduced by German Reform Judaism.

2. Adolf Kober, "Jewish Preaching and Preachers: A Contribution to the History of the Jewish Sermon in Germany and America," *Historia Judaica* 7 (October 1945): 104–5.

3. Alexander Altmann, "The New Style of Preaching in Nineteenth-Century German Jewry," in his *Essays in Jewish Intellectual History* (Hanover: University Press of New England and Brandeis University Press, 1981). Altmann, Kober, and Michael A. Meyer have all written about the Christian influence on German Reform Judaism. These paragraphs draw on all three, particularly Meyer, "Christian Influence on Early German Reform Judaism," in *Studies in Jewish Bibliography History and Literature in Honor of I. Edward Kiev*, ed. Charles Berlin (New York: Ktav Publishing, 1971).

4. Meyer, "Christian Influence," 293.

5. Ibid.

6. Ibid.

7. Kober, "Jewish Preaching and Preachers," 105.

8. Ibid.

9. The journal, *Sulamith*, also frequently reprinted sermons.

10. The information presented in this paragraph is drawn primarily from Kober, "Jewish Preaching and Preachers," 106–7.

11. See Altmann, "The New Style of Preaching," 191–93, for a discussion of these changes.

12. Meyer, "Christian Influence," 295; Kober, "Jewish Preaching and Preachers," 109.

13. See Altmann, "The New Style of Preaching," 191–96.

14. Ibid., 191–200.

15. Ibid., 192.

16. This paragraph is based on Meyer, "Christian Influence," 295–96.

17. "Preaching," *Encyclopedia Judaica* (New York: McMillian, 1971), 13:1003.

18. The biographical details of Leeser's life presented in these paragraphs can be found in any standard history of American Judaism. See, for example, Peter Wiernik, *History of the Jews in America* (New York: Jewish Historical Publishing, 1931), 170–72; Joseph L. Blau and Salo W. Baron, eds., *The Jews of the United States: 1740–1840* (New York: Columbia University Press, 1963), 447–54; and the many references to Leeser found throughout such works as Henry S. Morris, *The Jews of Philadelphia* (Philadelphia: Levytype Co., 1884), and Learsi, *The Jews in America*. I am also indebted to Rabbi Lance Sussman, who is currently working on the first full-scale biography of Leeser, for sharing his insights with me in personal conversations.

19. Estimates on the Jewish population of the United States during this period vary widely. Most estimates for the year 1820 range between four and fifteen thousand. See, for example, Learsi, *The Jews in America*, 64.

20. Isaac Leeser, *Discourses on the Jewish Religion* (Philadelphia: Sherman and Co., 1867), 1:1. The ten-volume edition published in 1867, the final and most complete edition, includes sermons from Leeser's last years of preaching and a variety of speeches that were not given from the pulpit. The sermons are unchanged from edition to edition, nor has any of the prefatory material been changed in later editions. Hence, the ten-volume edition published in 1867 is definitive. All future references will be to this edition.

21. Ibid.

22. Ibid.

23. Leeser claimed that he had heard only about six sermons while growing up in Germany. See his introduction to *Jerusalem: A Treatise on Religious Power and Judaism*, by Moses Mendelssohn, printed as a "Complement" to *The Occident and Jewish Advocate* (1851), 9: 14.

24. A clear explanation of Leeser's motives, drawn from comments he made on several occasions, can be found in Jonathan V. Plaut, "Isaac Leeser and the Occident" (unpublished rabbinic thesis, Hebrew Union College-Jewish Institute of Religion, 1970), 86.

25. Ibid.

26. Leeser, *Discourses*, 1:2. It was not until 1843 that he actually received formal approval.

27. Lance Sussman, "Isaac Leeser and the Protestanization of American Judaism," *American Jewish Archives* 38 (April 1986): 1–21.

28. Leeser, *Discourses*, 1:65–66.

29. For an insightful analysis of Leeser's orthodoxy see Howard Shapiro, "Was Isaac Leeser an Orthodox Jew, A Modern Orthodox Jew or A Conservative Jew?" (unpublished typescript, Cincinnati, 1966), Isaac Leeser Papers, Box 2654, American Jewish Archives, Cincinnati, Ohio.

30. Leeser, *Discourses*, 1:4.

31. For examples of Leeser's attitude concerning politics and religion, see the following editorials or articles that he wrote for his paper: "Politics," *The Occident and Jewish Advocate* 13 (February 1855): 561–62; "The People and Their Ministers," *The Occident and Jewish Advocate* 20 (November 1862): 337; and "Remarks of Isaac Leeser on the Death of President Abraham Lincoln," *The Occident and Jewish Advocate* 16 (May 1865): 118.

32. Isaac Leeser, "American Congregations," *The Occident and Jewish Advocate* 8 (August 1850): 210–11.

33. Congregation Mikveh Israel, *A Review of the Late Controversies between the Rev. Isaac Leeser and the Congregation Mikveh Israel* (Philadelphia: Congregation Mikveh Israel, 1850), 4.

34. Leeser, "Complement," *The Occident and Jewish Advocate* (1851), 9: 14.

35. German and Hebrew were his first languages. He also studied Latin while in school in Germany. Since he had served a Sephardic congregation in Richmond and had come to a Sephardic congregation in Philadelphia, it is likely that he also had some knowledge of Spanish and/or Portuguese.

36. Leeser, "The People and Their Ministers," 345.

37. Ibid.

38. Ibid.

39. Ibid.

40. Virtually every public speaking textbook will make this point. For a concise survey of the research literature that supports it, see Bert E. Bradley, *Fundamentals of Speech Communication: The Credibility of Ideas* (Dubuque: Wm. C. Brown Co., 1978), 105–6.

41. The primary reason most public speaking textbooks stress the importance of maintaining eye contact is that it allows the speaker to adapt his message to any feedback he receives from the audience. See Bradley, *Fundamentals of Speech Communication*, 106, and Robert C. Jeffrey and Owen Peterson, *Speech: A Text with Adapted Readings* (New York: Harper and Row, 1975), 341–42.

42. Virtually every picture we have of Leeser, and there are several, illustrates this.

43. Perhaps significantly, Mikveh Israel did not grow appreciably after Leeser began to deliver sermons, as might be expected if they had stirred a strong positive reaction.

44. Leeser, "American Congregations," 210.

45. Ibid., 211.

46. Ibid., 212.

47. Leeser, "Complement," 14.

48. Isaac Leeser, "Opening Address for the Dedication of the Hebrew Educational Society School-House," *The Occident and Jewish Advocate* 13 (January 1855): 489.

49. Isaac Leeser, "The Press and the Pulpit—Pt. 1," *The Occident and Jewish Advocate* 15 (May 1857): 51.

50. Ibid.

51. Ibid., 52.

52. Ibid.

53. Ibid.

54. Leeser, "The People and Their Ministers," 346.

55. Leeser, *Discourses* 3:vi.

56. This discussion of Leeser's library is based on my examination of Cyrus Adler, *Catalogue of the Leeser Library* (Philadelphia: E. Hirsch and Co., 1883).

57. The book was William B. Wood's *Personal Recollections of the Stage* (Philadelphia, 1855).

58. Leeser mentions all three of these men in the introduction to the third volume of his *Discourses*, where he reviews the scope of English preaching.

59. According to Adler's catalog, the collection of Jacob Da La Motta's *Discourses* was dated 1820, and the E. N. Carvalho sermon that Leeser owned was his funeral eulogy for Gershom Seixas, delivered and printed in 1816. Moreover, Leeser owned at least one collection of German sermons printed four years prior to his own first effort.

60. Isaac Leeser, "Confidence in God," *Discourses* 1:2.

61. Ibid., 3.

62. Ibid., 4.

63. Ibid., 7.

64. Ibid., 7–11.

65. Ibid., 12.

66. Ibid., 13.

67. Ibid., 14.

68. Robert I. Kahn, "Liberalism As Reflected in Jewish Preaching in the English Language in the Mid-Nineteenth Century" (unpublished Ph.D. dissertation, Hebrew Union College, 1949), 68–69.

69. Leeser, *Discourses* 1:1–139.

70. This figure is based on examining Leeser's *Discourses*. Each page consists of thirty-three lines of print, each line containing fifty spaces or ten words, using the five-spaces-per-word rule of thumb. An examination of his first fifty sermons, preached between 1830 and 1837, indicates that the average sermon consisted of 16.24 pages of printed material, with each page consisting of 330 words (thirty-three lines of ten words), for a total of 5,359 words.

71. The three collections were selected because their widespread and enduring circulation suggests that they are indicative of contemporary rabbinic practices. The first collection was Rabbinic Council of America, ed., *Manual of Holiday and Sabbath Sermons* (New York: Rabbinic Council Press, 1952). This is a collection of thirty-eight sample sermons presented by the Rabbinic Council as models. These sermons total 253 pages in length, an average of slightly under 7 pages each. The second collection of sermons used were randomly selected volumes from the *Best Jewish Sermons* series. For many years, starting in 1953, Jonathan David Publishers issued a volume of outstanding Jewish sermons preached during the previous year, selected by Rabbi Saul I. Teplitz. The enduring popularity of this series suggests that Teplitz's selections are representative of contemporary practices. The specific volumes randomly selected were: Saul Teplitz, ed., *Best Jewish Sermons of 5721–5722* (New York: Jonathan David Publishers, 1962); and Saul Teplitz, ed., *Best Jewish Sermons of 5733–5734* (Middle Village: Jonathan David Publishers, 1974). The first volume contained thirty-one sermons, which totaled 238 pages. The average sermon was slightly under eight pages long. The second volume contained twenty-one sermons, which totaled 186 pages. The average sermon was slightly under nine pages long. The final collection used were all sermons that appeared in the two most recent issues of *The American Rabbi* at the time this work was being done. This widely circulated periodical contains sermons and articles directed primarily toward rabbis. *The American Rabbi* 15 (December 1982) and *The American Rabbi* 15 (February 1983) were used. These two issues contain twenty-five sermons, which total 110 pages. The average sermon was about four and a half pages long.

72. The pioneer work in this area was done by Rudolph Flesch, *The Art of Plain Talk* (New York: Harper and Brothers, 1946). For more contemporary applications of Flesch, see Jane Blankenship, *A Sense of Style: An Introduction to Style for the Public Speaker* (Belmont: Dickenson Publish-

ing, 1968), 97–98; and Carroll C. Arnold, *Criticism of Oral Rhetoric* (Columbus: Charles E. Merrill Publishers, 1974), 176–78.

73. All complete sentences on every fourth page of Leeser's sermon, starting with page one, were used.

74. A random procedure was used to select three sermons and one speech. Those selected were: "The Sin of Insincerity," a sermon delivered on July 19, 1833; "Recompense and Retribution," a sermon delivered on April 10, 1835; "The Covenant of Abraham," a sermon delivered on November 6, 1841; and "Union in Israel," an address given at a benefit dinner for Jew's Hospital of New York on January 26, 1854. The same procedure described in n. 74 was used to analyze these randomly selected samples of Leeser's later speaking.

75. Leeser, "The Press and the Pulpit—Pt. 3," *The Occident and Jewish Advocate* 15 (May 1857): 126–30.

76. Ibid., 129. Here Leeser is highly critical of clergymen who deviate in any fashion from what he perceives to be the purpose of sermons: "expanding the tennents and duties of religion." He claims that those who attempt to do otherwise in order to entertain or amuse their audiences "demean themselves."

77. Leeser, *Discourses* 1:10.

78. Kahn, "Liberalism As Reflected in Jewish Preaching," 59.

79. Leeser, "American Congregations," 212.

Chapter 3: Jewish Preaching in a House Divided

1. Kagnoff, "The Traditional Jewish Sermon in the United States," 51.

2. Ibid., 49–50.

3. Kahn, "Liberalism As Reflected in Jewish Preaching," 36–37.

4. Ibid., 31–32.

5. Learsi, *The Jews in America*, 64.

6. Letter from D. F. J. (no other identification) to the editor, printed under the headline "Preaching" in the *The American Israelite* 1 (January 26, 1855): 230.

7. Unsigned article reprinted from the New York *Herald Tribune* under the headline "A Great Jewish Need" in *The American Israelite* 18 (July 7, 1871): 6.

8. Ibid.

9. Kagnoff, "The Traditional Jewish Sermon," 54, claims that English became the dominant language sometime during the decade 1850–60. Kahn, "Liberalism As Reflected in Jewish Preaching," 53, suggests that it was not until the latter 1860s, after the Civil War, that English sermons became the rule and German sermons became the exception. Clearly definitive evidence is simply not available.

10. Biographical details of Raphall's life can be found in any standard source. See for example "Morris Jacob Raphall," *Encyclopedia Judaica* (New York: McMillian, 1971), 13:1551.

11. See Maxwell Whiteman, "Jews in the Anti-Slavery Movement," introduction to Peter Still and Vina Still, *The Kidnapped and the Ransomed: The Narrative of Peter and Vina Still after Forty Years of Slavery* (Philadelphia: Jewish Publication Society of America, 1970), 97.

12. Ironically, Raphall's lectures were published in book form by Moss and Brothers of Philadelphia, publishers of antislavery material.

13. The details in this account of Raphall's delivery of the opening prayer for the House of Representatives are drawn from the excellent study "The First Jewish Prayer in Congress," in Bertram W. Korn, *Eventful Years and Experiences: Studies in Nineteenth Century American Jewish History* (Cincinnati: American Jewish Archives, 1954), 98–124.

14. Quoted in Korn, "The First Jewish Prayer in Congress," 109.

15. Ibid., 113.

16. For additional reaction to Raphall, from which these samples are drawn, see Korn, "The First Jewish Prayer in Congress," 101–8.

17. Whiteman, "Jews in the Anti-Slavery Movement," 25–31. Also see Bertram Korn, "Isaac Mayer Wise on the Civil War," in his *Eventful Years and Experiences*, 125–50.

18. Morris Jacob Raphall, *Bible View of Slavery* (New York: Rudd and Carleton, 1861), 11.

19. Ibid., 13.

20. Ibid., 14.

21. Ibid., 16.

22. Ibid.

23. Ibid., 17.

24. Ibid., 19.

25. Ibid., 19–25.

26. Isaac Mayer Wise's comments on Raphall's speech can be found in a short untitled article published in *The American Israelite*, January 18, 1861, p. 230. Most Jewish scholars would reject Raphall's claim. For a representative reaction of a contemporary scholar, see Matitiahu Tsevat, "Slavery and the Jews: The Jewish Position toward Slavery" (typescript, American Jewish Archives, Miscellaneous File).

27. Raphall, *Bible View of Slavery*, 26–28.

28. Ibid., 28–29.

29. Ibid., 29.

30. Ibid., 29–30.

31. Ibid., 30.

32. Ibid., 38.

33. Ibid., 36.

34. Ibid., 34–36.

35. See Tsevat, "Slavery and the Jews," 10–11, for a clear discussion of the relationship between Raphall's explanation and that of most Hebrew commentary.

36. Raphall, *Bible View of Slavery*, 39–41.

37. The best short discussion of American preaching on slavery is Herbert Vance Taylor, "Preaching on Slavery," in *Preaching in American History*, ed. DeWitte Holland (Nashville: Abingdon Press, 1969), 168–83.

38. For an example of a Christian apologist for slavery who does utilize the Old Testament see Thornton Stringfellow, "A Scriptural View of Slavery," in *Slavery Defended*, ed. Eric L. McKitrick (Englewood Cliffs: Prentice Hall, 1963), 86–98.

39. Among the more widely read Christian sermons that illustrate the use of the New Testament to support slavery is James H. Thornwell, "The Rights and Duties of Masters," in *Sermons in American History*, ed. DeWitte Holland (Nashville: Abingdon Press, 1971), 219–34.

40. See each of these papers for January 5, 1861.

41. See n. 18 for a full citation of the most widely distributed pamphlet edition. The most widely distributed sermon anthology that carried Raphall's sermon was *Fast Day Sermons: Or the Pulpit on the State of the Country* (New York: Rudd and Carleton, 1861), 227–46.

42. Both papers are quoted in Bertram W. Korn, *American Jewry and the Civil War* (New York: Atheneum, 1970), 18.

43. Only one of Felsenthal's sermons, delivered in 1865, has been preserved. We do not know exactly when he started to preach against slavery, though we do know that he was active in the Republican presidential campaign of John Freemont in 1856. Shortly after that campaign he turned down a rabbinic position in Mobile, Alabama, claiming that he could not live in a slave state. See Korn, *American Jewry and the Civil War*, 23.

44. The best biography of Heilprin is Gustav Pollak, *Michael Heilprin and His Sons: A Biography* (New York: Dodd Mead and Co., 1912). Also see Simonhoff, *Jewish Notables in America*, 358–59.

45. Raphall's sermon and the replies of Heilprin, Mielziner, and Einhorn have all been reprinted in Ella McKinna Friend Mielziner, *Moses Mielziner: A Biography with a Bibliography of His Writings* (New York: no publisher indicated, 1931). While the replies and Raphall's sermon can be found in a variety of other sources, the collection of them in this single volume is highly convenient. Heilprin's response, taken from the *New-York Tribune* of January 15, 1861, can be found on pp. 224–34. Hereafter, this copy will be used and cited as Heilprin, "Antislavery Answer to Raphall."

46. Heilprin, "Antislavery Answer to Raphall," 226–27.

47. Ibid., 228–32.

48. At least one contemporary biblical scholar has raised serious questions about Heilprin's response. See Tsevat, "Slavery and the Jews," 12.

49. The best biography of Mielziner, from which the information presented here is drawn, is Ella McKinna Friend Mielziner's *Moses Mielziner*.

50. See Mielziner, *Moses Mielziner*, 20–23, for a full discussion of the European history of Mielziner's work and the circumstances that caused it subsequently to be published in the United States.

51. See the *American Theological Review* 8 (April 1861): 232–60, and *American Theological Review* 8 (July 1861): 423–38.

52. *American Theological Review* 8 (April 1861): 232.

53. *Evangelical Review* 13 (January 1862): 311–55.

54. Ibid., 311.

55. Mielziner, *Moses Mielziner*, 23.

56. Ibid.

57. Moses Mielziner, "Slavery amongst the Ancient Hebrews" (Ph.D. dissertation, University of Giessen, 1859), translated by the author in 1885 and reprinted in Mielziner, *Moses Mielziner*, 64–103.

58. Ibid., 88–89.

59. The best study of Einhorn, who has not been the subject of a major biography, is Kaufmann Kohler, "David Einhorn, the Uncompromising Champion of Reform Judaism." This fifty-five-page essay was written for the one hundredth anniversary of Einhorn's birth in 1909 by his son-in-law, then the president of Hebrew Union College. It was in the 1909 yearbook of the Central Conference of American Rabbis and subsequently widely reprinted. Any standard history of American Judaism or standard reference work will also provide basic biographical details. See, for example, "David Einhorn," *Encylopedia Judaica* (New York: McMillian, 1971), 6:352.

60. Quoted in Kohler, "David Einhorn, the Uncompromising Champion," 12.

61. *Sinai* 6 (February 1861): 2–20; 6 (March 1861): 45–50; 6 (March 1861): 60–61; 6 (April 1861): 99–100.

62. This article has been translated by Einhorn's daughter, Mrs. Kaufmann Kohler, and the translation is reprinted in Mielziner, *Moses Mielziner*, 234–50. Hereafter, this version will be cited as Einhorn, "Antislavery Answer to Raphall."

63. Einhorn, "Antislavery Answer to Raphall," 235.

64. Ibid., 241.

65. Ibid., 242.

66. Ibid., 243.

67. Ibid., 249.

68. Ibid., 249–50.

Chapter 4: Isaac Mayer Wise and the Americanization of the Jewish Sermon

1. See Bertram Korn, "The First American Jewish Theological Seminary: Maimonides College, 1867–1873," in his *Eventful Years and Experiences*, for discussions of these two institutions.

2. The Jewish Theological Seminary was opened in 1886. The Rabbi Isaac Elchanan Theological Seminary, which subsequently evolved into Yeshiva University, was opened in 1896.

3. The definitive biography of Wise is Max B. May, *Isaac Mayer Wise: The Founder of American Judaism* (New York: G. P. Putnam's Sons, 1916). For additional biographical information see Dena Wilansky, *Sinai to Cincinnati: Lay Views on the Writings of Isaac M. Wise, Founder of Reform Judaism in America* (New York: Renaissance Book Co., 1937), 1–34, and David Philipson and Louis Grossmann, eds., *Selected Writings of Isaac M. Wise with a Bibliography* (Cincinnati: Robert Clarke Co., 1900), 1–113. Wise's autobiographical *Reminiscences*, trans. David Philipson (Cincinnati:

Leo Wise and Co., 1901), is also exceptionally helpful in detailing many of the rhetorical influences on Wise.

4. Philipson and Grossmann, *Selected Writings*, 2–3.

5. Details of Wise's education can best be found in May, *Isaac Mayer Wise*, 25–31.

6. Ibid., 33.

7. Ibid., 37.

8. Isaac Mayer Wise, "Fiftieth Anniversary As a Rabbi Sermon," *The American Israelite*, October 26, 1893, p. 4.

9. See Richard Henry Lee, "Letters from the Federal Farmer," in *Empire and Nation*, ed. Forrest McDonald (Englewood Cliffs: Prentice Hall, 1962), 87–173.

10. May, *Isaac Mayer Wise*, 40.

11. Wise, "Fiftieth Anniversary Sermon," 4.

12. Philipson and Grossmann, *Selected Writing*, 15.

13. Wise, *Reminiscences*, 46.

14. Ibid., 58.

15. Ibid.

16. Ibid., 134.

17. Isaac M. Wise, "The World of My Books," trans. Albert H. Friedlander, in *Critical Studies in American Jewish History*, ed. Jacob R. Marcus (Cincinnati and New York: American Jewish Archives and Ktav Publishing, 1971), 151.

18. Ibid.

19. Isaac Mayer Wise, "The College," *The American Israelite*, November 2, 1860, p. 40.

20. Letter, Isaac Mayer Wise to Julius L. Mayerberg, May 23, 1888, Wise Correspondence File, American Jewish Archives, Cincinnati, Ohio.

21. Wise, "The World of My Books," 151.

22. David Potter, "Foreword" to Hugh Blair, *Lectures on Rhetoric and Belles Lettres*, ed. Harold F. Harding (Carbondale: Southern Illinois University Press, 1965). This reprint of the original 1783 edition of Blair's *Lectures* is considered definitive by rhetorical scholars and is the most accessible edition. All future references will be to this edition of Blair.

23. Blair's biography can be found in any standard biographical source or literary history. The details presented in this paragraph are all drawn from Harold Harding's outstanding introduction to Blair, *Lectures in Rhetoric and Belles Lettres*.

24. For an excellent study that places Blair in the context of the rhetorical theory of his day, see the editors' introduction to James L. Golden and Edward P. J. Corbett, eds., *The Rhetoric of Blair, Campbell and Whately* (New York: Holt, Rinehart and Winston, 1968), 1–21. I have utilized Golden and Corbett's analysis of the four schools of rhetorical thought current in late eighteenth-century England for the organizational structure of this section.

25. Isaac Mayer Wise, "Some Rules on Preaching Sermons," *The American Israelite*, May 10, 1894, p. 4.

26. Ibid.

27. Letter, Isaac Mayer Wise to Max Heller, September 5, 1886, Wise Correspondence File, American Jewish Archives, Cincinnati, Ohio. Also see Wise, "Some Rules on Preaching Sermons," 4.

28. See Isaac Mayer Wise, "Varieties," *The American Israelite*, June 4, 1872, p. 8, and Wise, "Some Rules on Preaching Sermons," 4.

29. See Isaac Mayer Wise, "Preaching and the Preacher," *The American Israelite*, July 30, 1891, p. 4.

30. Blair, *Lectures* 2:108–9.

31. Wise, "Some Rules on Preaching Sermons," 4.

32. Blair, *Lectures* 2:114.

33. Ibid.

34. Isaac Mayer Wise, "Rules for Public Speakers," *The American Israelite*, July 12, 1872, p. 8.

35. Ibid.

36. Blair, *Lectures*, 1:iv.

37. See his letters to Mayerberg and Heller.

38. Wise clearly worked to improve his command of English and his ability to speak. He was especially fond of listening to outstanding speakers.

39. Blair, *Lectures* 2:180–81.

40. Wise, "Rules for Public Speakers," 8.

41. See Blair, *Lectures* 2:218–25, for Blair's criticism of the elocutionists.

42. Isaac Mayer Wise, "On Scholastic Education," *The American Israelite*, January 26, 1855, p. 228.

43. Wise, "The Theological Faculty," *The American Israelite*, May 2, 1873, p. 4.

44. Ibid.

45. Wise, "Preaching and the Preacher," 4.

46. Ibid.

47. Ibid.

48. Blair, *Lectures* 2:3–4.

49. Wise, "Preaching and the Preacher," 4.

50. Blair, *Lectures* 2:10.

51. Wise, "Some Rules on Preaching Sermons," 4.

52. Blair, *Lectures* 2:117–18.

53. Letter, Wise to Heller, September 5, 1886.

54. Wise, "The World of My Books," 152–53.

55. Blair, *Lectures* 2:108–9. This is also implicit in Blair's many critiques of specific sermons.

56. Isaac Mayer Wise, untitled editorial, *The American Israelite*, September 21, 1899, p. 4.

57. Isaac Mayer Wise, untitled editorial, *The American Israelite*, November 9, 1899, p. 4.

58. Isaac Mayer Wise, "The Outlines of Judaism," in Philipson and Grossmann, *Selected Writings*, 212.

59. Isaac Mayer Wise, "Men More Instructive Than Works," in *The American Jewish Pulpit* (Cincinnati: Bloch and Co., 1881), 185–86. Although no editor for this anthology of sermons is indicated, the anthology itself includes six of Wise's sermons, more than from any of the approximately

fifteen other rabbis represented. Additionally, Bloch and Co. was a Wise family firm. Hence, it is possible, if not probable, that Wise himself may have edited this anthology.

60. Wise, "Some Rules on Preaching Sermons," 4.

61. Isaac Mayer Wise, "Hebrew Monotheism," in *The American Jewish Pulpit*, 199–208.

62. Ibid., 199.

63. For a clear explanation of topical organization see Stephen Lucas, *The Art of Public Speaking* (New York: Random House, 1986), 149–50.

64. Wise, "Hebrew Monotheism," 200–207.

65. Ibid., 208.

66. Robert D. Kully, "Isaac Mayer Wise: His Rhetoric against Religious Discrimination" (unpublished Ph.D. dissertation, University of Illinois, 1956), 230.

67. Wise, "The World of My Books," 151.

68. Ibid., 152.

69. Ibid., 153.

70. Letter, Wise to Heller, September 5, 1886.

71. Kully, "Isaac Mayer Wise: His Rhetoric," 273–75.

72. Ibid., 275.

73. For example see "The Dearth of New Poets," *The American Israelite*, March 15, 1867, p. 5.

74. Letter, Wise to Mayerberg, May 23, 1866.

75. Kully, "Isaac Mayer Wise: His Rhetoric," 261.

76. See his criticisms of Max Heller's preaching in his letter to Heller, September 5, 1886. Also see Wise, "Rules on Preaching Sermons," 4.

77. The major events of Lilienthal's life can be found in any good history of American Judaism. See, for example, Learsi, *The Jews of America*, 68, 93, 117–18. The best biography of Lilienthal is David Philipson, *Max Lilienthal: American Rabbi* (New York: Bloch Publishing, 1915).

78. See Philipson, *Max Lilienthal*, 12–16, for an account of how Lilienthal was selected by Uvarov.

79. For an excellent study that details the Russian treatment of the Jews during this period and is the best source on Lilienthal's activities in Russia, see Michael Stanislawski, *Tsar Nicholas I and the Jews: The Transformation of Jewish Society in Russia 1825–1855* (Philadelphia: Jewish Publication Society of America, 1983).

80. See Stanislawski, *Tsar Nicholas I and the Jews*, 85–96, for an explanation of Lilienthal's failure to return to Russia.

81. Quoted in Philipson, *Max Lilienthal*, 49–50.

82. Ibid., 46–55, for a discussion of Lilienthal's early years in the United States, with emphasis on the reforms he instituted.

83. Ibid., 100.

84. Although a significant public figure in Cincinnati, Vickers is best known today for his ecumenical attitudes and efforts, which were well ahead of his day. See Barnett R. Brickner, "The Jewish Community of Cincinnati: Historic and Descriptive" (unpublished Ph.D. dissertation, University of Cincinnati, 1932), 60.

85. Evidently, Lilienthal's congregation was not as ecumenically minded as was Vickers's church.

86. "Religious Notices," *Cincinnati Daily Gazette*, March 2, 1867, p. 3.

87. Philipson, *Max Lilienthal*, 97–98.

88. Ibid.

89. This and all future references to the sermon are drawn from "Religious Liberality," *Cincinnati Daily Gazette*, March 4, 1867, p. 1. This front-page story carried Lilienthal's sermon text. The *Cincinnati Weekly Gazette* of March 6, 1876, also carried a sermon text. However, the weekly, as its name implies, simply reproduced and edited articles from the daily. The text found in the *Cincinnati Weekly Gazette* is identical to the first text, which appeared intact until the last five paragraphs, where it gives evidence of having been edited to improve its artistic merit. The first version, published on March 4, 1867, seems likely to have been a more accurate version of what Lilienthal actually preached. Hereafter, all references will be to the text appearing in the *Cincinnati Daily Gazette*, March 4, 1867, and cited as Lilienthal, "Sermon of March 3, 1867."

90. This statement is based on comparing this sermon with others that Lilienthal delivered. Lilienthal's sermons can be found in a variety of Jewish sermon anthologies, such as *The American Jewish Pulpit: A Collection of Sermons*; the collection of Lilienthal sermons and other writings in the appendix of Philipson, *Max Lilienthal*; and in the holdings of the Hebrew Union College-Jewish Institute of Religion Library. Since Lilienthal was a member of the first faculty of Hebrew Union College, that school has an extensive file of his sermons, many privately printed, available through the library of its Cincinnati campus.

91. Lilienthal, "Sermon of March 3, 1867."

92. He even makes reference to it in the text of his sermon.

93. See the accounts of the service found in the articles published under the headline "Religious Liberality," in the *Cincinnati Daily Gazette*, March 4, 1867, and in the *Cincinnati Weekly Gazette*, March 6, 1867.

94. Lilienthal, "Sermon of March 3, 1867."

95. Ibid.

96. His best-known and most complete statements on the topic were occasioned in 1869, when the Cincinnati school system was involved in a heated legal controversy over Bible reading and hymn singing in the schools. See his letters to *The Jewish Times* (New York) of December 10 and 17, 1869. These letters were subsequently privately printed and are perhaps most readily available today in the appendix of Philipson, *Max Lilienthal*, 474–87.

97. Lilienthal, "Sermon of March 3, 1867."

98. Ibid.

99. Ibid.

100. Ibid.

101. Ibid.

102. Ibid.

103. The aforementioned publisher of the *Cincinnati Daily Gazette* and *Cincinnati Weekly Gazette*.

104. For a summary of the reaction to Lilienthal, which includes both criticism and praise, see "Solemn Protest," *The American Israelite*, April 5, 1867, p. 4.

105. "Domestic Record," *The American Israelite*, March 15, 1867, p. 6.

106. Ibid. The extensive description of Vickers's speech that is presented in this article is signed by Maurice Fluegel, a Jew who was in attendance.

Chapter 5: American Jewish Preaching and Zionism

1. For accounts of the presidential campaign of 1900, see Charles S. Olcott, *William McKinley* (Boston: Houghton Mifflin Co., 1916), 2:262–95; Louis Koenig, *Bryan: A Political Biography of William Jennings Bryan* (New York: G. P. Putnam, 1971), 318–46; or John A. Garraty, *The American Nation* (New York: Harper and Row, 1971), 720–31.

2. Israel Cohen, *The Zionist Movement* (New York: Zionist Organization of America, 1946), 20.

3. Any good history of Zionism should detail the essentially apolitical nature of the movement prior to Herzl. See, for example, the entry "Zionism," *Encyclopedia Judaica* (New York: McMillian, 1971), 16:1031–162. Also see J. Mitchell Rosenberg, *The Story of Zionism* (New York: Bloch Publishing, 1946), 1–31; or Cohen, *The Zionist Movement*, 19–71.

4. Quoted in Rosenberg, *The Story of Zionism*, 36.

5. Quoted in Cohen, *The Zionist Movement*, 77.

6. Bernard G. Richards, "Zionism in the United States," chap. 20 in Cohen, *The Zionist Movement*, 334.

7. Nathan Glazer, *American Judaism* (Chicago: University of Chicago Press, 1957), 60.

8. Ibid.

9. Ibid., 62.

10. Ibid., 60.

11. Anita Lebeson, "Zionism Comes to Chicago," in *Early History of Zionism in America*, ed. Isidore S. Meyer (New York: American Jewish Historical Society and Theodor Herzl Foundation, 1958), 155–64.

12. For recollections of many of the founders of Chicago's Zionist movement, which include descriptions of Felsenthal's activities, see Lebeson, "Zionism Comes to Chicago," 163–64.

13. Glazer, *American Judaism*, 63.

14. Ibid., 64.

15. Ibid., 64–65, for amplification of this point.

16. Any good history of Judaism or immigration in New York City will illustrate this development in that city. For two good studies of other cities see Lebeson, "Zionism Comes to Chicago," and Maxwell Whiteman, "Zionism Comes to Philadelphia," in Meyer, ed., *Early History of Zionism in America*, 191–218.

17. Robert Gordis, "Origins and Development of Conservative Judaism," *United Synagogue Review* 37 (Fall 1984): 1.

18. For a summary of the Conservative movement's perception of Reform and Orthodox, see Gordis, "Origins and Development," 13–15.

19. Abraham J. Karp, "The Conservative Rabbi—Dissatisfied but Not Unhappy," *American Jewish Archives* 35 (November 1983): 198.

20. Samuel Halperin, *The Political World of American Zionism* (Detroit: Wayne State University Press, 1961), 103.

21. Ibid.

22. Quoted in Herbert Rosenblum, *Conservative Judaism: A Contemporary History* (New York: United Synagogue of America, 1983), 89.

23. Rosenberg, *The Story of Zionism*, 38.

24. Quoted in David Polish, *Renew Our Days: The Zionist Issue in Reform Judaism* (Jerusalem: World Zionist Organization, 1976), 230.

25. See Polish, *Renew Our Days*; Howard R. Greenstein, *Turning Point: Zionism and Reform Judaism* (Chico: Scholars Press, 1981); and also Halperin, *The Political World*, 71–100.

26. Quoted in Halperin, *The Political World*, 71.

27. Ibid., 72.

28. This paragraph relies heavily on the interpretation of Howard R. Greenstein. See his *Turning Point*, 1–3.

29. Isaac M. Wise, "Zionism," *The Hebrew Union College Journal* 4 (December 1899): 47.

30. Polish, *Renew Our Days*, 49

31. James G. Heller, "The Home of the Jewish Spirit," *Hebrew Union College Monthly* 2 (March 1916): 188–89. For details concerning the controversy caused by this sermon, see David Polish, "The Changing and the Constant in the Reform Rabbinate," *American Jewish Archives* 35 (November 1983): 280–81.

32. These figures are drawn from Michael A. Meyer, "A Centennial History," in Karff, ed., *Hebrew Union College-Jewish Institute of Religion at One Hundred Years*, 130.

33. The most informative single volume on Wise's life is his autobiography, *Challenging Years: The Autobiography of Stephen Wise* (New York: G. P. Putnam's Sons, 1949). Also see Carl Voss, *Rabbi and Minister: The Friendship of Stephen S. Wise and John Haynes Holmes* (New York: Association Press, 1964).

34. Quoted in Myles Martel, "A Rhetorical Analysis of the Zionist Speaking of Rabbi Stephen S. Wise" (unpublished Ph.D. dissertation, Temple University, 1974), 27. Without question, Martel's work is clearly the definitive study of Wise's speaking and warrants the serious attention of any scholar interested in Wise. Martel deliberately limits himself to an analysis of Wise's major public speeches on zionism and hence does not treat any of his sermons.

35. Voss, *Rabbi and Minister*, 33.

36. Martel, "A Rhetorical Analysis," 1.

37. Wise had previously turned down the opportunity to serve as rabbi of Temple Emanu El in New York City, perhaps the wealthiest and most prestigious temple in the United States. He did so because of his perception that the lay leaders of Emanu El might seek to limit his freedom in the

pulpit. See Wise, *Challenging Years*, 82–95, for a full account of his perceptions.

38. Quoted in Martel, "A Rhetorical Analysis," 939.

39. Martel, "A Rhetorical Analysis," 943–44.

40. Martel claims that numerous Zionist sermons delivered by Wise have been examined and that those examinations reveal "no major differences" between Wise's sermons and the nonsermonic or public speeches that Martel studied. See Martel, "A Rhetorical Analysis," 950.

41. Martel, "A Rhetorical Analysis," 945.

42. See Stephen Wise, "The War and the Jewish Question," *Free Synagogue Pulpit* 3 (April 1915): 57–78; and Stephen S. Wise, "Theodor Herzl: The Man and His Cause," *Beth Israel Pulpit* 1 (January 1905): 1–12.

43. Wise, "The War and the Jewish Question," 72–73.

44. Wise, "Theodor Herzl," 9.

45. See Martel, "A Rhetorical Analysis," 947–50.

46. Ibid., 949.

47. Topical organization is the speaker's imposition of an arbitrary order in discussing the subtopics of the overall subject, rather than use of a chronological, spatial, problem-solution, or similar organizational pattern. See Lucas, *The Art of Public Speaking*, 149–50, or any public speaking textbook.

48. Stephen Wise, "The Jewish Question," *Free Synagogue Pulpit* 5 (1918–19; otherwise no date): 53–58.

49. For example, in his sermon "Theodor Herzl: The Man and His Cause," Wise does not preview the organizational pattern he will follow for the first half of the sermon. Midway through the sermon (p. 7) he provides a one-sentence preview of what he will do during the remainder of the sermon. But even this limited suggestion is not signposted or distinguished in any fashion. Hence, it is hard to imagine an audience being alerted to his organization structure for the second portion of the sermon, based on this one sentence.

50. Stephen Wise, "Zionism and Zion," *Free Synagogue Pulpit* 5 (1918–19; otherwise no date): 62.

51. Although Wise does have a propensity to use long sentences, his average sentence length is only twenty-five words. Moreover, when he does use long sentences, the structure is easy to follow, making even his longer sentences easy to understand.

52. A balanced sentence "is constructed so that similar or contrasting ideas are expressed in reasonably equal clauses." See Blankenship, *A Sense of Style*, 99–103.

53. Wise, "The War and the Jewish Question," 70.

54. Martel, "A Rhetorical Analysis," 947.

55. Wise, "Theodor Herzl," 12.

56. Uri Herscher, "Stephen S. Wise: His Character and Values Manifest in Speech" (unpublished rabbinic thesis, Hebrew Union College-Jewish Institute of Religion, 1970), 44–54, has drawn together the firsthand impressions of many of those who heard Wise. The comments in this paragraph are drawn primerily from the accounts reported in Herscher.

57. Wise, *Challenging Years*, 129.

58. Ibid., 121.

59. The best short biography of Silver is the entry in the *Encylopedia Judaica* (New York: McMillian, 1971), 14:1543–44.

60. Abraham Feldman, "Abba Hillel Silver—Necrology," *American Jewish Historical Quarterly* 54 (June 1965): 474–77.

61. Polish, *Renew Our Days*, 117.

62. For a biographical account that focuses on Silver's training and experiences as a speaker, see the first chapter of Francis R. Wolpaw, "A Rhetorical Analysis of Doctor Abba Hillel Silver's Speaking on Zionism" (unpublished Ph.D. dissertation, Case-Western Reserve University, 1968).

63. Feldman, "Silver—Necrology," 117.

64. Quoted in Polish, *Renew Our Days*, 117.

65. For a fuller discussion of Silver's views on Reform Judaism and Zionism, see his paper presented to the Central Conference of American Rabbis on June 27, 1935, titled "Israel." This paper was published in the *CCAR Yearbook* 45 (1935): 1–31. Also see Polish, *Renew Our Days*, 116–19.

66. For an excellent study of Silver's August 30, 1943, speech to the American Jewish Conference, which justified these claims and is considered by many to have been the single speech that most unified American Judaism behind active support of Zionism, see Jereome B. Polisky and Frances R. Wolpaw, "Jewish Statehood Legitimized: Abba Hillel Silver at the American Jewish Conference," *Quarterly Journal of Speech* 58 (April 1972): 209–16.

67. Silver's election was also remarkable for the fact that his Zionist activities at this time were so demanding that he delegated many of his responsibilities to his lifelong friend, Abraham Feldman, at that time vice president of the CCAR. Surely those who voted might have anticipated that he would be unable to devote the normal amount of time to the job.

68. The best examination of Silver's speaking is Frances Wolpaw, "A Rhetorical Analysis of Doctor Abba Hillel Silver's Speaking on Zionism."

69. This list is a slight rewording of Wolpaw's findings. See Wolpaw, "A Rhetorical Analysis of Doctor Abba Hillel Silver's Speaking on Zionism," 138.

70. Ibid., 185.

71. See, for example, Abba Hillel Silver, "Zionism: What Is It?" Address delivered at The Temple, Cleveland, Ohio, undated. Privately printed, available at the HUC-JIR Library, Cincinnati, Ohio, or see virtually any speech in Abba Hillel Silver, *Vision and Victory: A Collection of Addresses by Dr. Abba Hillel Silver* (New York: Zionist Organization of America, 1949).

72. Wolpaw, "A Rhetorical Analysis of Doctor Abba Hillel Silver's Speaking on Zionism," 215.

73. Ibid., 208.

74. His wife often followed his speech texts as he was speaking. She is the source for this statement, quoted in Wolpaw, "A Rhetorical Analysis of Doctor Abba Hillel Silver's Speaking on Zionism," 206.

75. Ibid., 205–6, for a report of an interview in which Silver discusses his speaking preparation.

76. These statements reflect the author's conclusions after listening to tapes of Silver speaking.

Chapter 6: American Jewish Preaching 1945–70: Representative Voices

1. The basic biographical information in this section is drawn from Jacob Chinitz, "A Memoir of Rabbi Morris Adler," in Morris Adler, *The Voice Still Speaks: Message of the Torah for Contemporary Man*, ed. Jacob Chinitz (New York: Bloch Publishing, 1969), xiii–xviii; Louis Finkelstein, "Foreword," in Adler, *The Voice Still Speaks*, ix–xi; Lily Edelman, "Foreword," in Morris Adler, *May I Have a Word with You?*, ed. Goldie Adler and Lily Edelman (New York: Crown Publishing, 1967), xi–xiv; and the entry for Adler in *Encyclopedia Judaica* (New York: McMillian, 1971), 2:283.

2. Finkelstein "Foreword," ix.

3. Ibid.

4. Edelman, "Foreword," xiii.

5. Chinitz, "A Memoir," xiv.

6. Edelman, "Foreword," xi.

7. Chinitz, "A Memoir," xvii.

8. Ibid.

9. The largest widely available collection of Adler's sermons is *The Voice Still Speaks*. Other sermons, as well as samples of other types of speeches and writing, can be found in *May I Have a Word with You?* Adler's sermons were also regularly printed in *The America Rabbi*.

10. See, for example, Bradley, *Fundamentals of Speech Communication*, 187, and Lucas, *The Art of Public Speaking*, 173.

11. Morris Adler, "The Sanctuary: Dimensions and Limitations," *The American Rabbi* 2 (December 1966): 36–41.

12. Morris Adler, "The Battle Within," in Adler, *The Voice Still Speaks*, 89.

13. See examples in Adler, *The Voice Still Speaks*: "Sanctuary or Conservatory," 175–78; "What Is Genius?" 254–58; "Jacob and Israel: The Natural and the Supernatural Jew," 346–50. Also see "First Service," in *May I Have a Word with You?*, 147–48.

14. Of the fifteen sermons randomly selected from Adler's published works for this study, eight were topically organized. Topical organization results when the speaker divides the speech subject into subtopics, each of which becomes a main point in the speech. The main points are not part of a chronological, spatial, problem-solution, causal, or other recognizable pattern of organization. Rather, the speaker has imposed his own organizational pattern on the material. Because the audience does not sense the organizational pattern early in the speech, as it typically does when the speaker uses one of the abovementioned recognizable patterns, it is exceptionally important for the speaker using topical organization to provide a thorough preview to his audience, normally at the end of the introduction. See Lucas, *The Art of Public Speaking*, 149–50, and Bradley, *Fundamentals of Speech Communication*, 171–72.

15. Of the fifteen sermons examined in this study, three utilized problem-solution organization and two were organized chronologically.

16. See Lucas, *The Art of Public Speaking*, 173–83, and Bradley, *Fundamentals of Speech Communication*, 196–203, for discussions of techniques for concluding speeches effectively.

17. Adler, "Soviet Jewry: Yet Again," in *May I Have a Word with You?*, 58–59.

18. The basic biographical information in this section is drawn from the entry for Freehof in *Encyclopedia Judaica* (New York: McMillian, 1971), 7: 121; the dedication found in Walter Jacob, Frederick C. Schwartz, Vidgor W. Kavaler, eds., *Essays in Honor of Solomn B. Freehof* (Pittsburgh: Rodef Shalom Congregation, 1964), v–vii; Vigdor W. Kavaler, "Solomon B. Freehof," in Solomn B. Freehof, *The Sermon Continues*, ed. Vigdor W. Kavaler (Pittsburgh: Rodef Shalom Congregation, no date of publication but internal evidence indicates post-1982), 1–4; and the private special edition of *Key* (November 11, 1984), celebrating the fiftieth anniversary of Freehof's service at Rodef Shalom (Freehof Collection, Box 1, American Jewish Archives, Cincinnati, Ohio).

19. Frederick C. Schwartz, "The Scriptural Presentation," in Jacob, Schwartz, and Kavaler, eds., *Essays in Honor of Solomn B. Freehof*, 3.

20. Ibid.

21. See such works of his as *Modern Jewish Preaching* (New York: Bloch Publishing, 1941) and "The Literary Lecture," in Solomn B. Freehof, ed., *Israel Bettan Memorial Volume* (New York: Central Conference of American Rabbis, 1961), 132–46. A complete bibliography of Freehof's work, including sermons, can be found in Jacob, Schwartz, and Kavaler, eds., *Essays in Honor of Solomn B. Freehof*, 53–96.

22. Frederick C. Schwartz and Walter Jacob, both of whom worked closely with Freehof at Rodef Shalom, draw heavily on their conversations with him. See Schwartz, "The Scriptural Presentation," and Jacob, "The Pulpit Lecture," both in Jacob, Schwartz, and Kavaler, eds., *Essays in Honor of Solomn B. Freehof*, 3–52.

23. Schwartz, "The Scriptural Presentation," 5.

24. Ibid. Also see Jacob, "The Pulpit Lecture," 35.

25. Schwartz, "The Scriptural Presentation," 5.

26. Ibid.

27. Ibid., 30–31.

28. Virtually all of his sermons at Rodef Shalom were taped and then transcribed, hence transcripts of literally hundreds of his sermons exist.

29. Schwartz, "The Scriptural Presentation," 30.

30. Jacob, "The Pulpit Lecture," 51.

31. In addition to those found at Rodef Shalom, copies of over two hundred of his sermons can be found in the Freehof Collection of the American Jewish Archives. Rodef Shalom periodically published a number of Freehof sermon anthologies. The most recent is *The Sermon Continues*, which honored Freehof's ninetieth birthday and includes sermons delivered up to 1982.

32. Solomn B. Freehof, "Land That I Love—Its Religious Prejudices," in *Rodef Shalom Pulpit* (Pittsburgh: Rodef Shalom Congregation, 1957), n.s. 25, no. 5: 3–16.

33. On this point see Jacob, "The Scriptural Presentation," 9.

34. Solomn B. Freehof, "Jewish Missionaries," in *Rodef Shalom Pulpit* (Pittsburgh: Rodef Shalom Congregation, 1957), n.s. 26, no. 4: 3.

35. Ibid., 7.

36. Ibid., 11.

37. Ibid., 11–12.

38. See Freehof, "The Literary Lecture," 133–34, for a discussion of the purposes of this type of speech and the functions it might serve for the congregation.

39. See, for example, "The Heart of Shakespeare," a collection of three sermons delivered in March and April of 1959 on Shakespearean plays. *Rodef Shalom Pulpit* (Pittsburgh: Rodef Shalom Congregation, 1959), n.s. 28, nos. 3–5.

40. Jacob Feldman, *The Jewish Experience in Western Pennsylvania* (Pittsburgh: Historical Society of Western Pennsylvania, 1986), 286.

41. Sound recordings of Freehof are available in the Freehof Collection of the American Jewish Archives.

42. *Intermountain Jewish News*, May 25, 1979. Found in clipping file, Gordis Collection, American Jewish Archives, Cincinnati, Ohio.

43. *B'nai Brith Messenger*, July 21, 1972. Found in clipping file, Gordis Collection, American Jewish Archives, Cincinnati, Ohio.

44. *The New York Times*, April 3, 1976. Found in clipping file, Gordis Collection, American Jewish Archives, Cincinnati, Ohio.

45. The basic biographical information in this section is drawn from the entry for Gordis in *Encyclopedia Judaica* (New York: McMillian, 1971), 7:790; B'nai Brith, *Directions for the American Jewish Community* (Washington: B'nai Brith, 1964), 21–22; and from the clipping file in the Gordis Collection at the American Jewish Archives, Cincinnati, Ohio.

46. Robert Gordis, *Leave a Little to God* (New York: Bloch Publishing, 1967), xiii.

47. Ibid.

48. Ibid.

49. Ibid.

50. Ibid.

51. Eight of the nineteen sermons included in *Leave a Little to God* treat this topic area.

52. Gordis, *Leave a Little to God*, ix.

53. Robert Gordis, *Understanding Conservative Judaism* (New York: The Rabbinical Assembly, 1978), 190.

54. Ibid., 179.

55. Ibid. Freehof, who often treated best-sellers and Shakespearean plays in his Sunday morning sermons, is explicit in claiming that the rabbi is not a literary critic and "must relate" the ethical and spiritual ideas of his heritage to any books he discusses, whether he is in or out of the pulpit. See Freehof, "The Literary Lecture," 139.

56. Gordis, *Understanding Conservative Judaism*, 180.

57. For years Temple Beth El published his high holiday sermons, distributing them to the congregation at Hanukkah. These sermons are held by a variety of Judaica libraries. The most readily accessible collection of

Gordis's sermons is *Leave a Little to God*, a group of sermons that was revised for publication. However, a comparison of the texts distributed by Temple Beth El and the texts found in *Leave a Little to God* suggests that the revisions were very slight, primarily reflecting changes in the timeliness of material between the date the sermon was originally preached and the publication of the collection.

58. Robert Gordis, "What Is Worse Than Death?" in *Between Two Worlds* (Rockaway Park: Temple Beth El, 1964), 12–22. This sermon can also be found in Gordis, *Leave a Little to God*, 111–25.

59. Ibid., 13.

60. Robert Gordis, "The Passover Theme in the Twentieth Century" (Rockaway Park: Temple Beth El, 1960). Pamphlet in the Gordis Collection, American Jewish Archives, Cincinnati, Ohio.

61. Robert Gordis, "The Revolution in Man," in *Between Two Worlds*, 4. This sermon can also be found in Gordis, *Leave a Little to God*, 28–40.

62. Gordis, "The Revolution in Man," 9–11.

63. Robert Gordis, "Leave a Little to God," in Gordis, *Leave a Little to God*, 4.

64. The best short biography of Kahn is found in the opening section of Robert Kahn, *May the Words of My Mouth* (Houston: Emanu El Foundation, 1984). Unless otherwise noted, all the biographical information in this section is drawn from this source.

65. Kahn, "Liberalism As Reflected in Jewish Preaching in the English Language in the Mid-Nineteenth Century."

66. His lectures were privately printed by the Department of Midrash and Homiletics under the title *Aspects of Jewish Homiletics*. They are available through the Hebrew Union College-Jewish Institute of Religion Library.

67. Robert Kahn, "The Occasional Sermon," in Freehof, ed., *Israel Bettan Memorial Volume*, 147–64; Kahn, "Foreword," *May the Words of My Mouth*, xi–xxiv; Robert Kahn, "The Funeral Sermon," *The American Rabbi* 2 (April 1967): 27–38.

68. Kahn, *May the Words of My Mouth*, xv.

69. Ibid., xx.

70. Ibid., xvi.

71. Ibid., xix.

72. Ibid., xx.

73. Kahn, *Aspects of Jewish Homiletics*, 43.

74. Ibid., 44.

75. Ibid.

76. Ibid.

77. Ibid., 17–43.

78. Kahn, "The Funeral Sermon," 27–38. Also see Kahn, *Aspects of Jewish Homiletics*, 26–43.

79. Kahn, *May the Words of My Mouth*, 290–98.

80. Ibid., 291–92.

81. Kahn, "The Need for Reasonable Dialogue," in *May the Words of My Mouth*, 248–55.

82. Norman Lamm, "Eulogy for Rabbi Joseph H. Lookstein," in *Rabbi*

Joseph H. Lookstein Memorial Volume, ed. Leo Landman (New York: Ktav Publishing, 1980), 8.

83. The biographical information in this section is drawn from the entry for Lookstein in *Encyclopedia Judaica* (New York: McMillian, 1971), 11:487, and the eulogies and appreciations for Lookstein found in Landman, ed., *Rabbi Joseph H. Lookstein Memorial Volume*.

84. Haskel Lookstein, "Joseph: The Master of His Dreams," in Landman, ed., *Rabbi Joseph H. Lookstein Memorial Volume*, 17.

85. Joseph H. Lookstein, *Yesterday's Faith for Tomorrow* (New York: Ktav Publishing, 1979), xi.

86. Ibid., xii.

87. These three sermon types are discussed in "What Is a Sermon?," the introductory essay in *Yesterday's Faith for Tomorrow*, xii-xiv.

88. Joseph H. Lookstein, *Faith and Destiny of Man* (New York: Bloch Publishing, 1967), viii.

89. Lookstein, *Yesterday's Faith for Tomorrow*, xv.

90. Joseph H. Lookstein, "The Erosion of Authority," in *Yesterday's Faith for Tomorrow*, 122–30.

91. Ibid., 127.

92. Joseph H. Lookstein, "Gloom and Doom: Are There No Other Alternatives?" in *Yesterday's Faith for Tomorrow*, 183–89.

93. Ibid., 186.

94. Ibid., 188.

95. Lamm, "Eulogy for Rabbi Joseph H. Lookstein," 9.

96. Kahn, *Aspects of Jewish Homiletics*, 2–4.

97. Ibid.

Epilogue: Current Homiletic Training in American Rabbinic Seminaries and the Future of American Jewish Preaching

1. *Hebrew Union College-Jewish Institute of Religion Catalogue: 1985–1988* (Cincinnati: Hebrew Union College-Jewish Institute of Religion, 1985), 39. It should be noted that there are slight differences in offerings among the HUC-JIR campuses. This discussion will focus on the Cincinnati campus, which is the oldest campus of the now merged HUC-JIR and remains the central campus containing the major administrative and research facilities of the institution.

2. The discussion of this course is based on "Homiletics Core Course: Syllabus and Class Schedule 1984–1985" (unpublished handout) and discussions with Rabbis Michael Cook and Mark Washofsky, who teach the course.

3. Ibid., 2.

4. "Speech II: Syllabus and Class Schedule 1984–1985" (unpublished handout). The author has taught this course on the Cincinnati campus for the past seven years, while serving as visiting professor of communication.

5. Course descriptions of all of these courses can be found in *HUC-JIR Catalogue: 1985–1988,* 39.

6. A three-page, seventeen-question survey was distributed by the author to all full-time or part-time faculty teaching homiletics and speech courses on the Cincinnati campus in academic year 1984–85. Eighty percent, or four out of five, responded. Follow-up interviews were also utilized. Hereafter, references to the results of this survey will be cited as HUC-JIR Homiletics Survey.

7. Respondents were asked to fill in the blank in the statement "I would anticipate that the average rabbinical student at my institution has delivered approximately——— sermons prior to taking his first full time position as a congregational rabbi." The lowest figure mentioned was thirty, and the most commonly mentioned figured was forty.

8. HUC-JIR Homiletics Survey.

9. Ibid.

10. Ibid.

11. *The Jewish Theological Seminary of America Academic Bulletin: 1984–1985/5745* (New York: Jewish Theological Seminary of America, 1984), 34, 37.

12. Interview with Rabbi A. C. Felner, course instructor, March 20, 1985.

13. "Homiletics 7210X—Fall 5743: Syllabus" (unpublished handout), 1.

14. The same three-page, seventeen-question survey utilized to survey the faculty at HUC-JIR was submitted to all full-time or part-time faculty teaching homiletics in the academic year 1984–85 at the Jewish Theological Seminary of America. It was also distributed to several administrators who were involved with the program at the time of its most recent revision, or currently. Seventy-five percent, or six out of eight, responded. Follow-up interviews were also utilized. Hereafter, references to the results of this survey will be cited as JTS Homiletics Survey.

15. Respondents were asked to fill in the blank in the statement "I would anticipate that the average rabbinical student at my institution has delivered approrimately——— sermons prior to taking his first full time position as a congregational rabbi." The lowest figure mentioned was fifteen and the highest was fifty.

16. JTS Homiletics Survey.

17. Charles S. Lieberman, "The Training of American Rabbis," in *The American Jewish Yearbook: 1968* 69 (1969): 3–112, ed. Milton Fine and Morris Himmelfarb (New York: Jewish Publication Society, 1969).

18. "Rabbi Isaac Elchanan Theological Seminary: Requirements and Regulations," flier distributed to prospective students, academic year 1984–85, p. 2.

19. "RIETS Four Year Program—5744" (unpublished handout).

20. Lieberman, "The Training of American Rabbis," 33.

21. HUC-JIR and JTS Homiletics Surveys.

22. Interview with Rabbi Akiba Lubow, director of programming, Rabbinical Assembly Homiletics Service, March 18, 1985.

23. HUC-JIR and JTS Homiletics Surveys.

24. HUC-JIR Homiletics Survey.

Glossary of Hebrew and Rhetorical Terms

Adon Olam "Eternal Lord."　　Hymn of unknown authorship extolling the unity, timeliness, and providence of God. Recited in a variety of services.

Agodda (aggadah)　　Nonlegal contents of the Talmud and Midrash, including ethical and moral teachings, theological speculation, legends, and folklore.

bar mitzvah　　Ceremony at which a thirteen-year-old boy becomes an adult member of the community for ceremonial purposes, including that of making up a minyan.

credibility (speaker credibility)　　The degree to which an audience finds a speaker to be believable, based on the audience's knowledge of the speaker's competency, character, and motives.

drashah　　Sermon; originally, a sermon based on scripture.

extemporaneous delivery　　A method of speech presentation based upon extensive preparation and practice. Following preparation and practice, the speech is actually delivered from a very brief outline or less.

haftorah　　Prophetic writings read after the Torah readings take place in the service.

halakah　　Jewish law from the talmudic and later periods, dealing with religious, ethical, civil, and criminal matters.

hazzan　　One who chants the religious service.

homiletics　　Art of preaching, instruction in the art of preaching.

invention　　The finding or generating of ideas for a speech.

Kashruth　　Dietary laws, kosher.

Kol Israel　　All the people of Israel.

meturgeman　　Translator who, in ancient times, rendered each Torah verse into the idiom spoken by the people.

Midrash   The discovery of meanings, other than those that are literal, in the Bible. Literature that interprets scripture to find its full meaning.

minyan   Minimum quorum of ten, traditionally adult males, required for congregational prayer.

mohel   Ritual circumciser.

sabbath   Saturday, the seventh day of the week named in the Ten Commandments as a day of rest and worship. Traditionally observed from sundown on Friday until sundown on Saturday.

Sabbath Hagadol   The Sabbath falling immediately prior to the Passover holiday.

Sabbath Shuvah   The Sabbath falling between the holidays of Rosh Hashanah and Yom Kippur.

Sephardic Jews   Jews of the Iberian peninsula, or descendants of such Jews. The customs and rituals developed by Spanish and Portuguese Jews stem from Babylonian scholars and differ slightly from those of other European Jews.

Shema   The declaration of faith in the unity of God: "Hear O Israel, the Lord Our God, the Lord is One."

shohet   One who slaughters cattle and fowl in the ritual way to provide observant Jews with kosher meat.

tallith   Prayer shawl.

Talmud   A uniquely comprehensive work resulting from eight centuries of study and discussion of the Bible, halakah, and Midrash in the academies of Palestine and Babylonia. In the evolution of Judaism the Talmud is the sequel to the Bible, and the study of its contents has been the basis of Jewish religious life.

topical organization   An organizational pattern resulting when the subject of the speech is divided into subtopics, each of which becomes a main point. The main points do not lend themselves to chronological, spatial, problem-solution, or other common organizational patterns.

topoi (commonplaces)   A list of topics that can be used to generate ideas about any subject being spoken upon. For example, morality and efficiency are contemporary topoi used to generate ideas about such diverse current subjects as tax reform, abortion, and foreign policy.

Torah   The five books of Moses: Genesis, Exodus, Leviticus, Numbers, Deuteronomy.

tzedakah   Charity.

yarmulka   Polish word denoting the head covering worn by men during Jewish services. The Hebrew equivalent is *kippah*.

yeshiva   "Torah academy." Institution of higher learning for the study of Judaism.

Zion   Jerusalem; Jewish homeland. The spiritual capital of the world.

Select Bibliography

Specific sermons mentioned in the text, as well as newspaper citations and personal papers utilized in the text, are not included in this bibliography. All such material is fully cited in the endnotes, which include, where appropriate, the manuscript collections and libraries where they can be found. Major sermon anthologies are included in this bibliography, as well as scholarly books and articles.

Adler, Cyrus. *Catalogue of the Leeser Library*. Philadelphia: E. Hirsch and Co., 1883.

Adler, Morris. *May I Have a Word with You?* Ed. Goldie Adler and Lily Edelman. New York: Crown Publishing, 1967.

———. *The Voice Still Speaks: Message of the Torah for Contemporary Man*. Ed. Jacob Chinitz. New York: Bloch Publishing, 1969.

Altmann, Alexander. *Essays in Jewish Intellectual History*. Hanover: University Press of New England and Brandeis University Press, 1981.

Arnold, Carroll C. *Criticism of Oral Rhetoric*. Columbus: Charles E. Merrill Publishers, 1974.

Bailey, Thomas A. *A Diplomatic History of the American People*. New York: Appleton-Century-Crofts, 1964.

Bettan, Israel. *Studies in Jewish Preaching*. Cincinnati: Hebrew Union College Press, 1939.

Bitzer, Lloyd. "The Rhetorical Situation." *Philosophy and Rhetoric* 1 (January 1968): 1–14.

Blair, Hugh. *Lectures on Rhetoric and Belles Lettres*. Ed. Harold F. Harding. Carbondale: Southern Illinois University Press, 1965.

Blankenship, Jane. *A Sense of Style: An Introduction to Style for the Public Speaker.* Belmont: Dickenson Publishing, 1968.

Blau, Joseph L., and Salo W. Baron, eds. *The Jews of the United States: 1740–1840.* New York: Columbia University Press, 1963.

Bradley, Bert E. *Fundamentals of Speech Communication: The Credibility of Ideas.* Dubuque: Wm. C. Brown Co., 1978.

Brickner, Barnett R. "The Jewish Community of Cincinnati: Historic and Descriptive." Unpublished Ph.D. Dissertation, University of Cincinnati, 1932.

Campbell, Karlyn Kohrs, and Kathleen Hall Jamieson, eds. *Form and Genre: Shaping Rhetorical Action.* Falls Church, Va.: Speech Communication Association, 1977.

Cohen, Abraham. *Jewish Homiletics.* London: M. L. Cailingold, 1937.

Cohen, Israel. *The Zionist Movement.* New York: Zionist Organization of America, 1946.

Cohen, Naomi W. "Pioneers of American Jewish Defense." *American Jewish Archives* 29 (November 1977): 116–50.

Cremin, Lawrence A. *American Education: The Colonial Experience 1607–1783.* New York: Harper and Row, 1970.

Feldman, Abraham. "Abba Hillel Silver—Necrology." *American Jewish Historical Quarterly* 54 (June 1965): 474–480.

Feldman, Jacob. *The Jewish Experience in Western Pennsylvania.* Pittsburgh: Historical Society of Western Pennsylvania, 1986.

Feldstein, Stanley. *The Land That I Show You: Three Centuries of Jewish Life in America.* New York: Anchor Press/Doubleday, 1978.

Flesch, Rudolph. *The Art of Plain Talk.* New York: Harper and Brothers, 1946.

Freehof, Solomn B., ed. *Israel Bettan Memorial Volume.* New York: Central Conference of American Rabbis, 1961.

———. *Modern Jewish Preaching.* New York: Bloch Publishing, 1941.

———. *The Sermon Continues.* Ed. Vigdor W. Kavaler. Pittsburgh: Rodef Shalom Congregration, no date of publication.

Friedenberg, Robert V. "Isaac Leeser: Pioneer Preacher of American Judaism." *Religious Communication Today* 6 (September 1983): 22–28.

———. "Rabbi Isaac Mayer Wise and American Judaism's Rhetorical Indebtedness to the Reverend Hugh Blair." *Religious Communication Today* 7 (September 1984): 11–19.

———. "The Status of Homiletic Training in America's Rabbinical Seminaries." *Journal of Communication and Religion* 10 (March 1987): 26–34.

Garraty, John A. *The American Nation.* New York: Harper and Row, 1971.

Glazer, Nathan. *American Judaism.* Chicago: University of Chicago Press, 1957.

Golden, James L., and Edward P. J. Corbett, eds. *The Rhetoric of Blair, Campbell and Whately.* New York: Holt, Rinehart and Winston, 1968.

Gordis, Robert. *Between Two Worlds.* Rockaway Park: Temple Beth El, 1964.

———. *Leave a Little to God.* New York: Bloch Publishing, 1967.

────. *Understanding Conservative Judaism*. New York: The Rabbinical Assembly, 1978.

Grayzel, Solomon. *A History of the Jews*. Philadelphia: Jewish Publication Society of America, 1947.

Greenstein, Howard R. *Turning Point: Zionism and Reform Judaism*. Chico: Scholars Press, 1981.

Gurlock, Jeffrey. "Resisters and Accommodators: Varieties of Orthodox Rabbis in America, 1886–1983." *American Jewish Archives* 35 (November 1983): 100–187.

Halperin, Samuel. *The Political World of American Zionism*. Detroit: Wayne State University Press, 1961.

Herscher, Uri. "Stephen S. Wise: His Character and Values Manifest in Speech." Unpublished rabbinic thesis, Hebrew Union College-Jewish Institute of Religion, 1970.

Holland, DeWitte, ed. *Preaching in American History*. Nashville: Abingdon Press, 1969.

Jacob, Walter, Frederick C. Schwartz, and Vidgor W. Kavaler, eds. *Essays in Honor of Solomn B. Freehof*. Pittsburgh: Rodef Shalom Congregation, 1964.

Jeffrey, Robert C., and Owen Peterson. *Speech: A Text with Adapted Readings*. New York: Harper and Row, 1975.

Kagnoff, Nathan. "The Traditional Jewish Sermon in the United States from Its Beginnings to the First World War." Unpublished Ph.D. dissertation, American University, 1960.

Kahn, Robert I. "Liberalism As Reflected in Jewish Preaching in the English Language in the Mid-Nineteenth Century." Unpublished Ph.D. dissertation, Hebrew Union College, 1949.

────. *May the Words of My Mouth*. Houston: Emanu El Foundation, 1984.

Karff, Samuel E., ed. *Hebrew Union College-Jewish Institute of Religion at One Hundred Years*. Cincinnati: Hebrew Union College Press, 1976.

Karp, Abraham J. "The Conservative Rabbi—Dissatisfied but Not Unhappy." *American Jewish Archives* 35 (November 1983): 188–262.

Kober, Adolf. "Jewish Preaching and Preachers: A Contribution to the History of the Jewish Sermon in Germany and America." *Historia Judaica* 7 (October 1945): 103–34.

Koenig, Louis. *Bryan: A Political Biography of William Jennings Bryan*. New York: G. P. Putnam, 1971.

Korn, Bertram W. *American Jewry and the Civil War*. New York: Atheneum, 1970.

────. *Eventful Years and Experiences: Studies in Nineteenth Century American Jewish History*. Cincinnati: American Jewish Archives, 1954.

Kully, Robert D. "Isaac Mayer Wise: His Rhetoric against Religious Discrimination." Unpublished Ph.D. dissertation, University of Illinois, 1956.

Landman, Leo, ed. *Rabbi Joseph H. Lookstein Memorial Volume*. New York: Ktav Publishing, 1980.

Learsi, Rufus. *The Jews in America: A History*. New York: Katv Publishing, 1972.

Leeser, Isaac. *Discourses on the Jewish Religion.* 10 vols. Philadelphia: Sherman and Co., 1867.

Lieberman, Charles S. "The Training of American Rabbis." In *The American Jewish Yearbook: 1968* 69 (1969): 3–112. Ed. Milton Fine and Morris Himmelfarb. New York: Jewish Publication Society, 1969.

Lookstein, Joseph H. *Faith and Destiny of Man.* New York: Bloch Publishing, 1967.

———. *Yesterday's Faith for Tomorrow.* New York: Ktav Publishing, 1979.

Lucas, Stephen. *The Art of Public Speaking.* New York: Random House, 1986.

Mahler, Raphael. "American Jewry and the Idea of the Return to Zion in the Period of the American Revolution." *Zion* 16 (1951): 105–34.

Marcus, Jacob Rader. *The Americanization of Isaac M. Wise.* Cincinnati: Privately printed, 1931.

———. *The Colonial American Jew: 1492–1776.* 3 vols. Detroit: Wayne State University Press, 1970.

———. *The Handsome Young Priest in the Black Gown: The Personal World of Gershom Seixas.* Cincinnati: American Jewish Archives, 1970.

Martel, Myles. "A Rhetorical Analysis of the Zionist Speaking of Rabbi Stephen S. Wise." Unpublished Ph.D. dissertation, Temple University, 1974.

May, Max B. *Isaac Mayer Wise: The Founder of American Judaism.* New York: G. P. Putnam's Sons, 1916.

Meyer, Isidore S., ed. *Early History of Zionism in America.* New York: American Jewish Historical Society and Theodor Herzl Foundation, 1958.

Meyer, Michael A. "Christian Influence on Early German Reform Judaism." In *Studies in Jewish Bibliography History and Literature in Honor of I. Edward Kiev.* Ed. Charles Berlin. New York: Ktav Publishing, 1971.

Mielziner, Ella McKinna Friend. *Moses Mielziner: A Biography with a Bibliography of His Writings.* New York: no publisher indicated, 1931.

Miller, John C. *Alexander Hamilton and the Growth of the New Nation.* New York: Harper and Row, 1959.

Morris, Henry S. *The Jews of Philadelphia.* Philadelphia: Levytype Co., 1884.

Olcott, Charles S. *William McKinley.* 2 vols. Boston: Houghton Mifflin Co., 1916.

Parzen, Herbert. *Architects of Conservative Judaism.* New York: Jonathan David, 1964.

Philipson, David. *Max Lilienthal: American Rabbi.* New York: Bloch Publishing, 1915.

———. *My Life as an American Jew.* Cincinnati: John G. Kidd and Son, 1941.

———, and Louis Grossmann, eds. *Selected Writings of Isaac M. Wise with a Bibliography.* Cincinnati: Robert Clarke Co., 1900.

Phillips, Naphtali. *Eulogy to the Memory of Rev. Gershom Mendes Seixas.* New York: J. H. Sherman Printer, 1816.

Polish, Daniel. "The Changing and the Constant in the Reform Rabbinate." *American Jewish Archives* 35 (November 1983): 263–341.

———. *Renew Our Days: The Zionist Issue in Reform Judaism.* Jerusalem: World Zionist Organization, 1976.

Polisky, Jereome B., and Frances R. Wolpaw. "Jewish Statehood Legitimized: Abba Hillel Silver at the American Jewish Conference." *Quarterly Journal of Speech* 58 (April 1972): 209–16.

Pollak, Gustav. *Michael Heilprin and His Sons: A Biography.* New York: Dodd Mead and Co., 1912.

Rosenberg, J. Mitchell. *The Story of Zionism.* New York: Bloch Publishing, 1946.

Rosenblum, Herbert. *Conservative Judaism: A Contemporary History.* New York: United Synagogue of America, 1983.

Sarna, Jonathan, Benny Kraut, and Samuel Joseph, eds. *Jews and the Founding of the Republic.* New York: Markus Weiner Publishers, 1985.

Shain, Samson. "The Sermon and Modern Hebrew Literature." *Yearbook of the Central Conference of American Rabbis* 63 (1953): 519–23.

Silver, Abba Hillel. "Israel." *Yearbook of the Central Conference of American Rabbis* 45 (1935): 1–31.

———. *Vision and Victory: A Collection of Addresses by Dr. Abba Hillel Silver.* New York: Zionist Organization of America, 1949.

Simonhoff, Harry. *Jewish Notables in America 1776–1885.* New York: Greenberg Publishers, 1956.

Stanislawski, Michael. *Tsar Nicholas I and the Jews: The Transformation of Jewish Society in Russia 1825–1855.* Philadelphia: Jewish Publication Society of America, 1983.

Stringfellow, Thornton. "A Scriptural View of Slavery." In *Slavery Defended.* Ed. Eric L. McKitrick. Englewood Cliffs: Prentice Hall, 1963.

Sussman, Lance. "Isaac Leeser and the Protestantization of American Judaism." *American Jewish Archives* 38 (April 1986): 1–21.

Voss, Carl. *Rabbi and Minister: The Friendship of Stephen S. Wise and John Haynes Holmes.* New York: Association Press, 1964.

Whiteman, Maxwell. "Jews in the Anti-Slavery Movement." Introduction to Peter Still and Vina Still, *The Kidnapped and the Ransomed: The Narrative of Peter and Vina Still after Forty Years of Slavery.* Philadelphia: Jewish Publication Society of America, 1970.

Wiernik, Peter. *History of the Jews in America.* New York: Jewish Historical Publishing Co., 1931.

Wilansky, Dena. *Sinai to Cincinnati: Lay Views on the Writings of Isaac M. Wise, Founder of Reform Judaism in America.* New York: Renaissance Book Co., 1937.

Wise, Isaac M. *Reminiscences.* Trans. David Philipson. Cincinnati: Leo Wise and Co., 1901.

———. "The World of My Books." Trans. Albert H. Friedlander. In *Critical Studies in American Jewish History.* Ed. Jacob R. Marcus. Cincinnati and New York: American Jewish Archives and Ktav Publishing, 1971.

Wise, Stephen. *Challenging Years: The Autobiography of Stephen Wise.* New York: G. P. Putnam's Sons, 1949.

Wolpaw, Frances R. "A Rhetorical Analysis of Doctor Abba Hillel Silver's Speaking on Zionism." Unpublished Ph.D. dissertation, Case-Western Reserve University, 1968.

Index

About the Author

Robert V. Friedenberg is Professor of Communication at Miami (Ohio) University. He received his B.S. degree from Towson State College in Baltimore and his M.A. in American history and Ph.D. in speech communication from Temple University.

About the Series

STUDIES IN RHETORIC AND COMMUNICATION
General Editors:
E. Culpepper Clark, Raymie E. McKerrow, and David Zarefsky

The University of Alabama Press has established this series to publish major new works in the general area of rhetoric and communication, including books treating the symbolic manifestations of political discourse, argument as social knowledge, the impact of machine technology on patterns of communication behavior, and other topics related to the nature or impact of symbolic communication. We actively solicit studies involving historical, critical, or theoretical analyses of human discourse.